Taken from the Paradise Isle

THE GEORGE AND SAKAYE ARATANI
Nikkei in the Americas Series

Series editor Lane Hirabayashi

This series endeavors to capture the best scholarship available illustrating the evolving nature of contemporary Japanese American culture and community. By stretching the boundaries of the field to the limit (whether at a substantive, theoretical, or comparative level) these books aspire to influence future scholarship in this area specifically, and Asian American Studies, more generally.

The House on Lemon Street, Mark Howland Rawitsch

Starting from Loomis and Other Stories,
Hiroshi Kashiwagi, edited and with an introduction by Tim Yamamura

Taken from the Paradise Isle: The Hoshida Family Story,
edited by Heidi Kim and with a foreword by Franklin Odo

Taken from the Paradise Isle

THE HOSHIDA FAMILY STORY

by George and Tamae Hoshida

EDITED BY HEIDI KIM
FOREWORD BY FRANKLIN ODO

UNIVERSITY PRESS OF COLORADO
Boulder

Published by University Press of Colorado
5589 Arapahoe Avenue, Suite 206C
Boulder, Colorado 80303

The University Press of Colorado is a proud member of
Association of American University Presses.

The University Press of Colorado is a cooperative publishing enterprise supported, in part,
by Adams State University, Colorado State University, Fort Lewis College, Metropolitan State
University of Denver, Regis University, University of Colorado, University of Northern Colorado,
Utah State University, and Western State Colorado University.

∞ This paper meets the requirements of the ANSI/NISO Z39.48-1992 (Permanence of Paper).

ISBN: 978-1-60732-339-6 (cloth)
ISBN: 978-1-60732-526-0 (paperback)
ISBN: 978-1-60732-344-0 (ebook)

This publication was made possible with the support of Naomi, Kathleen, Ken, and Paul Harada,
who donated funds in memory of their father, Harold Shigetaka Harada, honoring his quest
for justice and civil rights. Additional support for this publication was also provided, in part, by
UCLA's Aratani Endowed Chair, as well as Wallace T. Kido, Joel B. Klein, Elizabeth A. Uno, and
Rosalind K. Uno.

Library of Congress Cataloging-in-Publication Data

Hoshida, George, 1907–1985.
  Taken from the Paradise Isle : the Hoshida family story, 1912–1945 / by George and Tamae
Hoshida ; edited by Heidi Kathleen Kim.
     pages cm. — (Nikkei in the americas)
  ISBN 978-1-60732-339-6 (hardback : alkaline paper) — ISBN 978-1-60732-526-0 (pbk. : alkaline
paper) — ISBN 978-1-60732-344-0 (ebook)
1. Hoshida, George, 1907–1985—Diaries. 2. Hoshida, George, 1907–1985—Correspondence.
3. Hoshida, Tamae, 1908—Correspondence. 4. Hoshida, George, 1907–1985—Family. 5. Japanese
Americans—Evacuation and relocation, 1942–1945. 6. Jerome Relocation Center (Ark.) 7. Japanese
Americans—Hawaii—Biography. I. Hoshida, Tamae, 1908– II. Kim, Heidi Kathleen. III. Title.
D769.8.A6H66 2015
940.53'17767825—dc23
[B]

2014026690

Cover illustration by George Hoshida

George Hoshida's original acknowledgments

Dedicated To:
The Memories of
My Late Wife Tamae
and
Our Late Eldest Daughter Taeko
And
To My Present Wife Grace Ayame
for her Encouragements and
Assistance in
Making the Reproduction of
Autobiography possible.

Contents

Figures

Foreword

Franklin Odo
January 2014

Heidi Kathleen Kim has crafted an elegant book from diary entries, letters, and artwork left to us by George and Tamae Hoshida. These precious sources, supplemented with documents and enriched by memoirs left by other Japanese American camp survivors, are direct voices from the WWII years when the Hoshida family was unceremoniously torn from its quietly improving circumstances on the Big Island of Hawai'i in the Territory of Hawai'i. George was an immigrant from Japan, arriving at age four, in 1912. His early years were spent working on sugar plantations and a cattle ranch, but this period served primarily as a backdrop to the war and incarceration and may need to be revisited at another time for a prequel! George's artwork is detailed and sensitive; these sketches deserve wide circulation—together with his writings they provide an unusually direct and effective link to the historical experience.

This volume reminds me of a much more modest project for which I wrote an essay: in 1994 the Honolulu Academy of Arts published a catalogue, *Reflections of Internment: The Art of Hawaii's Hiroshi Honda*, which featured

Honda's polished sketches and paintings. The internment was dramatic and traumatic for both men and their families. Honda eventually left his family and embarked on an art career in New York City; Hoshida stayed with his, working and reworking his memoir. Fortunately for us, Kim has fashioned the raw materials into a remarkable portrait of a man living through extraordinary hardship, accused in Kafkaesque fashion, without charges or trial, sentenced without judge or jury to indefinite detention in undetermined locations and with unfathomable outcomes.

George Hoshida was among some 1,000 Japanese Americans in Hawai'i who were targeted years before the December 7, 1941, attack on Pearl Harbor by Imperial Japanese military forces. These men (and a few women) were presumed dangerous to US national security because of their proximity to Japanese cultural traditions and not because of any evidence of espionage or sabotage. The traditions included religious affiliations like Buddhism or Shinto, the Japanese language, and especially martial arts like judo or kendo. These 1,000 targets included some who were accompanied into American concentration camps by family members. The relatively small number of individuals thus impacted by forced removal and incarceration, as contrasted to the 120,000 Japanese Americans incarcerated on the US mainland, is sometimes hailed as a modest triumph of reason on the part of military and civilian authorities controlling Hawai'i. But there are issues with this conclusion, at least for those directly impacted. The mass ethnic cleansing on the West Coast made it evident to the entire Japanese American community that they had all been indiscriminately and unjustly treated. But it made life more complicated for those 1,000 souls in Hawai'i because it appeared that they were selectively arrested for some justifiable albeit unknowable reason. The FBI provided itself with fig leaves of cover by inviting their targets to hasty and ridiculous "hearings." Fortunately, Professor Kim was able to provide the complete transcript of George Hoshida's hearing in an appendix. Hoshida even had token support from a haole (white) male who had known him over the years. But of course there was no way to refute phantom charges or innuendoes—such as those probably lodged against Hoshida by a Japanese American informant within the community. As we now know, some of these allegations came from individuals harboring personal animus against the targets.

Most internees were simply assumed dangerous because of their connection to Japanese culture. I recall reading the very brief transcription of a hearing for Shunichi Odo, a writer for a Japanese-language newspaper in Hawai'i and my father's first cousin. It was no more than a few pages long and perfunctory, leading inevitably to its foregone conclusion. In this respect, Hoshida's experience was quite different, with meticulous and detailed questioning, including at least one interesting outburst vehemently protesting a "prejudiced" misrepresentation of bushido by one of his interrogators. In addition, Hoshida was able to submit his own "statement" to the Board of Inquiry in which he explored at some length his feelings for his country of birth and his overwhelming debt to his country of life. As an alien legally prohibited from naturalization in the United States, a status limited only to those from Asia, Hoshida and his fellow Issei might be forgiven for harboring complex reservations about "loyalty." These sentiments bubble over occasionally, as when he writes his wife, Tamae, at a particularly depressed point during his internment that he might consider repatriating to Japan. This remark unleashed a torrent of protest from Tamae, who foresaw only two possible outcomes: either life entirely separated from her husband or a desolate future in postwar Japan. He quickly eliminated that option.

Perhaps less desperate but nonetheless angry, on October 10, 1942, George wondered about the possibility of mutual understanding—even between Axis and Allied peoples—and reminded Tamae of the excesses of the British Empire and that it was Pearl Buck who mentioned the "treatment the negroes are receiving in this land of liberty, equality and justice." In the same letter, he concluded that the camps in which Japanese Americans were confined were "actually concentration camps, regardless of whether they are aliens or citizens." Letters were carefully censored, from Japanese Americans in any of the many varieties of confinement camps on the mainland or from the Territory of Hawaii, but this did not deter Hoshida from exclaiming in his diary at 11 p.m. on December 31, 1942 ("only an hour remains before this year is gone"): [The US] had been caught unprepared. Who's to blame? Greek [sic] and Rome fell when they reached what seemed their height in prosperity. Is history repeating here in America too?" These are probably modest examples of incarcerated Issei sufficiently educated about the pre-WWII histories of the United States and the Western powers. The book ends with their release and trip back to Hawai'i and with George Hoshida's own words. Heidi Kim's editorial decision to provide maximum latitude for the language directly from George and Tamae seems both generous and wise. The pages come alive in a way no modified voice, however eloquent, could have conveyed.

Kim notes that the Hoshidas had been making slow but discernible economic progress in the years before Pearl Harbor, although their first child, a daughter, had been grievously injured in an automobile accident. She had to be left behind in Honolulu in a permanent state of disability when Tamae and the three other daughters eventually joined George on the mainland. While the family was incarcerated during the war, they learned that Taeko had drowned in a bathtub in 1944 in an accident that smacked of negligence. Kim also notes that the US government established a Japanese American Evacuation Claims Act in 1948 that invited requests from those who had suffered concrete economic losses due to the incarceration. The Hoshidas submitted a claim for $9,632.50. They were reimbursed for $275.00 in 1952.

On August 10, 1988, President Ronald Reagan signed HR 442, which provided an official apology and $20,000 in redress checks to every Japanese American who had been incarcerated and was still alive at the signing—about 60,000, one-half of the total, qualified, but not Tamae or George; she died in 1970, he in 1985.

FRANKLIN ODO is Founding Director of the Asian Pacific American Center at the Smithsonian Institution and Chief of the Asian Division, Library of Congress. He has taught at the University of Hawai'i, the University of Pennsylvania, Hunter College, Princeton University, and Columbia University. His book, *No Sword to Bury: Japanese Americans in Hawai'i during World War II*, was published by Temple University Press in 2004. *Voices from the Canefields: Folksongs from Japanese Immigrant Workers in Hawai'i* was published by Oxford in 2013. He has a Lifetime Achievement Award from the Association for Asian American Studies and a Distinguished Service Award from the Asian American Justice Center.

Acknowledgments

This book would obviously not have been possible without the support of the Hoshida family, particularly Tamae and George Hoshida's three surviving daughters, June Hoshida Honma, Sandra Y. Hoshida, and Carole Hoshida Kanada. I thank them for entrusting their family's story to me. They and grandson Gary Kanada have been immensely helpful in giving me important family history with which to cross-reference the memoir and briefly narrate what the Hoshidas did after the war. Grandson Scott Honma provided family photographs.

I also thank the staff of the Japanese American National Museum in Los Angeles, particularly former archivist Jane Nakasako, for help with my research and permission to publish the artwork and letters. Archivist Sherman Seki at the University of Hawai'i and various staff members at the National Archives were also extremely helpful in my retracing of the Hoshidas' journey. Mary Matayoshi, Kathryn Matayoshi, and Lisa Monhoff at the Charles M. Schulz Museum and Research Center as well as the staff of Art Instruction Schools provided information for the introduction and footnotes. Thanks to my research assistant, Laura Broom, for transcribing many of the letters, and Emma Calabrese, who also assisted with this task.

It is a delightful coincidence that Franklin Odo should write the foreword for this volume, not only because of his research and expertise in the Japanese American experience in Hawai'i, but because his teaching and mentoring of my brother at Princeton University filtered into my life, making me aware of ethnic studies and Asian American history at a very young age. I am therefore grateful to him not only for his foreword but for the early intellectual influence that brought me to work on projects such as this.

I thank the editors and staff of the University Press of Colorado, especially editor Jessica d'Arbonne and series editor Lane Hirabayashi for their support, and readers Greg Robinson and Arthur Hansen for their constructive criticism. Other colleagues who have been encouraging at key moments include Jennifer Ho, Eric Muller, and Gary Okihiro.

Finally, my last and most important tribute must be to Tamae and George Hoshida, whose courage and strength during the incarceration were truly inspiring.

Funding for this work was provided by the University of North Carolina at Chapel Hill's Faculty Partners Grant, R. J. Reynolds Junior Faculty Development Grant, and University Research Council's Small Research Grant.

Introduction

"Please daddy when the war is over do not forget to come for I am waiting [for] you every day," six-year-old June Hoshida wrote to her father George, held at Kilauea Military Camp on the island of Hawai'i. He was on his way to being interned on the mainland during World War II, one man in the mass federal incarceration of approximately 120,000 Japanese Americans.

The incarceration was one of the major domestic events of World War II, an egregious violation of civil rights enabled by a wartime climate of fear and a hostility toward or, at best, a lack of understanding of the Japanese American population that had been fostered by decades of discriminatory legislation against them. Executive Order 9066, signed by President Franklin D. Roosevelt on February 19, 1942, enabled the incarceration, although it did not explicitly outline it. Without trial or any concrete evidence of disloyalty, all Japanese Americans within 100 miles of the West Coast were first subjected to curfew and various restrictions, then incarcerated by the military in temporary assembly camps and, for the duration of the war, in camps away from the military zone. About two-thirds of them were US citizens, a fact often lost in the erroneous political and popular discussion of them as "prisoners of war" or enemy aliens. The other third were immigrants ineligible for citizenship under the laws of the time, which explicitly barred Asians from naturalization.

In the camps, Japanese Americans endured not only the mental and emotional pain of ruptured lives, but physically harsh conditions due to the barren locations and poorly built accommodations. Eventually, the incarcerees themselves and the War Relocation Authority (WRA), the civilian agency that administered the camps for most of the war, made some improvements. Life in the camps was often characterized by the Japanese saying *shikata ganai,* meaning "it cannot be helped," a philosophical attitude that helped the Japanese Americans to make the best of the situation and establish large agricultural operations, hobby classes, sports, and shops to cling to a semblance of normal life. However, there was also unrest, anger, and, on occasion, violence. After the Supreme Court's ruling on the suit *ex parte Mitsuye Endo* in 1944, Japanese Americans who were US citizens gained the right to be released to their homes on a case-by-case approval basis (some had already gone east through the WRA's "resettlement" program), and the camps were permanently closed at the end of the war. Many memoirs, fictional accounts, poetry, and documentary accounts of camp life and the difficult return home have been published. The most famous camp narrative is probably still Jeanne Wakatsuki Houston's 1973 memoir *Farewell to Manzanar,* written with her husband James Houston; it tells the story of her family and their incarceration in Manzanar, the large California camp. It is only recently that accounts of camp life have expanded to include the non-WRA camps run by other divisions, such as the Immigration and Naturalization Services (the Department of Justice) and the military.

Because so few Japanese Americans from Hawai'i were incarcerated, and fewer still in WRA camps, they have not had a loud voice among camp narratives in the past. They were, however, highly represented in the most popular and redemptive narrative of Japanese American patriotism during the war and lasting to the present day. The famed all-Japanese American soldiers of the 442nd Regimental Combat Team and the 100th Battalion, lauded by military comrades and mainstream media, drew almost half of its manpower from Hawai'i, a staggering total of 12,250 men. Originally, the 100th Battalion was drawn exclusively from Hawai'i and fought attached to other divisions before it was eventually permanently merged with the 442nd in Italy. As has been often cited, the 442nd had the highest per capita casualty rate in US military history, lauded by military officials and greeted upon their return by President Harry S. Truman, who said to them, "You fought not only the enemy, but prejudice—and won." The achievements and heroism of the 442nd and 100th have been recorded in journalism, memoir, histories, and even a Hollywood movie, *Go for Broke* (after the 442nd's motto, a Hawaiian pidgin expression). Perhaps the most famous veteran of the 442nd was the long-serving US senator from Hawai'i, Daniel Inouye, who lost an arm serving in Italy. He and his fellow veteran and senator, Spark Matsunaga, were important leaders in the fight for redress and reparations to Japanese American incarcerees in the 1980s. Other Japanese Americans served in the Military Intelligence Service and other, less publicized divisions. However, their political activism, popularity, and the continued honors that these veterans have deservedly received may have accidentally obscured the fates of the incarcerated minority of Japanese Americans from Hawai'i. In this volume, military stories are in the background; the citizen nephews of the Hoshidas write to them, visit them, and support them in every way possible, while George muses on the injustice of the treatment of Japanese American citizens and the need for them to prove that Japanese blood is "good blood"—something he was unable to do because of his alien status.

George and Tamae Hoshida, with three of their four children, were only five of the approximately 2,000 Japanese Americans from Hawai'i incarcerated on the mainland. Those initially arrested were held by the military or Department of Justice's Immigration and Naturalization Services. Their families who followed them into incarceration were sent to the WRA camps because of the citizenship status of the children and some spouses, and their status as voluntary, nonarrested incarcerees. Hawaiian residents have been mentioned relatively little in camp accounts because of the small total number of incarcerees (1 percent of the ethnic Japanese population of Hawai'i). Most Japanese Americans of Hawai'i, due to both the sheer logistical difficulty of incarcerating a third of the population and the more liberal policies of the military leadership there, were not incarcerated. However, they were subject to curfews and other restrictions, as George details, as well as the psychological pressure of propaganda urging them to abandon all Japanese

heritage and the anxiety caused by the removal of most of the heads of the
ethnic community. The increasing numbers of available memoirs and oral
histories tell of the personal tragedies suffered, illuminating the emotional,
psychological, physical, and economic toll of the incarceration in Hawai'i.
In particular, the perspectives of Yasutaro Soga's memoir *Life Behind Barbed
Wire* and the recently released *Family Torn Apart: The Internment Story of the
Otokichi Muin Ozaki Family* (as well as the forthcoming third volume in the
series) can be combined with this volume to offer a fuller picture of the experience of Hawaiian incarcerees. George knew Soga and read the Japanese-
language release of his memoir in the 1950s, which inspired him to return
to his own narrative; he also knew and drew Ozaki in the camps. Some of
George's drawings were published to illustrate some of Soga and Ozaki's
poetry in the collection *Poets Behind Barbed Wire* in 1983. The three men offer
some overlapping accounts of the same events.

The Hoshidas' remarkable narrative gives an intimate account of the
anger, resignation, philosophy, optimism, and love with which they endured
their separation and incarceration. George (a Japanese national, though he
had immigrated at the age of four) was separated from his wife and children
for almost two years after he was arrested in February 1942 and incarcerated
for his Buddhist and judo activities, passing through military and INS camps
at Kilauea, Sand Island, San Antonio, Lordsburg, and Santa Fe before being
paroled to join his family at the WRA camp in Jerome. Tamae, a US citizen
by birth, and their three younger daughters June, Sandra, and baby Carole,
born after George's arrest, followed him into the camps expressly to try to
avoid a lengthy separation; they and other families were also possibly "evacuated" all the more speedily from Hawai'i under the military policy of removing those who were on welfare or otherwise "nonproductive." Families went
in the hope of reuniting, but never expected that it would take almost a year
after their own departure. Because of the lack of specialized facilities in the
camps, Tamae had to leave their disabled eldest daughter Taeko behind in
a nursing home. Tragically, they never saw her again, as she drowned in a
bathtub there in 1944. According to Carole Hoshida Kanada, the lasting grief
made her parents more willing than most to speak openly of the incarceration and wartime. George's affectionate descriptions of Taeko, as well as his
original dedication, show that her memory was one of the chief motives for
his writing project.

This volume compiles an edited version of George's memoir, which includes his wartime diary (written chiefly in English, though he later also practiced his Japanese in it and translated it for the memoir), selected family letters from 1942 and 1943, George's wartime artwork, and official documents for context. His artwork, here collected and published in substantial amounts for the first time, is preserved and exhibited online at the Japanese American National Museum. There have been a few camp narratives told through both art and text, but usually by professional artists such as Miné Okubo, whose art and text formed the first published memoir of the incarceration. Hoshida's admittedly less technically proficient drawings have, however, the advantage of bringing in more unstudied, spontaneous depictions of the incarceration, and his memoir and correspondence are extensive, giving us great insight into the artist's environment and state of mind.

While George did not design all his works to be published together, his art and memoir combine powerfully. He had taken only correspondence courses on drawing and illustration but found this and other hobbies such as woodwork to be crucial sources of comfort in the camps. The style of his art bears testimony to his training through the very popular Federal School in Minneapolis, later called Art Instruction (now Art Instruction Schools). The school's most famous alumnus was Charles Schulz, creator of *Peanuts*, who, as a shy, out-of-place high school senior in 1940, enrolled in the correspondence course as well. For young George, the $10 a month must have represented an even more enormous sacrifice than it did for the hardworking Schulzes; in his more prosperous years before the war, his salary was $100 plus a car allowance each month ($10 covered his rent), but in his teenage years of hard labor it was certainly substantially lower. The magazine ads for Federal School, however, were ideally suited to appeal to an ambitious teenager forced to drop out of school to work; they suggested that "Drawing is a Way to Fortune," a means to find "Your Future." Readers were flattered by assurances of their talent and tempted by the possibility of salaries of as much as $150 a week. The ads appeared in popular magazines among advertisements for facial soaps, piano courses by mail, and etiquette books, a veritable cornucopia of self-improvement.

George enrolled in these and other courses while working at the Kukaiau Ranch (see chapter 8), about 1925. He describes his studies in a passage not included in this edition of the memoir:

During this time Yoshio continued with his studies on the correspondence course in Commercial designing, Illustration and Cartooning, and also that of the Japanese Intermediate Language Course. He sent home for several books on various subjects also in English and Japanese and studied these as much as he had time. Seeing Yoshio so studious, the boss, Mr. Haemura, gave him special considerations and offered him the southeast corner of the barrack. This corner, although the front was open, was partitioned by a wall from the rest of the barrack into a room of about ten feet wide and gave privacy from other occupants.

Yoshio was delighted. He built a study desk out of some scrap lumber which he found around the camp, and a chair out of an apple box to which he attached a back rest and runners on each side of the bottom to stabilize it. He also made a book case to keep his things in order. A private kerosene lamp gave him sufficient illumination to study during the nights. So, while the others spent their time in card games and idle gossips, Yoshio concentrated on his studies.

Both "Commercial designing" and "Illustrating and Cartooning" clearly refer to the Federal School courses of instruction. Describing this in the 1970s, George almost repeats the scenario of the wartime years, in which he sketches incarcerees at play; his time was more often spent writing letters for himself and others, reading, and drawing.

Like Schulz, George used art as an escape in his adolescence and a channel for his dreams of a better future. After George got married and grew busier with his sales career and family responsibilities, these studies drop out of his account but resurface during the war as a means of documentation as well as a way to pass the time. In his diary he even muses about becoming a cartoonist afterward, but never managed it, though he did later design and produce rubber stamps. He requests in a letter to Tamae that his "Federal School" books be sent to the camp to help him teach an art class. These were probably the Divisions 1–12 Modern Illustrating and Cartooning course, authored by famous artists, which took the student from line perspective through the drawing of human beings.

Some stylistic resemblances to *Peanuts* stemming from their common training can be seen in George's few cartoon-like drawings: large round heads, snub noses, and a close attention to the child-like proportions of the body for which Schulz became so famous. (Schulz's own drawings during World

War II, right after his correspondence schooling and before the development of *Peanuts*, show his interest in recording everyday experience during the war, but as cartoons.) But George's drawings had by the war mostly turned away from cartooning to realistic portraiture and landscape drawings, his intense historical interests driving him to document the experience as fully as possible. Jimmy Mirikitani, another young artist of the incarceration whose work was showcased in the documentary *The Cats of Mirikitani*, also used an art correspondence school—quite possibly the same one—and his drawings are similar to George's in the use of line, careful proportion, and strong color contrasts.

George's full-color drawings are beautifully finished and tend to show landscapes or large events rather than individuals. However, the sketches, sometimes hastily done on any available paper, capture bleak moments in the loneliness of the incarceration; they often betray more depression than his writing. While at Lordsburg, he was able to experiment with more advanced techniques such as oil and painting on cloth, though these have not been preserved. George did not at the time intend for these to be published or exhibited (aside from some amateur art shows within the camps), but he did enjoy drawing portraits for camp staff, soldiers, and fellow incarcerees; judging from various episodes, he used portraiture as a means to open communication across a racial barrier with camp administrators, soldiers, and, in one case, African American passengers in the "colored" cars of trains. He saved all of these drawings for himself and his family. Early in the correspondence, he sent several small sketches to his second daughter June, some of which appear here, but censors ruled against allowing any type of drawing in incarcerees' mail late in 1942.

George worked on his memoir over several years in the 1970s, and therefore the first two sections of this volume, on his and Tamae's childhoods and their early married life, were written much later than the wartime section. Notably, the wartime diary often reveals depression or concerns that he hid in cheerful letters to Tamae and June; Tamae often hid worrying situations from him as well. There is a marked contrast in tone between her letters to him describing life in the Jerome camp and her despairing plea for a speedy family reunion, addressed to multiple government officials (see Document 3). Tamae's letters and George's depiction of her experiences offer the point of view of a Japanese American wife and mother, quite rare among incarceration memoirs.

The memoir and letters are all the more remarkable considering that George had only an eighth-grade education and Tamae a fourth-grade education; Tamae was not fond of writing, and her earlier letters were occasionally written for her by her brother or nephew. Their correspondence also had to contend with censorship and significant time delays due to censoring and transportation difficulties; they often had to use their available letter quota (George was limited to two a week while at Lordsburg) to cover business details, including what to do with their Hawai'i home, small expenditures for necessities or hobby items, and their ongoing petitions for reunion. Tamae's exit clearance records reveal that officials were not simply censoring but reading and recording some of the content of their personal letters, noting favorably her stance against "repatriation" to Japan. (This government offer to send Japanese Americans to Japan, rather than keeping them in camp for a war of unknown duration, briefly tempted George, who saw little or no opportunity in a country that would arrest and imprison him. Tamae, who had never been to Japan, was resolutely opposed to the idea.)

George's early memories of immigration and his detailed description of the housing and working conditions of canefield workers illuminate the largely unrecorded experiences of Asian migrant laborers. The day-to-day detail, only part of which is reprinted here, is highly informative, but also notable is how swiftly his narrative moves from a small boy's confrontation with racial and linguistic difference for the first time to an almost matter-of-fact depiction of class and social separation of the races. Also not included are some formative personal episodes from George's childhood and adolescence in which he accidentally injured schoolmates and learned a deep caution and respect for others' physical health and safety, a concern that shows in his narration of his wife and daughter's severe injuries in a car accident and that arises again during the war when he cares for fellow incarceree Kinzaemon Odachi. His accounts of the canefield workers' camps eerily echo his own adult encounter with roughly built makeshift housing in the incarceration camps, while his meeting with a father who had left Japan before he was born is also repeated when George meets his youngest daughter, Carole, for the first time in Jerome when she is a year old.

George's story of Tamae's early life is slightly less detailed; here, the personal dominates, as Tamae's early injury and deformed hip shaped her career choices and her whole life, but it offers some details about the Hawaiian social structure of that time and the career options of young Japanese American women. Her struggles when left behind in Hawai'i and then on her own in the Jerome incarceration camp with three small children were, as George notes, much more difficult to endure than his, and are still a source of admiration to her children and grandchildren. Tamae's narrative provides details of the crushing labor of everyday life in the camps, from washing and drying diapers by hand in a damp climate to keeping the wood stove supplied and stoked. The plight of the single mother in the incarceration was rarely told from her own perspective, though glimpses of it appear in famous memoirs such as *Farewell to Manzanar*. Tamae's strength is evident in every line of her carefully composed letters, and never more so than when she resolutely opposed George's fleeting consideration of repatriation to Japan. Her determination to keep the family together and return to Hawai'i never wavered.

Adding to the Hoshidas' own records of their time in camp, government documents that show the official perspective on the Hoshidas, found in the National Archives and the University of Hawai'i archives, are reprinted here, including George's original detention hearing, Colonel Karl Bendetsen's memo on the Hawaiian transport that took Tamae and the children to Arkansas, and the responses to their petition letters. In particular, the military memorandum on George's judo club, the Butoku kai, defines it as a deeply dangerous military society. His membership almost certainly led to his indefinite incarceration as the argument over it during his hearing shows. While the Hoshida children had always heard the family story that George's argument with one of the judges (reproduced here in the appended hearing transcript) probably sent him into the camps, the negative report of the anonymous "informant" included in the hearing materials and the Butoku kai memo show that he had little or no chance of release, regardless. Another negative perspective on the incarcerees is the WRA report on the Hawaiians in Jerome; feeling more singled out, the Japanese Americans from Hawai'i were apparently a troublesome population for the WRA and were viewed as disloyal and pro-Japanese, though Tamae does not record any such sentiments.

Many memoirs of the incarceration, particularly those published quite soon after the war, such as Monica Sone's *Nisei Daughter* (1953), offer forced endings of reconciliation between Japaneseness and Americanness, sometimes smacking of an outright forgiveness or justification of the incarceration.

FIGURE 0.1. A photograph of the family during difficult times after their return. Pictured left to right are June, Sandra, and Carole with George at China Hill. This photo was taken several days after the April 1, 1946, tidal wave. Since their water supply had been cut off, they had gone up the hill to find a place to wash.

FIGURE O.2. This studio portrait was taken around 1962, when the family was living in Los Angeles. From left to right: Carole, Sandra, June, Tamae, and George.

George's memoir, however, offers no such easy resolution; throughout the memoir, he does not hesitate to critique the United States for its hypocrisy in the treatment of racial minorities and, even at the very end, he fears for his family's uncertain future which has been so damaged by their wartime incarceration. The resolution that he finds is a unique one, optimistic like other camp narratives but drawn from his Buddhist beliefs, so denigrated during the rush to Americanize during the war, and the support of loved ones. For this reason, I judged it best to let his own words close his memoir, rather than adding a traditional editorial afterword.

After the war the Hoshidas struggled to rebuild their finances in Hawai'i, since they had had to sell their house and possessions at a loss and had spent a substantial amount of their savings in camp. They stayed in a commercial college, with Tamae's sister, and finally at a Naval Air Station before finding suitable housing.

George could not get his job at Hilo Electric back, and repaired appliances from his sister-in-law's home for a while before he eventually took a sales position at Moses Company. Tamae worked as a seamstress from home, in a garment factory, and for a dry goods store. In 1959 George and Tamae moved to Los Angeles, where June was already living; Carole finished high school there while Sandra remained behind to attend the University of Hawai'i. Tamae worked in the Frolic Times garment factory, while George sold appliances for another hardware store and then became a clerk and occasional translator for the Los Angeles Traffic Court. George continued to be very active in the Buddhist church and created Sunday School curricula for the church in Gardena that were later used in many churches in Hawai'i.

Tamae passed away in May 1970, and in 1973 Carole and George returned to Hawai'i, Carole to live on Maui with her husband and George to Pearl City to live with Sandra. George participated in a few media features, art exhibits, and the University of Hawai'i's oral history project in the 1980s, and worked on his memoir for many years. He remarried in 1977 and lived on Oahu until his death in 1985, having always retained his firm conviction that the story of the incarceration needed to be told. In the introduction to his original volume, George wrote that he hoped to leave a record of his life to his descendants and also "mark [his] footprints on the sands of time." Fortunately, his entire family's story can now find a wide audience for the first time.

HEIDI KATHLEEN KIM
University of North Carolina at Chapel Hill

Editorial Notes

I have attempted to preserve George and Tamae's own writing in order to reflect their backgrounds and linguistic patterns, silently correcting some spelling and grammar errors for the sake of clarity (more aggressively in the memoir) but leaving the rest. More significant changes or additions have been marked with square brackets [ ]. It is important to note that the Hoshidas employ the terminology of the 1940s, using terms such as "relocation center," "internee," or "evacuation" in talking about the incarceration, and I have left this for the sake of historical accuracy. Also, George refers to himself in the third person as Yoshio, his original Japanese name, although he was using George commonly (as evidenced in the official documentation and his letter headings). Why exactly he does this is unclear, though it may be to underscore the fact that he officially adopted George as a name when he naturalized as a citizen after the war. He wrote in third person, he explains in his original introduction, because he felt that he "could be more objective in describing [his] actions, especially in some intimate scenes."

Unfortunately, for reasons of space, many interesting episodes, particularly from the Hoshidas' prewar lives in Hawai'i, have had to be excised; also, only selected letters are included here. (While not every letter was preserved, a large number of them, as well as George's artwork and a copy of the original memoir, are available for viewing at the Japanese American National Museum.) I have sought to preserve the most important aspects of their incarceration experience: concern for the children, George's care of Kinzaemon Odachi, the debate over petitioning for family reunion, and the general tenor of day-to-day life in the camps. George's memoir writing was somewhat repetitive and often also recapitulated the letters he had received, so I have cut large passages, paragraphs, and sometimes sentences within paragraphs to create a more readable narrative. Large cuts are marked by section dividers. I have also cut the letter headings except when they move to new camps. The censor's cuts in the letters are indicated by the bracketed word [CENSORED].

On a few occasions, I have inserted some explanatory sentences to bridge cuts that I made or to recount a particularly interesting recollection that one of the Hoshida daughters provided from their family stories; these are indicated in curly brackets: { }.

George's title for his memoir was *Life of a Japanese Immigrant Boy in Hawaii & America: From Birth thru WWII, 1907–1945.* (He contemplated a second volume.) The title I have given this collected edition actually takes a phrase from one of Tamae's letters, the "Paradise Isle." I wanted a title that encompassed both of their experiences and focused on Hawai'i, where part of this narrative takes place and for which they both had such a deep affection, but also referred to the incarceration, which is the topic of the bulk of the volume.

Note from the original memoir (unedited):

APOLOGIES AND REQUESTS

This book is a direct reproduction of the original manuscript and lacks the polish and refinement of regularly published book. Due to my failing health problem, I had to do these copies for private distribution before anything can happen to prevent my doing so. Therefore, although I had gone through the manuscript several times for corrections and revisions, I found more defects each time I went through it.

I should have someone to proof-read this but fearing that it would delay my having these reproductions done in time, I had not done so. Therefore, I believe that you will find numerous defects in these copies. However, since sometimes editing by others may change the true original meaning of the narration, this manuscript, no matter how poor it may be, should convey my true thoughts and sentiments. In this sense, I would like to apologize to you for the errors and request that you take a pen in your hand as you go through this manuscript and do your own corrections for the sake of future readers. Thank you.

GEORGE Y. HOSHIDA

Taken from the Paradise Isle

CHAPTER ONE

Departure to Hawaii

It was the summer of the year 1912. The sky was blue and the sea calm as the *Siberia Maru* plowed southeast toward its destination. The ship had left the port of Kobe five days earlier with many immigrant laborers, together with some women and children, bound for the sugarcane fields of Hawaii.

In the third class hold of the ship was Eno with two children—both of them boys—one around 11 or 12 and the younger one about four. The strain of the trip in the stuffy hold could be seen on both the mother and the younger son. The air was foul—smelling of cooked food and cheap coffee from the nearby ship's kitchen. Sitting at the foot of their cots on the floor, Eno listened to the murmuring talks of these men and women and thought of her husband who had preceded them to Hawaii before Yoshio was born—about 5 years ago. He had been sending some small amount of money once in a while but it wasn't enough to sustain them, and she had to work hard and long to keep her family of five going. He had seldom written, since he had no schooling, and could barely sign his name. When he did, it was written by someone whom he must have asked to do the favor. She too couldn't read nor write

DOI: 10.5876/9781607323440.c001

and had to run to a neighbor who could read. It wasn't clear, therefore, how he was getting along but it seemed that he wasn't doing too well. He had written some time ago that he had lost hope of being able to return in any near future and thought it would be better if the family would come over so that they both could work together and try for that elusive fortune.

Then a few months ago money came for the passage, but it wasn't enough for the whole family of four children and herself to go. Matsuo was the eldest, and the second child, Matsuye, was the only girl in the family. The third child, Masao, was seven. Yoshio was the youngest and father had left for Hawaii when she was still pregnant with him. It was a very difficult and heart-rending decision. But she finally decided to take the eldest since he would be taking over the name of Hoshida and also be of some help in Hawaii within a few years when he could start work. Then she couldn't possibly leave the baby of the family behind, Yoshio had to be taken along too. Fortunately her younger sister offered to take Matsuye, and Eno's husband's younger brother was to move into the house and the farm with his family on condition that he take care of Masao. So it was finally settled. Getting the necessary papers and having health check-ups and immunizations were troublesome, but Eno finally got through them.

It was dawn when word came that they had sighted more land. There was a small island in the bay, and Yoshio learned that it was Sand Island. The ship rounded the farther side of this little island and went into the harbor lined with some buildings built into the sea. People said this was the City of Honolulu where they were to leave ship and go on land at last.

They were all ready when the ship docked. But strange men came on board to check the passengers before they were finally allowed to get off the ship. Yoshio remembered being herded into a huge building. It had a large hall with benches placed around the walls where immigrants sat. The people were strange—some had brown hairs, fair skin and high narrow noses, while others had heavy features with dark brown skin. There were others who looked like their country people but they wore long, woven hair behind their backs and had dark jackets and long, loose pants made of thin materials. Mother said they were Chinese, and they spoke in high-pitched voices. Yoshio learned that the fair skinned men with brown hairs were called "haole" while the brown heavy-set people were called "kanaka." Everything was different here and Yoshio was uneasy.[1]

Then after sleeping there for one night and everybody was sitting on the benches the next morning, a man came in to call names. When the name Eno Hoshida was called, mother stood up and she called at Matsuo who was running around the large hall with some other children. Together they followed the man to a small room. A strange Japanese man was sitting on the other side. He was dark-skinned, slim and tall, and he smiled at them when they came in and sat. Mother smiled and bowed at him and called out "Otosan!" (Father). The man walked over to Matsuo first and said, "You must be Matsuo but you certainly have grown; do you remember me?"

Matsuo smiled shyly and replied, "Yes, I remember you, Otosan." Father then put his arms around Matsuo and hugged him.

"This is Yoshio. Yoshio, go to your father," said mother and pushed Yoshio toward the man.

Mother had spoken about father and had shown him his picture when at home, but he felt confused and shy at seeing this strange man standing before him. He clung to mother's hands and refused to let go. Then the man came and lifted Yoshio up and hugged him tightly. Yoshio struggled for a moment but when he realized that he couldn't budge, he hid his face against the man's shoulder and shut his eyes. Then he felt warm and comfortable. So this was father; he sure was strong!

NOTE

1. Haole is a native Hawaiian word meaning foreigner, and generally applied to white residents. Kanaka indicates native Hawaiians.

CHAPTER TWO

Hawaii Their Destination

(Family Journeys to the Big Island)

Piihonua [on the slope of Mauna Loa] had three or four camps which were originally built and owned by the Wainaku Sugar Plantation to which these two districts were affiliated. However, they were later sold to individual cane planters or leased to them so that people now living in these camps were mainly independent cane planters although, like our father, some were not fortunate enough to be able to buy their own and hired out as laborers to the cane planters. All of these people had come with the single purpose of making a small fortune and returning to their mother country to lead a life of ease.

Life as a plantation laborer wasn't easy. The camp houses where father lived were built of 1 × 12 rough pine boards on stilts and white-washed with lime. They usually were long bungalows with an open porch running the length of the barrack. They were partitioned with small rooms where two or three laborers slept together. Beds were built of rough lumber and thin grass-filled mattresses. The cracks between the wall boards were covered by slats on the outside but the floor boards had shrunk to expose wide cracks between them. Wind blowing through them made even the mild winter quite chilly and miserable. The camp was divided into sections with a community kitchen in each section with cooks who took care of their meals and lunches. The camp mainly consisted of single men, but for the few who had wives or families with children, larger individual bungalows with small kitchens were provided. But they too had to use the community bath house and laundry facilities.

Working conditions were cruel with lunas[1] who kept watch on the laborers, treating them like animals or slaves. Some of them carried whips and did not hesitate to use them on ones who were slow. These Oriental workers—including Chinese, Koreans, and later Filipinos—were used to hard lives at their homelands and persevered well, but sometimes when their patience was stretched too thinly, they rebelled. But punishments were swift and they found themselves penalized further with more strenuous work or stricter supervision. When they were sick and failed to report to work, the lunas would check up on them and, suspecting false pretenses, force them to get up from their beds to labor in the fields until they collapsed.

However, at the end of their contracts, they were free to do what they wished. Some returned to their homeland with savings which they had somehow accumulated, while others turned to farming on their own. Still other enterprising ones started some businesses of their own and laid the foundation for a successful future for themselves and their offsprings. But Father, with his taste for cheap sake[2] and occasional gambling—although he never admitted to them—was constantly in debt for aside from the debts he had incurred during the years he was here, he had borrowed money from some of his friends to send for his family.

When they topped the hill, they came upon a relatively level stretch with several houses visible beyond the cane fields which ended within a few hundred feet. This was Kaumana Five Miles where their home was to be. Father said there were many Portuguese families in Kaumana, especially in the lower section where they just passed, but very few Puerto Ricans. There were others who were Korean and Chinese, but they too were very few. The greater majority of people were Japanese, mainly from Hiroshima, Yamaguchi and their Kumamoto Prefecture. They came to a stop a few hundred feet from the main road in front of a small old shack to the left of the road. The shack looked more like a store house than a home. But father said that this was their home.

Mother showed her disappointment but quickly changed her expression and gave a sigh of relief, apparently because their long journey had come to an end. Father opened the door and carried the baggage into the house. The room was just a bare one with a floor covered with old Japanese reed mats. Some futon (cotton-filled comforters and mattresses) were piled in one corner and few clothing belonging to father hung on some nails on the wall. One long 1 × 12 board served as a shelf where some articles were placed. A small rectangular table with short legs completed the furnishings of the house.

Days went into months and a couple of years passed while the family settled into the routine of this new life. Things improved somewhat for the family, and they were able to move into a better house. Then came another addition to the family. It was a little brother to Yoshio, and they named him Takeo. Mother had to quit work for a while and care for the baby.

Notes

1. Lunas were plantation foremen, often though not always of European ethnicities. Reports of ill treatment were frequent. (Takaki, *Pau Hana*, 74–75, 77.)

2. An alcoholic beverage made by fermenting rice. However, the word used in a Japanese context may also refer more generally to any alcohol.

CHAPTER THREE

Father Becomes a Sugar Cane Planter

Three more years passed and the family moved to another house to the north side of the village by the edge of a cane field. This third family home was built high on stilts and even adults could walk under it and mother could hang the laundered clothes. There were two rooms and a kitchen here, with a large water tank behind the house which supplied enough water even for bathing.

About this time Father finally was able to purchase about five acres of virgin forest land. A footpath through the cane fields led to this land at the edge of the cultivated cane fields. But the land was a jungle covered by many species of tropical trees, shrubs, ferns, and other undergrowth. To open up this virgin jungle and cultivate it into cane fields was not an easy task. With a family to feed, Father had to keep working for others to earn money and it was only during the weekends that he was able to work on this land. It took two years before the crop could be harvested, and the whole family worked hard any spare time they had to take tender care of the growing cane. Usually fields which were old produced between 30 to 40 tons an acre, but their harvest produced about 60 tons, due chiefly to the rich virgin soil and also the

DOI: 10.5876/9781607323440.c003

loving care they gave all through the two years. So when father went down to the plantation office to receive payment for the crop, he received more pay than he expected even after clearing the debt he owed the company for all the expenses of growing and harvesting the cane. He brought back enough money to pay off much of their debt and then more to purchase some necessities and even some luxuries. Also, since Matsuo was working full time and could help out with the family budget, things started to look up.

CHAPTER FOUR

Boyhood Days in the Country

When Yoshio's family moved into their second home, Yoshio started to acquire some friends among the boys near his age. As they grew up together, they sought adventures Tom Sawyer and Huck Finn style. Silent movies were coming out about that time and cowboy and Indian pictures were their favorites. They made pistols out of wood and road [*sic*] horses of sticks. They galloped around over the lava rocks, hiding among the bushes and attacking each other with loud "Bang! Bang." They had great fun. Japanese Samurai movies were also shown at the large frame building owned by Mr. Yamanouchi, their schoolmaster. They copied the samurais also and made swords out of guava sticks, and they battled with each other with the sticks when they got tired of playing cowboy and Indian.

There were special celebrations on holidays during the year. First came New Year when everybody laid off work for at least two or three days and celebrated it to pray for good fortune during the year. Every house, following the custom from Japan, decorated their doorways with branches of pine, bamboo, and peach (called "Sho-chiku-bai"). Since there was no plum here,

DOI: 10.5876/9781607323440.c004

they used peach which looked the nearest to plum. Japanese emperor's birthday was one of the important holidays celebrated by the Japanese nationals. It was called "Tenchosetsu" and all the people of the village gathered at the Japanese school to begin with a ceremonial service. In the evening there were entertainment programs on the outdoor stage. Traditional Japanese dance called "No" was danced. One year Yoshio participated with a sword dance called "kenbu."

During this time great changes were taking place in America and some horseless carriages called automobiles started to appear downtown. There came a day when one of them chugged up the road to their village, scaring the wits out of the horses. Then men came from the light company for application to install electric lights. Some were hesitant about installing them since the cost might be too high for them, but finally most of them agreed to take them. Electric poles with wirings were installed along the streets and lead lines pulled to each house. When at last the current was switched on and the lamps lighted, it was like daylight come back into the dark night. A new era had come to this country village.

Yoshio started school a couple of years after arriving from Japan. Matsuo took him to school and registered him both in the Japanese and English schools. He came to like school after he got used to it. As he advanced through the grades, he found himself having fun reading story books outside of school, especially the Japanese fairy tales which brother Matsuo bought from the store for 5 cents each. While reading these books of tales, he found himself living in a world of fantasy and it sometimes led him to look for some magic events to take place in his real life.

Besides math, Yoshio enjoyed science, drawing, and writing. He was therefore able to maintain "A" grades quite consistently in classes. He joined a literary club during his 9th year and received recognition for writing quite well when he handed in a composition assignment from the club. Unfortunately, Yoshio's school[ing] ended after his graduation from the Junior High School. A letter arrived from Matsuo with sad news that he had fallen ill with rheumatoid arthritis. He continued to work in the hospital the best he could while receiving treatment, but the illness became so bad as to disable him completely. So it was that when Yoshio graduated from junior high school, his parents asked him to quit school and start working in order to help out with the family finances. It really was a sad day for Yoshio since he very much liked school and study and had set his mind on getting a proper education so that he could be somebody in the world. But now this hope was completely shattered and he could only see a dark hopeless future ahead of him.

CHAPTER FIVE

End of Schooling and Start of Work

Yoshio had been reading about many great men in the past who had attained success in spite of all their adversities. Abraham Lincoln hardly had any schooling, but he had set his mind and heart to educating himself. One quotation which struck Yoshio's heart deeply was: "I will study hard now so that when opportunity comes knocking, I will be ready!" Yoshio decided that even though he may not attain even a fraction of what Abe Lincoln did, he should be able to grasp better opportunities if he could prepare himself for them. Yoshio's enthusiasm for self-improvement continued throughout his later life. He went through numerous correspondence courses, night schools, seminars, and other special training programs. Looking back at half a century of struggle with many experiences, his not being able to have proper schooling may have been a blessing in disguise, for it gave him incentive to keep on studying throughout his whole life.

On the side of physical culture, Yoshio didn't care much about ordinary sports except basketball, in which he participated for couple of years during his adolescence. But "Shinyukai," a judo club in Hilo town, came up to

DOI: 10.5876/9781607323440.c005

promote judo among the young people of Kaumana. Yoshio received the third kyu and later, when he moved downtown to work there, he continued attending practices at the Shinyu Kai Dojo.

This perseverance led him ultimately into the attainment of higher rank to fourth class of black belt and enabled him to participate in the promotion and teaching of this art to many of the second and third generation youths. However, it became one of the reasons for being interned during World War II and sharing some of the sufferings which millions of people experienced.[1]

About a month after the first group of workers left Kaumana [for Kukaiau Ranch], the foremen for the contractor came back to recruit more workers. He brought word from Yoshio's parents for Yoshio to enlist and join them at the ranch construction site. While attending junior high school, Yoshio continuously used the facilities of the public library. In fiction he especially adored Zane Grey's western novels. When he read these books, he was so absorbed in them that during nights he would forget the time and keep awake in bed until he could finish them. The deserts, the canyons, buffalos, cowboys, rustlers, together with all the natural beauty and excitements of the wild western life was [as] real to him as if he had experienced them himself. This ranch, therefore, with its natural beauty and wide open range and western atmosphere, felt so familiar and intimate that he had the sensation of having lived it in his past life his heart melted into its warm embrace completely.

Since Yoshio had developed his body and muscles through the hard labor at construction work, instead of just going into cutting cane work, he decided to try out with "Happaiko" (packing cane bundles to the flume). After working on this for some time, the foreman requested him to go into sled packing. Yoshio went through this work somehow for the first day, but on the second day he suddenly felt his back give with a sharp pain and found himself unable even to stand. This going on and off the job continued for some time until Yoshio realized that he was no longer suited for hard labor. He, therefore, started to think about other occupations which would be more suitable for him.[2]

Yoshio found a position as a clerk at a store downtown called the Tanimoto Variety Store. Another young man started working also after Yoshio was there for a few months. His name was the same as Yoshio's but spelled "Yoshiwo." They hit together very well and soon became fast friends and, in fact, their friendship lasted for their lifetime. His parents and elder brother were devout members of the Hilo Hongwanji Mission, the foremost local Buddhist Temple, and it was he that induced Yoshio to attend and join the Young Men Buddhist Association. This also was one of the most important seeds which ripened into a most meaningful spiritual life to guide Yoshio through the turmoils of his whole life.

Yoshio [became] specialty salesman on various items for about 2 years until the local utility firm, The Hilo Electric and Gas Company, took notice of his sales activities and offered him a position as a regular appliance salesman. Yoshio was offered a salary of a hundred dollars a month plus 5% commission over the quota of a thousand dollars in sales. Thus started a regular selling career which was to continue for about eleven years until the start of World War II.

NOTES

1. See appendix C.
2. George's unedited memoir describes his experience at Kukaiau Ranch in detail, from the journey there to the details of plantation work. Kukaiau was (and is) a large, beautiful ranch on the slopes of Mauna Kea, with sea views of Maui that George loved. He did construction/road work with his father and occasionally worked in the fields. Hapaiko was the native term for carrying cane on the back and/or loading it onto train cars, a difficult and essential part of the all-important sugar industry. Here George refers more particularly to loading the cut and bundled sugarcane into the flumes so that it could be more easily transported down to the mill. In another narrative, a plantation laborer reminisced, "With my bare hands I helped build Hawai'i. . . I cut cane, I hapaiko, carried cane and watered sugarcane." (Felipe, *Hawai'i*, Kindle ed., Kindle locations 108–9.)

CHAPTER SIX

YBA Convention and Trip to Kauai

An orchestra was organized by Mr. Susami Yamasjita, a regular member of the county band. Yoshio had picked up violin playing to amuse himself while in his teens. He decided to join the orchestra. The orchestra consisted of about thirty members, and they practiced twice a week. When they became good enough to carry their parts, they gave performances at the church and eventually at other churches around the island. The ultimate glory came when they were invited to an interisland convention of the united Young Buddhist Associations (YBAs) of all main islands at Kauai in 1931.

However, when the time for departure arrived, one of the only two female members of the orchestra was not able to make the trip and left Teruko, the pianist, as the only female member to make the trip. Her parents, therefore, were reluctant to have her go. But this was solved when Tamae, Teruko's aunt who was only a few years older than her, was available and willing to go as chaperone. Yoshio was quite intimate with both families through his business dealing with them, and they were very happy to have Tamae go when Yoshio approached them for their consent.

DOI: 10.5876/9781607323440.c006

As the ship left the protection of the breakwater, the sea became choppy and rough. After a while, the rolling settled down into a steady rhythm. Yoshio walked to the railing and looked toward the shore and the dark outline of the peaks of Mauna Kea.

Yoshio felt the presence of someone approaching behind him. He turned around and saw Tamae.

"Tamae! I thought you were still sleeping. How are you feeling now?"

"Oh, I feel all right now but it was terrible a while back. I almost threw up but managed to hold back. I'm feeling better now, but how are you?"

"I got sick too and fed the fishes. But I'm fine now. Sure was rough!"

"What place are we passing now?" Tamae inquired as she came to the railing and looked at the twinkling lights on the dark shoreline. The moon, almost full, had risen behind them by this time. Tamae's face glowed softly in the moonlight. She was pretty and so sweet and gentle! She only came up to his shoulder beside him and he could feel her body warmth! What was she saying. . . Oh! the place.

"Ah. . . I think that cluster of lights going down to the shoreline must be Pauuilo. It's a nice country town. Hope I can visit it again someday."

Yoshio had known Tamae for almost four years, ever since he joined the YBA. She had a dressmaking shop in front of their Buddhist Temple at Kilauea Street in partnership with a close friend by the name of Masayo. Yoshio went to her shop at times between his sales calls and became very friendly with both of them. This most memorable voyage was to bring about great changes into the lives of Yoshio and Tamae.

CHAPTER SEVEN

Dawn of Romance and Marriage

Yoshio dated Tamae a few times and took her to shows, but always together with her niece Toshiko. Then, a couple of months later when Yoshio dropped in, her mother said that she had been hospitalized. It seemed that her pleurisy had become active again. Yoshio visited her whenever he had some time between his sales calls and brought her some magazines to read and other things to cheer her up. They had opportunities for more intimate talks, and Yoshio learned much about the turbulent life she had led from her early age.

Tamae's parents came to the islands a few years before the turn of the century from the Yamaguchi Prefecture in Japan and, like other immigrants, were contract laborers. Four children were born to them—first son, Riichi, second daughter Yoshino, then Kanemasa and Tamae the last. Tamae was born at the outskirts of Hilo at a camp belonging to the Waiakea Plantation on July 18, 1908—[not quite] a year after Yoshio's birthday of October 23, 1907. Her mother, Yumi, named her Tamae, which meant "a pearl child," since she was such a pretty adorable baby with a round face and clear pearly skin. She was born normal and healthy, but when she was three years old her father

DOI: 10.5876/9781607323440.c007

slipped down the front steps with her on his back and caused dislocation of her left hip joint. However, they didn't suspect this injury. [It was] only after several months, when she continued complaining and limped when walking, that they felt the need for a check-up and took her downtown to a doctor. He cut open the hip and found it festering inside. He cleaned it the best he could and had Tamae at the hospital for a period until the wound healed to some extent. There was nothing they could do to alleviate this condition, and Tamae suffered for many more years thereafter.

The family, in the meantime, purchased cane land at Papaikou Plantation and moved to an old [clapboard]¹ house which came with the farm at a place called Pueopako. Then one day a most tragic accident happened and plunged the family into turmoil. Tamae's father had gone to work in the field behind their home near the gulch. The family was worried about his lateness and were about to go out in search for him when they heard the splashing of water at the rain barrel behind the house. When they went out to look, they were horrified to find him naked except for his shorts and in terrible shape. From his condition they could see that he must have fallen into the gulch and then managed to struggle up the steep slope on hands and knees, and in the process must have torn off his clothing.

The doctor came over shortly and, after checking on him, said that he seemed to have a slight case of brain hemorrhage affecting his speech. He remained in bed for about three months and, although he seemed to improve at times, he gradually weakened until he lapsed into a coma. His heart finally failed but the passing was very peaceful. He was in his early sixties when he went.

A year after he passed away, a public nurse came to see Tamae and informed the family that there was a hospital opening soon at Honolulu by the Shriners, which was going to take care of such crippling cases as hers. It was free to needy people so that they need not worry about finances. Tamae's application was approved as one of the first cases to be taken up. When the time arrived, the nurse came for her, and Tamae was taken over to Honolulu.

It was such a drastic operation that the sight of the incision caused a nurse to faint. The hip joint of the left leg which fitted into the socket had completely rotted through with tubercular infection. The doctor did a thorough job of removing all the infected parts. It took about another six months after the operation before Tamae could return home. However, since Tamae's hip joint was completely removed and her leg was attached rigidly to the hip bone, she of course could not bend her leg at the hip. Also, her leg itself was about two inches shorter than the right leg, and she had to be fitted with an orthopedic shoe. But she could walk without the conspicuous limp she had previously. It was heavenly to be able to go around without being very conspicuous.

She continued going to school, but since she had missed so much time with these health problems, she had a very difficult time to keep up with her lessons. So when she reached the compulsory age of fifteen and got through the fifth grade, her sister Yoshino advised her that it would be better for her to take up sewing. Tamae was able to attend the sewing school for several years until she became proficient enough to open her own sewing shop in partnership with Masayo. They continued until Tamae was laid down with her first attack of pleurisy.

It was one of the characteristics of Japanese people that they, unlike the westerners, were very reticent about expressing their emotions openly. So, although Yoshio very much [would have] liked to hold Tamae in his arms and ask her for her lips, he never dared to put it into action.

However, as time passed and he felt secure of Tamae's affection toward him, he started to build enough confidence in himself to think about showing his affection more openly. Finally, he resolved to have it come true when they went to the Intermediate School Band Concert. Instead of driving home, he drove to the left, up toward his old home village of Kaumana. The hill nearest toward town was called Halai Hill. This was a favorite spot for lovers. Yoshio had driven up here several times with his friends and at times spotted couples necking, but this was the first time that he had ever taken a girl here himself.

He had seen scenes of marriage proposals in the movies and read about them in novels, but when faced with it himself, he was completely lost and didn't know how to proceed. They sat there talking about the beauty of the town lights, but finally they found themselves out of subjects to talk about and fell silent. His heart thumped wildly and he felt tension mount as they sat in an awkward silence. Finally, he could hold it no longer and, extending his arm over her shoulders, he held her nervously and blurted out, "Give me a kiss!" Tamae was silent but when Yoshio pulled her to him, she came without any resistance. Yoshio leaned over her and their lips met tenderly for the first time in consummation of a sacred vow of everlasting love and affection. When they finally separated from their close embrace and sat closely together, Tamae broke the silence and queried softly, "You aren't just playing with me, are you?"

"Of course not!" Yoshio answered passionately, "I love you and I want to marry you!"

The words were not a question but a statement, and there was no need of their confirmation, for they knew in their hearts that their kiss was the seal of their solemn vow. As Yoshio sat there with Tamae enfolded in his arms, he dreamed of the future with her. He pictured in his mind a pretty little cottage—one like those down there in the tract. It really would be heavenly, and they would be happy together no matter what came.

When the following year came around, they felt that they were in position to look forward to marriage, and they decided to set a date for the wedding. They went through the formal proceedings of requesting the hand of Tamae for Yoshio and then had exchanges of regular wedding presents, called Yuino, according to customs. The wedding date was set at April 23rd [1933].

Then there was the problem of living quarters for the new couple. They decided to go through the wedding first and then consider the problem of housing later. A very simple ceremony, with only the family members and close relatives in attendance, was performed at their temple and Rev. Teramoto officiated. Yoshio took Tamae home just as a gesture of their marriage, but having no sleeping quarters, not having enough to finance a honeymoon, they drove off to the beach at the Coconut Island[2] and spent an hour looking at the moon and dreaming of the day they could be together as man and wife in their own home.

Yoshio and Tamae started house hunting and, luckily, they were able to locate a newly built one-bedroom cottage in the southern section of town. It was quite difficult to manage with Yoshio's meager income, but they manipulated somehow and were happy as could be with their new life.

Time flew fast for them, and on the 30th of January of the following year, their first child arrived. It was a girl. After the baby was washed and wrapped, Tamae's mother brought her out in a blanket to show her to Yoshio. He took her gingerly as she gave her into his arms to hold for the first time. What a precious little thing it was with a small wrinkled red face and tiny little hands and fingers! She was so light, but Yoshio was afraid he might drop her. They named the baby Taeko, which meant "an exquisite child."

When Taeko was around two months old, they moved into an apartment next to Tamae's brother's home. There was a grocery store across the street at the corner, and their temple was only about a couple of blocks away. Also, with Tamae's mother nearby, she could come whenever needed to baby-sit and help out with extra housework. [Tamae's] Brother Riichi and other members of the family came over or took Taeko out to their home to play with her too. They were very happy there and it appeared that things were going to work out real fine.

NOTES

1. "Chapboard" in original text.
2. A small island on the east side of Hilo Bay.

CHAPTER EIGHT

Tragedy and Awakening to Reality

There is a quote in Japanese which says, "Tsuki ni murakumo, Hanani kaze," which translated means, "There's black clouds for the moon and stormy wind to the cherry blossoms." This indicates the cruel reality of life.

It was late afternoon on May 1, 1934, exactly three months after Taeko was born. Tamae was sitting by Yoshio's side in the front seat of their Model T Ford with Taeko on her lap as they drove down Kilauea Avenue to their new home. As they neared the lane leading into their driveway, Yoshio made a left turn signal and proceeded to make the turn when it happened!

With a splintering crash, a speeding sampan bus, driven by a young Portuguese boy, rammed into the rear of Yoshio's flimsy car! Yoshio's car spun around with the tremendous impact and crashed on the pavement upside down! As they went down, Yoshio heard Tamae scream, and he caught a glimpse of her and the baby hurtling out of the car!

Yoshio was stunned momentarily but when he regained his senses, he could see an opening in front of him through the windshield frame and he crawled out of the capsized car to safety. He looked around frantically for his

DOI: 10.5876/9781607323440.c008

wife and the baby; he caught sight of Taeko first, about thirty feet away on the middle of the street, her tiny hands pawing the air silently. He then found Tamae doubled up at the corner of the curbing. It was like a horrible nightmare and although his heart and mind raced toward them, his body seemed frozen to the spot [where] he was standing.

{Both Taeko and Tamae were found to have skull fractures at the hospital, and lay unconscious for several days. Tamae woke up after three days and recovered well.}

But Taeko didn't seem to get back to her old self and laid there in her crib without much movement. She had been giggling and laughing out loud before the accident when they took her in their arms and played with her. But now she lay blankly staring into space and didn't seem to recognize them or her environment. The doctor checked her carefully and shook his head saying, "I'm afraid you are right. You can try brain surgery but there is no doctor here who can do it. Even if it is done, I am afraid there's slim chance of her getting her eyesight back."

Added to their misery was the problem of finances. Franklin D. Roosevelt had taken over the country's reign a couple of years ago, but depression had set in and the country was in bad shape financially. The effect of this depression was a big blow on Yoshio's sales. There were times when he didn't have a nickel in his pocket with no hope of getting any sure income except from these elusive sales. However, there was one thing which helped him through this miserable plight and that was the trust which people had in Yoshio.

{Taeko had an operation that relieved her frequent epileptic convulsions, but she remained blind and partly paralyzed.}

But although Taeko remained blind and not able to talk, her sense of hearing was very keen. She could sense her father's and mother's voices and their presence around her, and she would reach for them at times as they went near her. She could even recognize the engine noise of Yoshio's car. She would cock her ear and when she recognized the car, she would express her joy by bouncing her body up and down and letting out happy laughing sounds. Since Taeko had become too heavy for Tamae in later years, she would be waiting for her father to come home and carry her around. Her greatest pleasure was to be carried around outside in the fresh air, and she showed her joy. Otherwise when she was left alone, she usually sat down silently with her head bowed down and her thumb in her mouth, lonely and pitiful. Yoshio's heart ached at times to watch her tragic figure, and he would reach for her to take her in his arms and hug her closely, while tears blurred his eyes. So, although she was so pitifully crippled, compassion for her made Yoshio love her the more, and he cuddled and cared for her as much as time permitted.

CHAPTER NINE

New Life and a New Home

The second baby arrived when Taeko was two and a half years old, on June 23, 1936. This one was an easy birth and she was born only about two hours after Tamae started her labor pains. Although it meant additional expense and care, Yoshio was happy that they were blessed with another girl. This perhaps would take Tamae's mind off Taeko's condition, and she might not worry about her too much. They named their second daughter June Mitsuko.

A few years passed and, after Taeko's operation, things in general began to brighten. Sales became easier for Yoshio also. Then they had a chance to buy a house. Yoshio got many varieties of plants and flowers from his friends and relatives and worked on landscaping his garden. The dream he had when he first proposed to Tamae that night on Halai Hill, picturing a house with picket fences, flowers, and children running around on the lawn had become a wonderful reality. In 1940 Tamae, in spite of their wish for a boy, had another girl, Sandra Yoshiko. He felt that his happiness was complete. The nightmare of those tragic days seemed to recede into the

DOI: 10.5876/9781607323440.c009

past in spite of the sad reminder of a crippled child still with them, and Yoshio and Tamae were able to enjoy peace and happiness for the first time since that incident.

CHAPTER TEN

World War II

On December 7th, 1941, while representatives from Japan were meeting with those of the U.S. at Washington DC, Japan launched a fierce surprise attack on Pearl Harbor and air bases in Oahu. Taken by surprise, the raid took a tremendous toll.

Yoshio had gone early to the temple that day for Sunday School, and it was around 10 o'clock that he learned of the attack. Many ministers and laymen were having a meeting at one of the school rooms when the office girl came to notify Mr. Nagao, his neighbor who was also there, of a phone call from his home. When he returned from the phone call, his face was pale and showed signs of shock. But when he announced that Japan had just attacked Pearl Harbor, the people there were stunned into silence. When they recovered from their initial shock and started to talk, there was disbelief in their speech and expressions. It couldn't be true! It must be a mock battle for practice and some people must have taken that for a real battle. Or perhaps the people who heard it over the radio must have misinterpreted.

DOI: 10.5876/9781607323440.c010

However, Mr. Nagao insisted that it was true and he also relayed a message to Yoshio from his wife to return home at once. But most of the people there didn't seem to realize or believe in the seriousness of the situation, and they decided to continue with their meeting. Yoshio drove home and later heard that most of the ministers who were present at the meeting were arrested on their way home or met FBI agents waiting for them at their home.

Tamae met him at the front door with a shocked expression. She had her radio tuned to Honolulu, but the regular program was missing. Frantic calls for doctors' help were being broadcast, and warnings and instructions in regard to the activities of the people were being given. When Yoshio tuned in on the local station, he heard announcements confirming the Pearl Harbor attack by Japanese planes. People were warned to stay indoors as much as possible.

"What's going to happen to us? Will Japan attack Hilo too?" Tamae queried, but Yoshio had no answer. He was stunned and confused. Here they were living so peacefully and happily, and although they had been hearing about wars going on at other parts of the world, they had been only news to them. What will happen to them if this island was attacked? More shocking was the fact that the enemy attacking his adopted country was his own country of birth! What will his position and others in a similar situation be? What will their relationship with people of other nationalities in this country be? Yoshio, although raised here in Hawaii since four years old, was nevertheless without any citizenship. He was legally an enemy alien now because the law of this country had not been allowed him to be a citizen. As a national of Japan born there, he was legally obligated and bound to Japan. However, of the 34 years of his life, he had lived here for 30 years and only 4 years in Japan, which he hardly could remember. He had his obligations toward this country for practically everything which he possessed now. Furthermore, his wife and their three children, being born here, were American citizens by their right of birth. But in spite of being husband and father to these citizens, this country does not recognize him as legally being a subject of the U.S., and he was still an enemy alien. It was not his fault that Japan had chosen to attack this country. Now, suddenly, he had become an enemy of the country which he had considered his only home.

At 4:25 that afternoon, Governor Poindexter announced that Hawaii was now under martial law and the control of the actions of the Hawaiian people were taken over by the military command under Major General Walter C. Short.[1] The military took over the civilian courts and put on a tight news censorship on the newspapers and any news going out of the territory, even on ordinary news. However, rumors leaked out about some tragic mistakes of antiaircraft gunners shooting down their own planes and their shots raining down in downtown Honolulu, destroying properties, and injuring or killing civilians. There was also foolish talk about Japanese paratroopers being dropped in the mountains of Oahu and Island Japanese-Americans blocking the roads to Pearl Harbor.

Many of the prominent Japanese people in business, churches, and other Japanese oriented activities were arrested the same day of the attack and also during the following days. FBI had been checking on these people and had them on their black list as undesirable aliens and potentially dangerous to the security of the islands.[2]

Yoshio was worried too because he had been active in the church. He was at that time the president of the United YBA of Hawaii and also of the Big Island Hongwanji Judo Association,[3] an association of all the judo clubs affiliated with the Buddhist temples in this island. These judo clubs were also affiliated with the judo headquarters in Japan through their teachers, mainly for convenience in obtaining official black belt ranks for the members. Actually, the affiliation was chiefly for convenience in recognition of official ranking. But with some members in the Japanese community here questioning points in the headquarters' constitution which might raise doubts in the minds of uninformed people, or more specially to the FBI, Yoshio too might be considered a potentially undesirable enemy alien.

People continued to be apprehended and taken up to the Kilauea Military Camp at Kilauea Volcano. The camp was usually used as a vacation resort for military personnel, but now it was temporarily requisitioned for these Japanese nationals arrested by the FBI.[4] Even prominent Japanese second generation American Citizens were being arrested on suspicion of being pro-Japan. Among them were ones active in politics, and one of them was a senator and another a representative in the territorial legislature.[5] Actually, it seemed that politicians in the opposite political camp had used this opportunity to eliminate their opponents.

Thus, people who were on very friendly terms before the war became suspicious of each other. There were talks about the Filipino people, whose homeland was also simultaneously attacked by the Japanese planes, planning to retaliate on the Japanese nationals here. It was rumored that they were sharpening their cane knives and preparing other weapons for the time they would go on a mass attack on the Japanese. Older Japanese were afraid to talk in their native tongue in public.

Military orders were issued constantly, restricting the actions of alien Japanese. They were not to hold meetings over certain numbers; they were not to go out of their districts without written permits; they were not to possess any shortwave radios. Yoshio took his radio, which had a shortwave circuit, to a specified radio shop and had the coil removed. Possession of swords and any other weapon by the Japanese aliens were prohibited also.

Blackouts were ordered, and windows and doors had to be covered with black tar paper to prevent any light from leaking out. At one time a guard knocked on Yoshio's front door at night. Their hearts jumped a skip since it didn't mean any good news. The guard said that lights leaked from the side of some of the windows and warned him that it should be remedied at once or there would be some penalties. Yoshio went outside with the guard and found thin line of lights showing from the sides of a couple of windows. He taped them down carefully and rechecked until no light showed out.

There was news of the FBI searching homes to look for some evidences of some undesirable connections with Japan so that they could arrest them. Yoshio became worried about the many Japanese books and articles they had at home. He checked into these and burned many volumes of books he prized. They had many Japanese dolls which their relatives and friends had given to their firstborn, Taeko, on Girl's Day. He burned them too and kept only a few better ones hidden in the ceiling.

Things were turning from bad to worse and, besides the anxiety for the prospect of arrest, sales were dropping from the uncertainty of the situation. Also with the rationing of gasoline and restrictions in travel, Yoshio found no incentive for prospecting. So, most of the time, he just hung around his home tinkering around on minor chores. This apparent leisure was no fun, for he was constantly nagged by the prospect of future financial difficulty and possible apprehension by the FBI. There was nothing he could do but to wait and see how things turned out as time went on.

NOTES

1. Joseph B. Poindexter, territorial governor of Hawaii, 1934–42. A summary of Poindexter's legacy can be found in Lane, "Joseph B. Poindexter and Hawaii during the New Deal," 7–15.

Major General Short, who had served in World War I, only stayed in command several more days before he was recalled to Washington, DC. He was investigated by a presidential commission, headed by Supreme Court Justice Owen Roberts, for a lack of preparation and dereliction of duty in not taking more seriously the possibility of a Japanese attack on the islands. He was retired from active duty in early 1942 and passed away in 1949. For more, see the 1995 Department of Defense investigation report, reprinted in Borch and Martinez, eds., *Kimmel, Short, and Pearl Harbor*, 23–91. Studies include Anderson, *Day of Lightning, Years of Scorn*; and Rosenberg, *A Date Which Will Live*. The amount of blame attached to these two men necessarily enters into the realm of various studies about the intelligence and foreknowledge of the attack on Pearl Harbor, treated in works such as Stinnett, *Day of Deceit*; Gannon, *Pearl Harbor Betrayed*; and the well-known memoir by Rear Admiral Edwin T. Layton, *"And I Was There."*

An excellent description of the situation in Hawai'i and the attitude toward Japanese Americans right after Pearl Harbor that reflects these mentions of Poindexter and Short appears in chapter 9 of Okihiro's *Cane Fires*.

2. In 1940–41, the FBI had been actively engaged in developing lists and dossiers of "subversives," both on the mainland and in Hawai'i. These were primarily male Issei, and often community leaders or those particularly affiliated, whether socially or through employment, with Japanese consulates or organizations such as Buddhist or Shinto temples or martial arts clubs, which were classified as military organizations. As on the mainland, those on the lists were arrested in the days and months after Pearl Harbor, long before the general incarceration order on the mainland. This reaping of the Japanese American leadership had profound effects on the community. (Okihiro, *Cane Fires*, 207–9.) For more, see Robinson, *A Tragedy of Democracy*; Kumamoto, "The Search for Spies"; Spickard, "The Nisei Assume Power"; and Okawa, "Putting Their Lives on the Line."

3. Hongwanji, now commonly anglicized as honganji, is a school of Jodo Shinshu Buddhism. It is used in the names of several different schools and associations with which the Hoshidas were associated. George was particularly active in Buddhist organizations, which certainly hurt his case, since any religion other than Christianity was perceived as a lack of Americanization by many government divisions.

4. Kilauea Military Camp was the army camp on the island of Hawai'i where all the arrested Japanese nationals were first housed. It is in the southeast area of the island, in Hawaii Volcanoes National Park, about thirty miles southwest of Hilo. It is still a military vacation site.

5. Refers to Sanji Abe, the first Japanese American state senator in Hawai'i, who was arrested in August 1942, and Thomas Sakakihara, a state representative, arrested in February 1942. (George's timeline is a little confused, probably because this section was written in the 1970s.) Neither was sent to the mainland, but they were held for several months in Hawai'i. For more information on them and other legislators, see Coffman, *The Island Edge of America*; and Whitehead, *Completing the Union*.

CHAPTER ELEVEN

Detention as Enemy Alien

Days went by and, as time passed, his anxiety toward being arrested lessened somewhat, for if he was on the FBI list, he would have been taken during the early part of the disastrous event. Then on February 6th, what Yoshio feared happened!

He had gone out in the morning to report on the office and then made a round of calls on his prospects, without any success, as expected. He returned home for lunch and decided to stay at home and do some chores around the house. The wire screen of his front door was torn, and he had been planning to repair it. So he took out some tools and [had] started on the repairs, when a car stopped in his driveway.

It was his brother-in-law Riichi's car. Riichi stepped out of his car and came up the concrete walk which led to the front steps. Yoshio greeted him as he came toward him but kept up with the repairs. But when Riichi came up the steps to him, he spoke hesitantly:

"Hossan,[1] you'll have to get ready; I've come to take you!"

DOI: 10.5876/9781607323440.c011

Yoshio couldn't quite grasp what he meant, but when he looked up at his face, it was very grave and serious and showed no trace of a smile. Then it came to him like a thunderclap! His brother-in-law had come to arrest him! Since Riichi was working as a detective for the police department and now that the islands were under martial law, the police department and all its personnel were under military command. They had to take their orders from the military in arresting enemy aliens too. Perhaps Riichi had volunteered to come for him since it would be easier on Yoshio than having unknown military soldiers or FBI agents come for him. But it was quite a jolt to Yoshio. He felt his blood draining from his face and his body chilled from this sudden catastrophe! He picked up his tools numbly and went into the house, unable to utter a word.

Tamae was in the kitchen where she was cleaning after the lunch. She saw her brother walking to the front door. She met Yoshio at the door to the living room with her brother Riichi following after him. She sensed at once that there was something seriously wrong. Then Riichi spoke from behind and said, "Tamae, Yoshio will have to go. Pack up enough clothing for a few days. I'll come for more if he is to stay. Believe he'll have to go to Kilauea Military Camp so put in something warm too. Just take your time; I'll wait outside."

Tamae was speechless. Yoshio's mind was filled with the enormity of the situation, and his thoughts raced through the question of what would happen to his family hereafter. He took down the old suitcase from the bedroom closet shelf for Tamae to pack while he changed into a suit. Although there was so much to be said, they could not find words to express them[selves], and they went about the packing numbly.

At last when the preparation was finished, Yoshio took Tamae's arm and said, "Take care of yourself and the children." Only then did Tamae burst into tears and, clinging to Yoshio, sobbed out, "Why are they taking you? You've done nothing wrong. What's going to happen to us?"

"Just don't worry about me, and talk things over with your brother. He'll help you. Also, get in touch with my mother and Takeo. I believe we can write to each other if I am to stay long. So we'll discuss things over then and decide what's best. I must go now."

He kissed her on her tear-stained cheeks and, taking the suitcase, walked out to the front door. Tamae followed him to her brother's car. Another detective, a Chinese who usually teamed with Riichi, was standing at the side of the car and mumbled some greetings gloomily. Yoshio knew him well. He must have felt badly about it and had his eyes cast on the ground. Yoshio climbed into the back seat while Riichi placed Yoshio's suitcase inside the car trunk. Riichi then took the wheel, and the other detective followed him into the front seat. Yoshio did not have the heart to look back at Tamae's distressed face and sat straight looking forward. They were silent as they drove off.

They stopped once at Matayoshi Hospital in the Villa Franca District.[2] There was a Caucasian man waiting there. He was an insurance man whom Yoshio knew well through this man's special interest in the Japanese art of judo and fencing. He had been very helpful in the promotion of these arts. Yoshio couldn't understand the reason for him being there. Yoshio caught his eyes through the car window and nodded to him, but he turned his eyes away as if he didn't recognize Yoshio.

Riichi stepped out off the car and, talking briefly to the man, he went into the hospital. A few minutes later he reappeared, accompanied by Dr. Matayoshi with a suitcase also in his hand. Dr. Matayoshi stepped into the back seat and greeted Yoshio with a slight smile and said, "So you are going too, eh!"

It dawned on Yoshio that judging from the presence here of the Caucasian insurance man, who had been closely connected with this organization and now the apprehension of Dr. Matayoshi, the reason for their arrest seemed to be their connection with this organization. The Caucasian man then must be working for the FBI, perhaps to avoid suspicion on himself, or he may have been working with them while pretending interest in the Japanese arts. It made Yoshio realize the hidden nature of men which manifested itself in such times of stress. People who appeared to be one's friends may not actually be so when things change to endanger their own welfare.

Yoshio's suspicions were confirmed when he arrived at the police station, which was now the military provost marshal headquarters. Two more of his friends, who were connected with the organization, were there also and four more brought in a little later.

They were asked to empty their pockets and their suitcases were checked. Yoshio's pen knife was confiscated and other possessions okayed to be taken with him. After their examination, the eight of them were taken together in a limousine and driven up to the Kilauea Volcano Military Camp. The men spoke little, and anxiety for their future fate showed in their faces. When

FIGURE 11.1. "Kilauea Military Detention Camp." The barracks of Kilauea Military Camp, showing the architecture that George also describes in great detail, with Mauna Loa in the background. This was finished after he left Kilauea, as by May 25, 1942, George was at Sand Island, Honolulu, getting ready for the long voyage to the mainland. First published in *Poets behind Barbed Wire*, ed. Nakano and Nakano.

Yoshio thought about all the overwhelming problems which had now shifted to the frail shoulders of his wife, and his heart was heavy. After about an hour's drive through cane fields, villages, and tropical jungles on thirty miles of winding road climbing upwards on the slope of Mauna Loa, they reached the volcano. The flagstaff with the American Flag, indicating the site of the military camp, came into sight. Guards checked the identifications of the officers who drove them up, and the car stopped in front of a large barrack.

The barrack was set about five or six feet above the gravel-covered ground. A long veranda enclosed by wire meshes ran the full length of the barrack front. When they were ordered to step out of the car, they caught sight of several familiar faces staring out of the screened windows of the barrack. As soon as they entered the barrack, they were surrounded by outstretched hands and joyous embraces. Rev. Tsunoda, the judo instructor at the temple, got to Yoshio first and, grabbing his hands tightly, shouted, "Welcome! Welcome! I've been waiting for you!" Others then got hold of Yoshio to welcome him with handshakes and embraces.

This overwhelming reception chased away all the anxieties and apprehensions about his arrest, and Yoshio felt at ease among these fellow detainees—as they were officially named. Most of them, being prominent businessmen, ministers, Japanese school teachers, and other active community leaders, were well-known to Yoshio. Some, however, being of higher status in the Japanese community, were not personally intimate people to him. But here, sharing together the same fate in this time of emergency, they were brought together closer as humans on an equal plane.

There were perhaps over a hundred people in here. The barrack was about a hundred feet long and fifty feet wide. A portion of the west end was partitioned off, and a doorway led into a spacious lounge with fireplace, lounging chairs, and couches. Books and magazines were furnished by the military for the inmates to relax.

It was late afternoon when Yoshio and seven of his companions arrived at the camp and, by this time, dusk was setting in. The detainees lined up along the long porch to wait for the signal from the officer of the guards to proceed. About ten guards with guns and fixed bayonets lined up in two rows facing each other to form a pathway through which the detainees were to march from the barrack to the mess hall. Seeing the solemn faces of the armed soldiers, Yoshio was reminded of the seriousness of the situation and, for a moment, he was chilled with the fear of the unknown fate which awaited him.

At a signal from the officer, the detainees filed down the steps to the ground through the pathway lined by the guards and up the steps of the mess hall. Yoshio remembered coming to this mess hall some years ago, when he was serving as temporary serviceman for his company, to service a large commercial refrigerator. The detainees picked up stainless serving trays and silverware from a table and marched single file in front of the serving table. The KPs dumped in food as they pushed their trays along the counter. The food didn't look very appealing to Yoshio but, since he was hungry, it tasted good. But he missed the rice since mashed potato was served in place of rice. Also, there were no fresh vegetables served, in spite of the fact that there were many farms around this volcano district with Japanese farmers producing plenty of first grade farm products. Yoshio found later that these were requisitioned by the military with priority going to the military personnel. With the influx of military personnel, there were not enough vegetables to go around, and hence the detainees were out of luck.

As they finished eating, they were free to go back to their barrack individually. Then they went out and through the path lined by the guards back again to their barrack. Mist blew across the compound, and the rows of small huts to the west of the grounds blurred from sight with the thickness of the mist. Although Hawaii is a tropical island, winter could be felt in the chilly air of this mountain slope. Ordinarily there was no need for any heavy coat down at Hilo, but here he felt the need acutely. Also, since the barrack had no provision for heaters, except for the fireplace in the lounge, it was necessary at this time to wear heavy clothing even inside the barrack.

The barrack interior was fairly well lighted and less gloomy than the mess hall. Yoshio walked around the barrack to familiarize himself with the facilities. Rev. Tsunoda advised Yoshio to take a shower before too many of the inmates came back from the mess hall, for once they started to take showers, they may run out of hot water and will have to wait until the heater caught up with them.

Yoshio was glad that he had taken the shower early, for although he had bathed together with others during the construction work at Kukaiau Ranch, he was still a bit shy about sharing the shower together with others. But it was unavoidable, and in time he became used to showering and sitting together openly with others on the toilet seats each day.

Four rows of cots ran the full length of the barrack, and Yoshio was assigned to a cot about fifth from the entrance to the lounge at the western end of the barrack. Enough blankets together with other linens were supplied to keep Yoshio warm and comfortable in bed, even in this chilly mountain weather. But when he went to bed the first night, he laid awake for many hours. Sandra and Taeko were taking naps in their cribs while June was with her grandmother when Yoshio left home, and he had come without seeing them. He should at least have looked in at Taeko and Sandra, but it would only have compounded the agony of leaving home if he had seen their innocent sleeping faces. Now he felt that he should have gone to see them, for it might be quite some time before he would be seeing them again. Thoughts of his loved ones and the dark and uncertain future which would be waiting for them all kept Yoshio awake for hours in the gloom of the dimly-lighted barrack.

At home he had been hearing unpleasant rumors about this camp. There were talks about some of them being treated harshly by the guards and one old businessman being shot and wounded when he absentmindedly wandered out of the restricted area. But this place didn't seem so unpleasant although the fact of confinement like a prisoner and [the] uncertain future laid heavily upon their hearts.

Judging from the fact that the eight who were taken in yesterday were fellow members of the organization which promoted Japanese martial arts, they agreed that it must have been the reason for their apprehension, although they could see nothing wrong in participating in their practices and promotion. Later, through talks of the other inmates who were in there before them, the reason became clear.

According to their story, there was an informer here who had been in contact with the FBI. It became apparent when hearings of these detainees was started at the federal building in Hilo. About half a dozen people were taken down to town each day for a hearing and, during the course of their questioning, members of the hearing board brought out facts which the detainees had talked about in their camp barrack. They had talked confidentially about things which they thought might be the reasons for their detention. Because there couldn't be any possibility of being overheard by outsiders, it was apparent that it couldn't be anyone except someone who may have been present with them when they talked. Finally they noticed that one man, an alien himself and very active in Japanese community activities, was called out each time FBI agents came up to the camp.

He was a representative of a Honolulu Japanese newspaper. He had been active also in the promotion of the organization of Japanese arts to which Yoshio and many others belonged. This informer himself was one of the charter members of this organization and, in fact, he was secretary to that organization at the time war started. After people became aware of his suspicious actions, they took care not to say anything while he was around so that he no longer became effective as an informer. Then about a week before Yoshio and the seven were arrested, he was released from confinement without any apparent reason. Thus their suspicion was definitely confirmed.

Yoshio himself had seen this man going around in company with a known FBI agent just before the war started. So it was plain that he must have pointed out Yoshio, with the other seven who were apprehended together, for arrest. The Caucasian man who was at Dr. Matayoshi's hospital was good friends with this man and it seemed that they cooperated in the arrests with the FBI. Many people came in later and reported that they had good reasons to believe that they were apprehended because of this informer.

This informer prospered during the war, but misfortune followed after the war and he eventually lost everything, including his prestige among the Japanese community. It is a very unfortunate fact of life resulting from the tragic war which left no one unaffected in this world. This man, sadly, was one of the victims also and should be pitied.

Letters were censored and any account of the camp was cut out. They were allowed only one page with a limited number of words. But they could write every day. So Yoshio and Tamae exchanged letters every day and he was quite well informed about his family. Letter writing became the main consolation and receiving them was a source of great pleasure to be looked forward to each day. However, letters had to be written in English, and most of the inmates were unable to read or write English. Yoshio, therefore, volunteered to write their letters and was kept quite busy doing this service. This brought him together in intimate terms with many of them, and their pleasant relationship continued even after the war.

First letter after arrest:

Feb. 7, 1942

Dearest:

I'm O.K. so do not worry about me. How's Taeko and the kids? Hope they are not giving too much trouble. Get my mother to take care of Taeko.

I have some Gas Company commission check coming to me so ask brother to get it for you from Fukumoto and mail it up to me so that I can sign and return it to you. I believe the welfare will take care of you so don't worry.

Please send me the following articles:

1. Envelopes
2. Laundry soap
3. Cleenex

4. Toilet paper 1 roll
5. 4 shirts (1 blue 3 white)
6. Aloha shirts
7. Buy & send grey sweat shirt
8. 2 or 3 Underpants & undershirt
9. Slipper ([I] think you have one new skin slipper [in] the closet. Send that one)
10. Finger nail clipper (in case)
11. 3 prs socks.
12. One blue necktie
13. Eyeglass (maybe in some coat pocket)
14. Fountain pen ink (in drawer)
15. Black shoes
16. Black & tan shoe polish and brush
17. Anasin or aspirin
18. Glass cup
19. Leather container for tooth brush, tooth paste & etc. (one I used when going to Honokaa[3])
20. Japanese playing card

You can send on Tuesdays and Fridays & have your brother take them. Pack in paper box and paste list of things you are sending. Ask brother about things you can send.

You might be lonely but keep your chin up as worse things can happen. We should be glad that we are all right now. Be cheerful so that the children will not get gloomy. If anything happens depend on your brother.

Telephone bill is paid so you can use it this month. Cut off next month if you think it not necessary. Water bill is not paid so pay it, $1.10.

Give my regards to our relatives and neighbors.

Above all don't worry and keep yourself health and look forward to the happy day when we can be together again.

With love

George

P.S. When answering always write in English and do not write about war or Military matters. You can write about business, family affairs or friends. Send letter to George Y. Hoshida c/o Provost Marshal Hilo.

The shock of her husband's arrest was like a terrible nightmare to Tamae. He had hardly spoken a word when her own brother took him away. What will the fate of their little ones and herself be? Tamae's mother came over, her face pale and clouded with concern.

"Tamae, I just heard that Hossan was taken, and of all things, by Riichi! I can't see why he should be taken. He had done nothing wrong. So I'm sure he'll be released and be coming home by nightfall."

"Yes, Mother. He's done nothing wrong. So I believe he'll be released right away. Anyway, when Brother Riichi comes home, we'll know how it will be. But what if he isn't released? I'm afraid, Mother!"

"Now, don't worry so much. I'm sure it won't be long. If he doesn't return soon, you'll have to be strong and take care of things. So, brace yourself and don't lose heart!"

Tamae felt better at this, but when she sat down to think about how she was going to manage if Yoshio wasn't released, her heart became heavy. She had heard rumors about people detained at the military Camp, about someone wandering away from the restricted grounds there and being shot and injured. The soldiers there were being very harsh to these people now regarded as undesirable aliens. What can she do without her husband to take care of things? After the war started, they couldn't even visit their friends as they had done before. Also, now that her husband has been taken, people will stay away from their home for fear they may become involved. People of other nationalities were also hostile toward them, and some showed it openly in public places.

Evening came, but there was no sign of Yoshio's return. Later in the night Riichi came over.

"Tamae, I am sorry but Yoshio has been taken up to the military camp with several other people, and I believe he won't be back for some time until he has a hearing. So you'll have to be patient and hope for the best. I believe he'll be released after the hearing, but it will take at least a month or so. Anyway, if anything happens I'll let you know, so don't worry too much. We are all here to help you. Just keep your spirits up and I am sure things will come out all right in the end. In the meantime, he will need some clothing and toilet things for daily use. Pack what you think he will need and I'll come for it later. Put in some warm things, for it's quite chilly up there."

After packing some things in a paper carton, Tamae took them over to [her] brother's home which was only two doors away. It was fortunate that his home was near. She also had her elder sister Yoshino too, and Brother Jimmie's home was only a few blocks away. Then there was Yoshio's family with his mother and two brothers. At a time like this, she had to depend on these close relatives.

The following day brother Takeo drove over with his mother.

"Tamachan! What a terrible thing! When was he taken?" Yoshio's mother showed deep concern and distress.[4]

"He was taken around noon yesterday. We thought he might be released soon and didn't want to worry you. So we didn't let you know."

They then sat around the dining table sipping tea and discussing about what best to do. They finally decided that since Yoshio's mother had nothing to do at present and Matsuo's family could get along fine without her help, she [would] stay with Tamae and help with the children's care and household chores.

In the meantime, Riichi and his wife Ayako came over too and joined into the discussion. It seems that at such emergency, the compassion and good in everyone showed, and Tamae felt a deep sense of appreciation and gratitude which eased the pain and distress of losing her husband's presence in this great crisis.

Nisei (second generation American-Japanese), although being American citizens, were brought in too.[5] This brought to the minds of the first generation inmates the hopelessness of their being released when even citizens were arrested, not because they were actually involved in subversive activities but just on the basis of their nationality and leadership in the second generation group. On the other hand, there were also many people who were just farmers or laborers in the country districts brought in. Some had recently taken trips to their homeland and hence suspected of acting as spies although none actually were even remotely connected with such activities. There were others who had worked to collect donations for Japan in her war efforts against China because they wished to carry out their duty as Japanese subjects.[6] Perhaps arrests of these may have been justified, although they had done it without any intention of ever harming the country of their adoption. But this was a serious situation and most of the detainees felt no resentment or bitterness against this country which had taken away their freedom.

About ten days after Yoshio's detention, the inmates were notified that their families were allowed to come up for a visit. However, since it would be quite impossible to accommodate all the families at one time, they were to be divided into two groups on separate days. A list of the family names was given them, and Yoshio found his family included in the first-day visitor list. This really was good news, and everyone looked forward to the happy day. The visiting time was to be for three hours, from 1 to 4 PM. Tamae wrote joyfully about it too and said that her brother Riichi would be bringing the whole family up.

The day arrived a week after its notification. Cars started to arrive soon after the inmates returned from lunch. Yoshio kept looking for his family, but even when the last of the cars had come into sight, he saw none that resembled his family. His heart ached with anguish at the thought that perhaps they had failed to come. However, at the very end of the line of cars he recognized Riichi's car and saw his wife and the little ones waving at him. June came out of the car first and ran into her father's waiting arms. Yoshio picked her up. He hugged her warm body and felt the surge of happiness in his heart. Riichi picked up Taeko from Tamae's lap and helped Sandra and Tamae out of the car. Tamae took Sandra's hand and walked up to Yoshio. They embraced each other briefly and Yoshio took over Taeko from the arms of his brother-in-law, thanking him for his help.

"Sorry we were late," said Riichi. "I had to take charge of this group and get them started so that I had to come the very last." As Yoshio led his family to his cot with Taeko in his arms, Taeko must have recognized him. She hugged his neck as she had been doing at home and showered his cheek and neck with kisses while uttering joyous whimpers. He felt his eyes become suddenly moist and he hugged her tightly with warm love and compassion. Being so attached to each other, Yoshio's mind was constantly on this unfortunate child. He dreamed of her several times after his confinement here.

June was hanging on to her father's arm as they walked toward Yoshio's cot. Tamae followed, leading Sandra by the hand. When Yoshio put out his hand to caress Sandra's head, she reached out to grasp his hands in warm affection. Yoshio realized how much he had missed them all during these several days of separation. He had never been away from his family except for a few days on business.

"Tamae, how are you doing at home? Believe it must be hard on you taking care of all the children and attending to household chores and problems."

"Yes! It is really hard without you and I miss you terribly. But since your mother and your brother, Takeo, is helping me, I am not having too much difficulty. Also, as I've written to you, the bank is suspending our payment on the house and as long as we pay interest on the loan, they are allowing us to live there. Welfare Department is taking care of household finances and, although it isn't much, I can manage to get along. My sister and brother too bring me extra food and some things we need, so don't worry about us. Only, please take care of yourself and keep healthy until you are released. Hope you don't have to stay here very long."

Sandra had slipped down from Yoshio's lap when June ran off with her friend. She toddled after June for a distance but came back when Yoshio and Tamae called after her. She was a little over a year-and-a-half old and could toddle around quite well. She had a soft round face with fair skin and cheeks now rosy in this cool climate. Her wondering large dark eyes with tiny full upper lips and tucked-in lower lip gave her an expression of seriousness. She seldom smiled unless induced, but when picked up, she would cuddle close in intimately warm affection.

Time was too short for this meeting of the loved ones. The heartbreak of separation was here again, and the officer in charge announced that the visiting was at an end. Yoshio and Tamae looked at each other in silent longing. There were tears in Tamae's eyes, and Yoshio felt his vision blurring. He called at June and Sandra to hide the tears which threatened to flow. He embraced Tamae briefly and stole a kiss. Then, picking up Taeko, he led his family into the stirring crowd of people leaving for the exit in farewell.

Brother Riichi met them at the doorway and took Taeko from Yoshio's arms. He tucked them into his car and then stood outside to direct the traffic in their departure. When finally the last car was sent on its way, Riichi started after the other cars. Tamae and the children waved frantically at Yoshio and Yoshio waved back, his heart heavy.

The return trip, in contrast to the exciting prospect of meeting with her husband, was bleak and sad. Mitsuko kept chattering away about what she saw and did in the barrack, but Tamae could hardly pay any attention to what she was talking about. Her heart and mind were immersed in her contact with him and what they had discussed. The brief joy she felt in meeting him was blotted out with the fear for the future fate of her husband and her children. Riichi questioned briefly about her meeting with Yoshio and reassured her of his early release. He talked about his plans to hire a lawyer for him at the hearing to give him a better chance of being released. After all, although he was born in Japan, he had come when he was only a little boy and grew up together with other Nisei who were born here, and there should be little difference. So there should be a very good chance for him to be released after the hearing. Tamae felt some sense of relief in his words.

After the excitement had died down, the army officer in charge came in to make a startling announcement. The inmates and the families had been forewarned that they were not to exchange any restricted items while visiting. But a couple of violations had occurred. One was a letter written in Japanese from an inmate to his family that was not able to visit him for some reason. Since letters had to be written in English and he [was] unable to write except in Japanese, [he] had to have his letters written by others. So he thought he would take advantage of this visitation and get someone to take his letter to his family. But this carrier had put his letter in his coat pocket, and when he left the barrack, he bent down to fix his shoelace and the letter slipped out of the pocket to the ground. Unfortunately a guard saw him picking it up and took it away from him. The letter was just a personal message from the inmate to his wife and contained nothing which would be detrimental to the security of the military. But this violation was one of the more important regulations, and they considered it a serious violation of privilege.

But the tragic thing was that the penalty was imposed on people who were having their families visit them the following day. Although they were allowed to visit the camp, they were prohibited from meeting inside the barrack. They could only talk to each other through the screen covering the barrack porch, with the family members on the ground looking up at the inmates on the porch. They were unable to touch or embrace each other nor talk intimately since they had to talk quite loudly in order to be audible. It was really pitiful to see them since this was the only chance they had to meet each other. They may not meet again for a long time; in fact, no one could predict that they would be able to meet again.

The violators were sincerely remorseful of their thoughtless actions. The representatives of the inmates met with the officers and pleaded with them to allow the second day visitors to meet with their husbands and fathers with promises that they would see to it that no further violations [would] be committed. But the authorities were firm in their stand.

New detainees were brought in continuously. Riichi came in with them quite often, and the strain seemed to show on him. One of the inmates, after observing him in the guards' office through a peephole, remarked, "Take (Takemoto in short) sure looks lonely and sad sitting by himself among the haole soldiers. It must be hard on him to be arresting his own nationals." It really must have been trying for him, for he remarked to some inmates that he too might be joining them one of these days. There was no guarantee that anyone of Japanese extraction would be spared.

Days dragged slowly for Tamae, but she gradually settled down into a resigned acceptance of her life without her mate. They continued correspondence, and his letters were the only source of joy and comfort which bolstered her spirit. Her brother came in to her at times to report about more people being arrested. Finally she had a call one day from her sister Yoshino that her husband Hisakichi was also apprehended. Although Tamae felt sorry for her sister, this news brought her some sense of lightening her spirits to think that now her own sister will be in the same boat with her, and Yoshio will also have close company.

However, as days went by, she started to notice some changes in her physical condition. With the passing of more days, she felt convinced that she was pregnant! She felt a sinking sensation when she thought what it would mean to her and her family to be burdened with another addition to the family at this crisis.

The time came when the smell of food induced in her nausea and vomiting. Not being able to keep this to herself, she finally confided this fact to the two mothers. They were shocked at first, but as they recovered from their shock, they advised Tamae not to worry too much about it but go to the doctor to check on this.

Tamae had been quite sure of her pregnancy, but now that the doctor had confirmed it, she felt an overwhelming sense of disaster. She had borne all the nightmarish events which had been piling up before her, but in her delicate condition now, things seemed to magnify tenfold and the problems blanketed her with disastrous fear and despair. Cold sweat oozed out of her pores and nausea overtook her. She went out of the doctor's office in a daze, hardly hearing what the doctor was saying. Riichi was waiting for her in the waiting room.

"What did the doctor say? Are you all right? You look so pale, what happened?"

"I'm all right. Yes, the doctor said that I was three months pregnant. Please take me home."

When Tamae returned home, the two mothers were waiting. When they heard that she was really pregnant, they congratulated her and advised her to take care of herself. But seeing Tamae so pale and weak, they took her into the bedroom to have her rest. Then, as she lay there in a daze, she felt the chill of cold sweat even under the comforter. Her flesh and skin started to quiver all over the body uncontrollably. She was in a nervous shock. She called out to the mothers, but her voice shook with fear and was hardly audible. But finally the two mothers, suspecting something, looked into the bedroom and found her huddled under the covers and shaking uncontrollably with cold sweat showing on her brow.

Alarmed, Tamae's mother took hold of her and shook her, crying out, "Tamae! What happened? Get hold of yourself!"

Yoshio's mother was frightened too and exclaimed, "I think we had better call the doctor. This must be something serious!"

The doctor came over in about 15 minutes and injected some tranquilizer to quiet Tamae's nerves, which took effect immediately. She then fell into a merciful sleep.

When Tamae opened her eyes, it was already dark outside. Tamae lay there thinking about the things which had happened so rapidly, one after another. When Yoshio was taken, she felt as though everything had come to an end. To be left with three little ones, including the crippled Taeko, and then having to think about another addition to the family, seemed too much of a burden to carry on her slender shoulders. But still she had borne them until today, and things surely couldn't get worse. She must brace herself and take things as they came and do the best she could. Thinking back to the times when her husband was home to manage all the difficulties they had to go through, she realized how much she had been depending on him. If she should give up now, there will be no hope for their family. And how can she face Yoshio when this is all over and he returns to them? She must do all in her power now to carry on no matter what happens! She felt strength welling up within herself as these thoughts surged through her body and mind.

Tamae's mother sat beside her. She looked up at her mother and smiled. "Please forgive me for worrying you. You are right! I must brace myself and I will promise you that I'll be all right from now on! I'll do my best to carry on until Yoshio returns. So please forgive me for all the troubles I caused you all!"

Her mother was greatly relieved and pleased to see the changes in Tamae. "I'm happy! Everything is how you take it, and I'm sure now that you've made up your mind, everything will turn out all right!"

Tamae felt completely refreshed. She pushed the comforter aside and sat on the edge of the bed. All the chills and nervousness were gone now, and she felt her strength returning to her.

"I'm all right now, Mother. I'll get up and go on with my work. Thank you, Mother."

Tamae wrote to Yoshio about her pregnancy. His answer came with a happy note although she could sense that he was concerned about this new development which would burden her further. But she reassured him that everything will come out all right and he need not worry about her. She didn't mention about her nervous breakdown, for it would only serve to worry him needlessly.

Mar. 13, 1942

Received your letter of 12th and cotton and folder today. Also the cash, $5.00. Sorry that I had to ask you for money but I believe this will last me for a long time.

I am very happy to hear that we are to have a new addition to our family. It will be hard for you but try your best and take good care of yourself. The Welfare is giving medical attention too so talk over with the representative from the department when she comes over and follow her advice. Above all try not to worry too much and do not be too particular about doing your housework. I hope it will be a boy this time and I believe it will be because we'll be needing lots of men after [illegible].

I am glad to know that mother is still with you. Give her my love and ask her to keep on helping. Your brother's family sent us some pickles. Please thank them and give our appreciation for their kindness. Send Taeko's picture when it's finished and send me some snapshots of you and the other two kids when and if you can have them taken by someone. I believe the Welfare takes a little time before they can start helping, so wait for it. I've sent back some candies through Mr. Richardson today. Hope you received it. Send me a package of Baking Soda anytime.

Well, take good care of yourself and give my regards to Grandma and folks.

Love,

George

Notes

1. Riichi is adding the Japanese honorific suffix -san to a shortening of Hoshida to address George, Hos + san. Tamae's mother also uses it later.

2. This is Dr. Zenko Matayoshi, a famous doctor and community leader, who began his medical work caring for plantation workers in Maui and then bought this hospital practice in Hilo and maintained it until his death in 1970. He was originally from Okinawa and attended Kumamoto Medical College in George's birth prefecture before he did his residency at the University of Michigan. These private Japanese American–owned hospitals catered to that population and also cost about half of a standard hospital stay. The Matsumura Hospital where Tamae delivers her baby (see chapter 14) is another such private hospital. (Nakano, *Kanda Home*, 78–79; Smith, *Japanese American Midwives*, 116; "Catalogue of the University of Michigan for 1919–1920," 666.)

Dr. Matayoshi was released after ten months in Kilauea and continued his medical practice. A military guard was posted at his hospital, but after the guard panicked, shot at nothing, and fled one night, it was not renewed. (Personal communication from Mary Matayoshi.)

3. A plantation community on the northeast shore of the island of Hawai'i. Honokaa is near Kukaiau Ranch, so George may be referring to a travel kit from his time there.

4. George's mother is addressing Tamae by her name appended with the affectionate suffix -chan, Tama(e) + chan.

5. First-generation Japanese Americans (Japanese-born immigrants) were known as Issei, while the American-born second generation were called Nisei. These Japanese words came into fairly common use during World War II. Other important terms included Sansei for the third generation and Kibei for the American-born second-generation individuals, usually men, who were sent back to Japan for education and spent many formative years there. While often viewed as troublemakers and the most loyal to Japan, the Kibei were also of great assistance in military intelligence because of their language skills. George rarely uses these terms in his narrative. His use of the terms Japanese, American Japanese, second-generation Japanese, etc., varies quite a bit.

6. The Second Sino-Japanese War, usually dated from 1937, then included in World War II.

CHAPTER TWELVE

The Hearing

The day for his hearing finally came, and Yoshio was taken down to the federal building in town with three other men.[1] The guards took them up to the third floor to a room at the northwest corner of the building. They instructed them not to talk and warned them to keep away from the windows.

Yoshio had heard that sometimes word leaked out somehow about the time the detainees were taken down for [their] hearing, and family members waited for them at the side entrance through which they were taken into the building. Seats were provided for them, but Yoshio stood against one of the back walls near a window, and when the guards' attention was slackened, he eased himself near the back window and peeped out. When he glanced down at the lawn, his heart skipped a beat! His family was there and their two mothers!

Tamae caught sight of Yoshio when he showed himself at the window, and she waved at him excitedly. She called the mothers and the children and pointed up at Yoshio. Although he was excited himself and felt like jumping out of the window, if that was possible, he didn't want to attract

DOI: 10.5876/9781607323440.c012

the attention of the guards. So he extended his forearm a bit and waved at his family with his hand. Tamae then pointed to her lower waist to indicate the slight bulge which showed the new life that was forming in there. June was jumping up and down and waving at him while Sandra stood staring up, perhaps not recognizing her father half hidden at the side of the window too high for her. Tamae, realizing this, picked her up in her arms and pointed her finger to Yoshio. She then seemed to understand and, raising her little arm, started to wave at him. Yoshio's eyes blurred with longing for his dear ones. When will it be before he would be able to hold them close to him again? But this meeting was abruptly brought to an end by the voice of one of the guards.

"Hey you there! Move away from the window. Didn't I tell you not to go near the window?" Yoshio gave a last wave to his family and retreated.

Then about twenty minutes later when he managed to peep out of the window again, they were gone. He learned later that another guard patrolling the grounds had ordered them off saying that this was a restricted area and civilians were not allowed here. They were not to meet again for over a year and a half.

Yoshio's turn for the hearing finally came. A guard led him through an empty courtroom and took him to a room opposite to the waiting room at the southeast corner of the same floor. The room must have been the judge's chamber and not very large. A long table was in the center with about three military officers and three civilians seated at one side and the ends of the table. A chair was placed at the center of the other side where Yoshio was asked to be seated. The hearing started with one of the board members, who appeared to be the chairman, checking with a file he had in front of him.

The hearing proceeded smoothly with questions about Yoshio's life history brought out from the file. Although Yoshio was born in Japan, and hence an alien, the fact that he had been educated here with other Hawaiian-born citizens seemed to have a favorable reaction from the board members. But then the question of judo came out. One of the members asked Yoshio whether there was anything else besides the art of Judo taught to the students. Yoshio answered that practice of judo promoted spiritual culture also. "Since judo came down from the martial arts of the olden day warriors, called samurai or bushi, this spiritual [culture] is called 'Bushido,' 'The Way of the warriors,' which is in essence the spirit of warrior ethics."

Then a civilian member who was the general manager of a large local firm spoke out and said, "Bushido is a way of killing people! It is this spirit which prompted the Japanese to attack Pearl Harbor, Manila and other places, killing thousands of people. Bushido is evil!"

This irritated Yoshio and he stood up and retorted, "Bushido is nothing like that! You are prejudiced!"

The man must have been angered by Yoshio accusing him of prejudice, and he reemphasized that bushido was indeed a spirit of killing people and it was evil!

The chairman then restrained them and said to Yoshio, "Well then, let's hear your explanation of bushido."

Yoshio said, "Bushido to me is something like sportsmanship; only it goes deeper than that. It will give fighting spirit in combat, but once the opponent is subdued, the spirit of Bushido will help the conquered with compassion so that true peace is brought about. However, some may not have the true spirit of Bushido and hence appear to abuse this spirit." But just then a clerk came in and whispered something to the chairman. The chairman addressed Yoshio then and said, "I just got word that a lawyer had been hired for you by your relative to defend your case. You may step out and meet him now. We will continue your case later."[2]

The guard took Yoshio out to the balcony where a Caucasian lawyer waited for him. He said that his brother-in-law Riichi had asked him to represent Yoshio in this hearing. They then huddled together at the bench and he questioned Yoshio in order to get as much facts as possible. He also looked over the statements which Yoshio had prepared and remarked that although there were some passages which might have been better left out, it did express Yoshio's position and thoughts quite well. So it might as well be presented to the hearing board.[3]

About half an hour later, the clerk came out to call in Yoshio and the counselor to the hearing room. The lawyer made a statement in defense of Yoshio and presented the papers Yoshio had prepared. However, in a military case like this with the lawyer not having time to prepare for the defense, it was doubtful whether he could have any favorable effect on the decision. Also, with the argument Yoshio had with the civilian board member, that person at least would not have any favorable opinion toward Yoshio. So when the list of detainees to be shipped out to Honolulu was announced about a month later, Yoshio was on it.

Apr. 25th, 1942

My dear wife:

I haven't received your letter yet as I believe they haven't brought it up yet. I believe it will be in the late afternoon before we'll receive them and since we will have to mail ours out today before 10 AM I'm writing now.

It's nine thirty now. I had my hearing finished yesterday and with the lawyer to help me I believe the result was very favorable. I am only to wait their decision now and I surely hope it will turn out all right. Still we cannot tell until they notify us and we can do nothing but hope and pray. I do hope I will be cleared for the sakes of you and the children. But, we should not be downhearted even if the decision is infavorable to us as we will have to consider it as fate and look forward to the day when we can be together again and consider us as fortunate in being able to have had this valuable experience. This in a way is unfortunate but if we try to take it the right way and try to gain out of this experience, we will have been very fortunate for being able to encounter this experience. The only thing is that we do the right thing, and keep on doing it, and wait until the misunderstanding towards us is cleared.

I had done nothing wrong intentionally and have no intentions of doing anything wrong in the future, and since people judging us are human and human is not God and cannot be expected to see everything clearly, it is natural of them to misunderstand. But if we are right, there will surely be a day when we will be rewarded, as God can see us for what we are. In the meantime, we should not think wrong of Uncle Sam even if we are not properly judged, but try all we can to do the right thing. After all, we owe a great deal more to him than can be off-balanced by this mistake he has committed through misunderstanding. This is your country and our children's country and although it is not my country legally, I owe 30 years of my life to her and I will have to repay for this obligation; and if it eases his mind to have me detained, at least I'll be helping him. So let us not complain even if I am not released and just hope that we will be more fortunate.

I am glad to know that mother is helping you again. You will not have to strain any more now, so just don't worry about things and take things one at a time. I am glad to have been able to get a glimpse of you when I was down and to see the children all healthy and lively. Only, how is Taeko? Hope her convulsions are not bad. Don't worry too much about her as we have done all we could and it's beyond our power. Everyone has his or her own life to live and it was destined to be her life and we can only hope that she'll be more fortunate after she had gone to another world. Until then let us try all we can for her.

Thank brother that I am very grateful for his kind help and will try all I can to repay him for it as soon as I am able. It was a great help for me and believe that it was the best help that we could have ever had. Hope everybody is all right in his family and give my love and regards to them.

I was glad to see the two grandmas healthy. Thank them for this help and tell them to be careful of themselves until I'll be able to see them again. Give my love to them.

Well, will wait for your letter today, and will write again next Wednesday. Until then take good care of yourself.

Love

George

P.S. Sorry wasn't able to see you yesterday. I was in court & out past 4.

P.S. By the way, will you please get for me an English Bible if you can. It won't have to be an expensive one. They have been allowing Bibles and I believe if you'll ask their permission they'll allow you to send it in. Send the dictionary also as I believe you'll be allowed to send it, if together with the Bible. I would like to study the Bible while I have time. Get a small pocket-size one if you can.

Apr. 28, 1942

Dear June:

Daddy was very glad to receive your letter and pictures too. You are getting better every time. If you keep it up, you will be a very bright girl when daddy can go home.

I am glad to know that you are having a typhoid injection. You will not get sick if you have the injection.

I was very glad to see the pictures too. June, Sandra, Taeko, Mama, and the grandmas all look nice. Write again.

Good bye. Love,

Daddy

In the meantime, her brother had applied for help to Tamae's family to the authorities, and in answer to it, a social worker visited her home one day. After taking all the information, she assured her that everything will be taken care of so that she could get along properly during this crisis. Also seeing Taeko, she suggested that it would be advisable to have her sent to Waimano Home in Oahu where the government had provided facilities to take care of such children. Tamae would have less [of a] burden to bear, especially now that she was now expecting another addition to the family.

It was heartbreaking to think that she cannot care for her any longer if she should be taken to the Home. The social worker assured her that the Home will take good care of her. But Tamae had her doubts about how much care and love they could give her. It certainly couldn't be like what parents could give. However, how would she manage when the new baby arrives with added care? It really was a very difficult decision for her to make.

Tamae wrote to Yoshio about this and received answer that he could understand how difficult it must be to care for Taeko now that he could not help. Perhaps when the war ends or when he could return home, they may be able to get her back and care for her themselves again. So, he advised her to talk it over with the relatives and decide on the best course to take.

However, it was a couple of months later that arrangements were finally made for Taeko to be taken to the Home. When the day came, Brother Riichi took Tamae down with Taeko to the police station where the social worker took over. But when Tamae handed over Taeko into the arms of the social worker, she felt as though her heart was being wrenched out of her. Tears welled out of her eyes as she kissed Taeko farewell. Taeko, without sight or normal sense, was oblivious to what was happening to her, and she sat on the car seat beside the social worker sucking her thumb with her head bowed down. It was a pitiful sight, and Tamae's heart ached at this sorrowful separation. When the car started away, she felt as though a part of her had gone with it. A few days later she received report from the Welfare Department that Taeko was safely placed in the Waimano Home at Pearl City and reassured her that she will receive good care there.

It was May 1, 1942 that she was sent out to Oahu in the care of a social welfare worker, coincidentally on exactly the same day that Taeko met with the tragic accident which incapacitated her, eight years ago on 1934. Yoshio never saw her again.

FIGURE 12.1. "Sandra, June, Mama, Daddy Very Fat." A sketch George included with a letter to June written on April 28, 1942. While imprisoned at Kilauea Military Camp, he joked in letters about getting fat due to the starchy food and lack of exercise, but he lost all of the weight gain and more through seasickness on the crossing to the mainland. The cartoon of his face shows traces of his Federal School correspondence training.

FIGURE 12.2. This photograph was taken in the back yard of the Hoshidas' house in 1942, probably after George was arrested. From left to right: George's mother, June, Tamae holding Sandra, Tamae's mother (back), and Taeko, the Hoshidas' disabled eldest daughter. This is the only known picture of Taeko. If George ever drew her, he did not save those images. The dog is Fly, Tamae's brother Riichi's German shepherd.

May 1, 1942

My dearest wife:

Received your letter of 30th. I believe it must be very lonely to be without one member of the family even though she was so crippled. I thought of her while I lay in bed at night and couldn't help feeling pity for her and wetting my pillows. She used to wait for me so much every noon and evenings. I believe I really couldn't have been able to stand the heartbreak of separation. I feel embarrassed even now as I write as tears kept on welling up and people might notice and wonder why I'm crying. But I guess they all understand as I couldn't help telling them about Taeko. They all feel pity for her and wonder how fate would be so cruel sometimes. But it's all in the way we take it, so let's not brood over it, and just pray that she'll get the best of care while she lives. Please thank everybody for their kind considerations towards her. I can imagine Sandra and June missing her but they'll get used to it and when we greet the new baby, he or she will take the place of Taeko, although we'll not be able to forget her.

I'm glad to know that mother is staying on. Be good to her for after all she's been very good to us and she herself had a very hard life although. I cannot do anything for her myself so do all you can for her. Tell her not to worry about myself as I am in perfect health and am spending my time pleasantly.

Give my regards to your mother also. I believe separating from Taeko must have hit her hardest as she had been thinking about her as much, and Taeko had loved her most. How's her leg? Hope she's not suffering too much from it. I could have massaged her if I was home but I guess I'll be able to some day soon. Tell her not to worry too much about Taeko as she'll get the best of care over there.

I guess today must be glorious. Hope you enjoyed it. I heard the band playing last time I was down there and felt like old times. Hope I'll be able to enjoy them soon.

Tell sister that brother is getting along very fine. He's getting healthier as he has quite a lot of exercises [CENSORED]

I'm enclosing a sample of looseleaf for my smaller folder. Will you try and get couple of packages of it? [. . .] Will you also send me some green things, a head of cabbage or lettuce and some "namasu" and pickles (home made). The others are very generous and bring them to me and I can eat all I want but it doesn't look good only to take and not give anything in return, so send me some once in a while if you can.

I have sent back yesterday two shirts addressed to you, for washing. Have your brother check out the Provost Marshal's office and bring it back for you. Send them back to me when you finish.

The sun is setting now over Mauna Loa and it's glorious. Everyone is looking out of the window at the beautiful scene. 6:45 P.M. We had our supper early tonight and are all ready for the night.

Well good night with love and kisses.

Yours,
George

May 7, 1942

Dearest Husband:

I haven't as yet received your wash so I wish you would find out about it. This time I am sending you 100 sheets of loose leaf paper, hair oil, 3 packages of bandages, 3 pairs of shoe strings, a box of bandages, adhesive tape, mercurochrome, shaving cream, listerine toothpaste, and a pair of B.V.D. which I made. If the B.V.D. is too large, send it back after marking the sides so I may be able to repair it.

It is a week now since our invalid daughter left for Honolulu. We all miss her, although everyone knows she is well taken care of.

Tomorrow we shall have the last typhoid injection and later we shall be vaccinated.

Mrs. Wong went to the Catholic church to get you a Bible, but there isn't any now and a new stock is to arrive soon so please wait.

The reason that I prefer a Bible from the Church for you is that it will be blessed by the ~~priest~~ Father.

Everyone is healthy and we are all praying and waiting for you.

With love,

Tamae

Please send back the empty boxes and jars if it is possible.

Mitsu is sending pictures to you and she will write a letter to you later.

May 8, 1942

My dear wife:

Today is Friday and [I] am waiting for your letter. Hope everything has been going along all right. We've had our injection and vaccination day before yesterday and I slept the whole day yesterday from the reaction, but I'm all right today. Hope it won't be worse on the second one. How did you and June come out? I guess you are stronger than I. Did Sandra get hers?

Do you still have the telephone? If you have I think you had better keep it for emergency. Be careful about locking the doors at night and do not open the door unless you are sure of the persons who are calling. Phone your brother or the police station in case you suspect anything. Be careful not to go out alone during the daytime. I wouldn't want anything to happen to you or the family. I'm always afraid of it as I cannot be with you to watch out and help you.

The shirts I sent back to you were taken to the laundry and have received them so do not worry about it.

5: PM

Have been ordered to go out to Honolulu suddenly this afternoon. Remember what I've said before and do not grieve. Wait for the day when we can be together again. Keep yourself healthy and watch out for yourself. Depend on the relatives and take their advices. Send me some money to Honolulu if you can [marginal note: "I have $5.00"]. Above all don't worry about me. God will watch out for me. Will be going out tonight or tomorrow. Give my best regards to all the relatives and friends.

Am sending back two packages of things I do not need. I have everything so do not worry. Will write from Honolulu if able. Do not worry even if I do not write and wait for the day when the war ends. The main thing is to be alive and healthy.

Send me a hat if possible. Be sure to make it good size. A little bigger than the old one at home. Send some woolen socks too. Size 11.

Well, watch out for your health. Be very careful and above all do not worry. This might be the best thing for us. Only the future will tell so just wait for the happy day when we can be together again.

Love and kisses,
Your husband

May 19?, 1942

Dearest Husband:

I have received your letter of May 8. I was so shocked to hear that you had left. My only regret is that we didn't meet before you left.

I am perfectly alright. I shall keep my telephone, and as you say, I am careful about everything. I can and shall depend upon my relatives; they are very kind to me.

I have received your two packages. I shall try to send you money, hat, socks, shawl, two flannel underwear, and a pair of pajamas if it is possible.

Our home is safe for the bank[,] out of kindness, will only take the interest of $11.07 per month.

I know you are more worried about me than of yourself. Please don't for I am quite brave about everything. I know we shall meet someday—the children, you, and I. The thing which comes to my mind now is how I will act and feel when you return home. This would be the happiest moment of my life. I shall only look forward to this day instead of thinking that which has happened.

Take good care of yourself. As for me I will take good care of the children and my coming "boy" baby. If you have a chance to write to me be sure to write. But if you cannot I shall not worry.

Again goodbye till we meet.
With love,
Tamae
P.S. I am sending you $25.00 with the letter. If you receive it please let me know.

Hilo, Hawaii

May 21, 1942

Dearest Husband:

I received your letter of the 17th. I am glad you received all the things which I sent you. I am very happy to know that you are in good health and having a wonderful time.

I was worried about your insurance, but my brother, Jim, said he shall [take] care of it and for you not to worry.

Again do not worry about me. I am healthy and gaining in weight. I am not suffering at all. The children are all fine and very healthy. I am more than able to take care of them. We have all had our injections and vaccinations.

I shall send you by mail the shorts which you asked for. I do hope you receive it in time.

If you are to go to the mainland please take good care of yourself. Try to write as often as you can so I may know your whereabouts and to know that you are healthy. After things settle down be sure to come home for we shall all be waiting for you.

With love,
Tamae

May 21, 1942

Dear daddy

How are you daddy. I hope you are fine and storng. I am storng and healthy too. I am still going to school. I am getting very smart girl now.

I play very nicely with my friends. I always obey mama and help her do things. so please daddy when the war is over do not forget to come for I am waiting you everyday.

Good-Bye

with love

you daughter

June

Yoshio, together with the group of detainees who failed at the hearing, were shipped out on May 7th on the interisland steamship. Since they were transported to the ship in covered army trucks on back roads, no family knew when their men were shipped out until a few days later when they received the remains of their possessions from the camp. The ship sailed on its way to Honolulu about 4 PM. As it glided out through the channel between the breakwater and the Coconut Island, the town of Hilo spread out along the crescent waterfront across the bay. Above the town, the emerald green of the cane fields spread upward to the dark rainforest of ohia trees and rose up toward the peaks of Mauna Kea to the right. Having resigned [himself] to his fate now that nothing seemed to change his destiny, Yoshio's heart was no longer in turmoil. But what will his fate be? Will he ever come back or will he ever see his family again? They were only about a mile away in distance from here, but how infinitely apart they seemed!

Detention Camp

Sand Island

Honolulu, T.H.

May 22, 1942

Mrs. Tamae Hoshida

Hilo, Hawaii

My dear wife:

Received your letter of the 18th and also the stamps. I received all the things you've sent me previously including the check for $25.00. I believe I can get along with it but will let you know when I need anymore.

We are leaving here tomorrow morning, so it will be good-by to Hawaii for a while. Hope it will be a pleasant trip. Take good care of yourself and be ready with our new "boy" when I come back. Let's look forward to that happy day and bid each other farewell with a smile. Watch out for Sandra and June and remember all that I had said before. Think that I'm just on a vacation and do not worry about me. I'll take good care of myself, so be sure to keep yourselves healthy and be ready for all emergency. I might not be able to write from now on but do not worry. I'll try & write if possible. Give my love and best regards and thanks and also farewells to your brothers, sister, grandmas and all the relatives and their families and ask their continued help.

Well, no matter what happens, just live and fight through and wait for me until the war ends.

Love and kisses,

George

Notes

1. The transcript of the hearing is in appendix B and includes the panel's deliberations before George enters the room; this adds quite a bit of information about the panel's perceptions of George, which were largely shaped by the report of an informant.

2. George's account of this dispute is fairly accurate, though here he gives himself the last word rather than the board member.

3. See appendix B for George's full statement.

CHAPTER THIRTEEN

Internment Camps

Yoshio had kept a diary while in the internment camps. It starts on August 15, 1942. Reading through it now, I find that it was quite well written, and in fact, being in the middle of these tragic times, his feelings have been expressed most realistically. So I have decided to copy it as written except in some passages where it will be necessary to add some important details missed in his diary.

GYH 9–11–73
At Lordsburg Internment Camp
Compound 2, Company 5, Barrack 4
August 19, 1942
By Yoshio Hoshida

I was transferred from Hilo to Honolulu with a group of internees, the second group to be sent out from the Kilauea Detention Camp. We left KMC at 7 A.M. on May 9th and set sail 3:30 PM the same day on the interisland steamer. Reached Honolulu the following day at 1:30 PM, having taken a course north of Maui to avoid possible attack from Japanese subs. The Japanese subs had

DOI: 10.5876/9781607323440.c013

been quite active in the channel between the islands of Hawaii and Maui and there [was a] news leakage of a couple of ships being attacked by them in the channel. In fact, Hilo Harbor itself was attacked some time after the war started and while I was still at home. I could recall vividly that event which shook the people of Hilo with fear.

When we landed in Honolulu, we were transported from the pier to the immigration station located at the waterfront. It was a two-story building and we were herded into a second floor room filled with cots stacked four high with only walking spaces between. There were already many internees there from Oahu and other islands. They each had stories to relate about their arrest and hearings. There were some incidents within this confinement. One had tried to commit suicide by cutting his wrist. He was discovered and received treatment in time but this caused the authorities to prohibit any razor blades and only provided them at certain times when they were given time to shave.

Other inmates kept coming in and it became really overcrowded. Toilet facility was not enough for the number of people there and we had to get in line for it. Also since there weren't enough sinks to do laundry, one of the toilet bowls was commissioned for that purpose so that relieving oneself became a problem too. After 2 days at the immigration station finger-printing and photographing, we were transferred across to Sand Island with a large barge. There were already about 200 inmates awaiting there. There was also another fenced in area where some women were detained in a two-story cottage. A haole woman was in charge of them and from what we heard she was the wife of the camp commander. But unlike the commander who was very strict and quite hard to the inmates, she was kind and well liked by the women inmates. They held Christian services on Sunday mornings and people in the men's camp who wished to attend the service were allowed to go there. Many men, although not Christians, applied to go to the service, mainly because they were starved for the sight of women. I attended it too and was treated to the warm welcome of the women folks.[1]

There was also a true Japanese prisoner of war confined in a cottage near the women's compound. He was one of those who came in to attack on that fateful day with the two-man submarine. He went into the Kaneohe marine base and was captured there unconscious in a damaged sub. However, he was sent over to mainland camp together with the first groups of internees and there were none there until more prisoners were sent in from various war fronts.[2]

After ten days at Sand Island, 110 of us were called out and sent aboard a large passenger ship, believed to be the old *Matsonia*, which had been commissioned for military service. After being confined below deck in the sweltering heat for a day and night, the ship set sail with a flotilla of ten other ships, convoyed by two destroyers. It was May 24th.

The trip was very smooth but in spite of it, being a very poor sailor, I was laid up and slept in the army bunk all through the trip. I hardly could eat and would throw up anything I ate. So having nothing to eat, when we were weighed at Angel Island, I was down to 165 pounds from 185 pounds I usually had before confinement. The trip from Hawaii to our destination, which happened to be San Francisco, normally took four days, but since the convoy took a zig-zag course in order to avoid the Japanese subs which might be waiting for them, it took 8 days. It was June 1st around 3 pm when we finally reached our destination. We were confined under the forward deck and through the portholes, we were given a thrilling sight of the famous Golden Gate Bridge for the first time. I enjoyed it in spite of the condition we were in. I had never hoped to see the mainland and to think that I was able to see it now without a cent, made me feel that being interned wasn't all bad. Only the future would tell but if it turns out all right in the end, this new experience should be one of the most valuable experiences in my life.

The ship sailed into the bay under the bridge and docked. There were many dock workers staring curiously at us. Going without bathing and also not [having] been allowed to shave, we must have presented a very miserable appearance. We had our suits on but they were all wrinkled and soiled. With army duffel bags on our shoulders, marching single file down the plank, guarded by soldiers with fixed bayonets, we must have appeared like real prisoner of war criminals. It truly was humiliating.

We were apprehensive about the train, for we had heard that the previous internees shipped out were taken to their inland camps aboard freight trains. But to our great relief, the train awaiting us was a passenger train and although it was quite old, the seats were wide and comfortable enough. We finally pulled out at 8:45 PM. Being summer it wasn't dark yet and we were able to enjoy the scenery for about half-an-hour as we went through the city and into the countryside. As darkness settled down along the track, we

NEVADA DESERT, 6-5-42

SALT LAKE, UTAH 6-5-42

FIGURE 13.1. "Nevada Desert" and "Salt Lake, Utah," June 5, 1942. George drew several pictures from his journey, which he chose to view optimistically as a tremendous opportunity to travel. He described these views in his diary, but they have been omitted here for length.

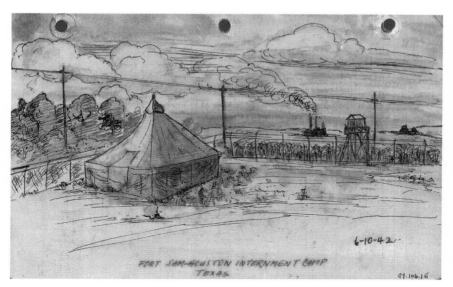

FIGURE 13.2. "San Antonio Texas/ Fort Sam Houston Internment Camp," June 12, 1942. The first of five camps where George would be incarcerated on the mainland: San Antonio, Lordsburg, Santa Fe, Jerome, and Gila River. He erroneously calls it Fort Worth Internment Camp in the memoir.

went through some beautiful spectacles of lighted cities. Some exclaimed that after the long blackout they went through, this trip was worthwhile even for this alone.

The area was about ten acres with the sign "Fort Worth Internment Camp" written on a board by the gate.[3] Inside the tents were set in several rows on bare graveled ground. It was around 10 o'clock now and the sun shone white and hot on the gravels.

So this was the camp where we are to be confined! It was really a disheartening disappointment. There was a German internee who had been sent to the Wisconsin Internment camp, through some oversight, and returned to Sand Island.[4] He had described the camp as situated in a beautiful spot among refreshing forests with mountain peaks in the background. The facilities there were well-planned and the internees were as comfortably confined as was possible under the circumstances. We may be all right if this was just temporary quarters. But we had no way of knowing how long we would be here, for the officers would not inform us about their future plans.

We could see quite a number of internees who had preceded us here and they crowded near the gate to greet us with warm welcoming smiles and waving of arms. But strangely ones who appeared to be our own nationals wore green uniforms, apparently old army uniforms dyed for our use and they were printed in white "PW" on the back of the shirts and also on the front of their pants. This was not right for we were not prisoners of war but just civilian internees. There were also quite a few other inmates of foreign features—apparently of German and Italian nationals. There were about 300 of them in all, and half of them appeared to be Japanese and the other half divided about equally between Germans and Italians. The Japanese, we learned later, were from Alaska and they were the ones with the pants and shirts or jackets marked PW. They said that they were taken and treated as such when they were arrested.

After standing there sweating miserably in the searing sun, we were finally assigned living quarters in the first two rows of tents at the east side of camp. I was given a tent marked 46 together with five other fellow internees. The camp was bound by barbed wires with another fence of meshed wire about five feet beyond. Civilian cars, passing our camp on the highway, brought us to the realization of our miserable plight most acutely. We had looked upon this country as our home, but to be treated as an enemy alien and dangerous to the security of this country and be segregated and confined behind barbed wires under guard was a rude awakening. We would have gladly relinquished our affiliation to the land of our birth and become citizens of this country of adoption but discriminating naturalization laws has denied us that privilege.

To us Hawaiians, coming from the temperate climate cooled by the northwest breeze, this heat was really hellish. We had to go under a cold shower several times a day in order to keep cool. The ration was poor and we were hungry long before the next chow bell in spite of the fact that we did no physical labor. We just lay on the cots or under them because it was too hot to move around outside during the day.

But as time passed, we got used to the heat and during the morning when it was cooler, we amused ourselves looking for fossils of shells and pretty stones. There was an army canteen operated by the internees there at the fort. But without any funds we were only able to purchase some bare needs

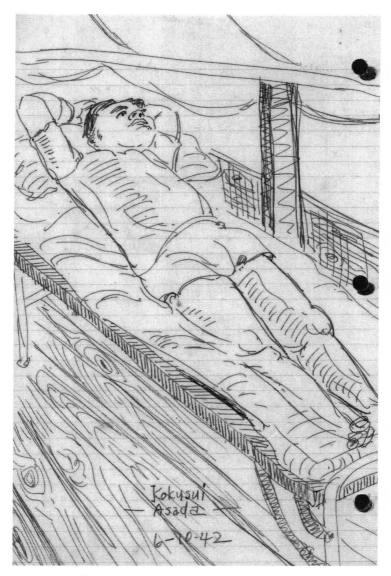

FIGURE 13.3. "Kokusui Asada," June 10, 1942. Enduring the midday heat in San Antonio's Fort Sam Houston camp. The digitized National Archives records of Hawaiian "Civilian Internees" do not list a Kokusui Asada. This may be Shigeru Asada, one of George's fellow prisoners from Hilo, whom he drew at other times. "Kokusui" may simply be a nickname or descriptor, since the word means "national essence or character."

when we could borrow from those who had spare [change] with them. On rare occasions some generous people would treat us with soda pops to refresh our parched throats.

The internees here, being confined and treated as enemies with no hope of ever being released in the foreseeable future, finally became resigned to being true enemy aliens. So, strengthened by the number of fellow sufferers, the feeling that they might as well act as the nationals of their homeland became strong. The German and the Italian internees started to march around the compound in formation singing their national anthems, proudly and loudly, with their right arms raised in salute to their homeland leaders. Soon the Japanese internees contracted their fever and started to follow them around enthusiastically singing their own national anthem and finishing the march with the pronouncement of "Banzai!" The guards didn't interfere and the soldiers across the fence looked on—some amused and others in disgust.

Hilo, Hawaii

June 19, 1942

My dear husband:

I received your letter of June 9th from Texas and was very much releived to know that you are safe and in good health. I am sure that trip was a treat for you. I certainly wish that I had traveled with you too. Yes, perhaps someday we'll travel together. Lets keep our fingers crossed.

I also received your two letters one from Frisco and the other from Sand Island the one you wrote the last.

Everyone home is in good health and doing very well. The children and I are very healthy and strong so do not worry. June had her 6th birthday. Sandra is going to be 2 years old soon. She has certainly grown now. I wish you could see her. She doesn't forget you, she always asks for daddy, especially when she sees your pictures. June has certainly grown too. She will be going to Kapiolani School from September for convenience. She can wait at the Hisanagas.

Takeo is staying with me since May and [it] is very nice to think that a man is in the house. The children and I feel safe with him and very convenient too. He goes odd things for us like yard work etc. and so you shouldn't worry at all and besides your mother does a lot for me too. She plant lots of vegetables and some other things, so we don't have to buy so much. She made a good garden all by herself. She is very nice to me so do not worry.

I am well taken care of by the Welfare Div. and in time of birth they are going to see that my expenses are paid etc. Hope its a boy, don't you? Nothing to worry really.

Remember don't leave there no matter what, the children and I love you and expect you to return to us as soon as everything becomes normal.

All the relatives are fine and very nice to me. Write to me when you are able to and I shall do the same. Take the best of care and I'll pray that you'll come back very soon[.] Be good now!!

Good-Bye

Yours with love

Tamae Hoshida

P.S. My mother sends her best regards and wishes you to come home soon.

The order to move to Lordsburg, New Mexico, came after nine days at this camp. However, the German and Italian internees were left behind and we from Hawaii and Alaska were ordered to move. Although together only for a brief time, the Germans and Italians must have felt some kinship with us, for they crowded near the fence to bid us farewell. We didn't hear the reasons were their being confined here but it must be on some suspicion of subversive actions. We never learned of their fate either. War plays untold tragedies. How sad.

We filed out of the camp gate on the afternoon of June 17, 1942. The fleet of army trucks took us back to the railroad depot for a night and a day's trip. The train came to a stop at the middle of a desolate desert. About two miles above a gentle slope, a fenced-in area could be seen with towers at regular intervals silhouetted against the cloudless shimmering sky. Rooftops of rows of what appeared like barracks appeared beyond the fence. As we watched, whirlwind of yellow dust rose among the barracks and blew downwind in a hazy mass. The temperature in the early afternoon must have been well over a hundred.

The camp was quite large and divided into three compounds—which we later learned were made to accommodate a thousand internees each. A separate fenced-in area apart from the internees' compounds was for the administration and guards' quarters. The train which transported us here was gone.

Only the desolate wasteland with the rail steel gleaming in the hot sun gave us the feeling of being left alone in the middle of nowhere and struck mercilessly into our miserable hearts.[5]

NOTES

1. Sand Island Detention Center was a military facility that held all those Japanese Americans arrested on Oahu as well as those in transit to the mainland, like George. In 1943, due to security concerns, the remaining prisoners were taken to a military facility at Honouliuli. Sand Island later became a POW camp. See Miyamoto, *Hawaii*.

2. The POW was Ensign Kazuo Sakamaki, the sole survivor of the five mini-submarines used in the Japanese attack on Pearl Harbor. Sakamaki's submarine, HA-19, was used in War Bonds drives during World War II and is currently on view at the National Museum of the Pacific War. In his memoir, he recalled nothing of his captivity at Sand Island except several suicide attempts, "my mind working only in a haze and in dark despair." He was later returned to Japan and became a pacifist. (Goldstein, "Kazuo Sakamaki, 81, Pacific P.O.W. No. 1"; Sakamaki, *I Attacked Pearl Harbor*, 49.)

3. George refers to this camp here as the Fort Worth Internment Camp but labels some pictures San Antonio or Sam Houston. It is certainly Fort Sam Houston (outside San Antonio), another military facility used as a temporary holding camp for Japanese Americans in transit.

4. The Wisconsin camp was Camp McCoy, also a military training facility, which was used to hold Japanese (and other) nationals temporarily, including POWs.

5. The Lordsburg camp, in southwest New Mexico, was a large military internment camp, designed to be permanent; it held at its height about 2,500 incarcerees, Japanese and German nationals, later released to the INS. It held German POWs from 1944.

CHAPTER FOURTEEN

Lordsburg Internment Camp

George Y. Hoshida (ISNHJ-1133-C1)
Co. 10—No. 4, Internee Camp
Lordsburg, New Mexico

June 21, 1942

Mrs. Tamae Hoshida,
483 Kalanikoa Ave.
Hilo, Hawaii
My dear wife:

Hope you've received my letters of [SEVERAL LINES CENSORED]. Everything is new and well arranged here. Only its very hot and dusty with temperature over [CENSORED] during the day time and we spend the day in indoors and cold showers. After all there's no place like Hawaii. I've sweat all the fat out of myself and have lost weight and feel very fine. Hope I can remain that way instead of going back to that [CENSORED] lb. baby elephant.

How's June and Sandra and the baby? Believe the baby must be full of pep and kicking. Hope everyone is all right too. Give my aloha to them all. Keep yourself healthy and wait for me with "sonny."

Sorry I couldn't meet Setchan. He might have been in Texas. Have you heard from him and also how's Itchan and Kazuo?[1] Send me some 20¢ stamps.

Adios with love,

George

July 13, 1942

My dear wife:

Haven't heard from you yet but hope you are all right. Believe Sandra must be very cute jabbering away. She'll be two by the time this letter reaches you, I believe. June must have grown quite a bit too, since it's over 5 mos. since I left home. Guess she's a good girl and helping mama. I believe you're getting heavier too. Don't strain yourself and don't worry about things so that we can welcome a very husky and healthy "boy." Give him or her whatever name you think good. I'm getting along fine too and feel much better with all my excess fat gone. Believe you'll like me better. [LINE CENSORED][2] I'm not certain that I'll be going but believe it better all around if I can. We'll have very little opportunities left in Hawaii after the war and believe will be better to start over in Japan. I'll write again when things are definite. Meanwhile take good care and give my love to all.

Love

George.

Hilo, Hawaii

July 19, 1942

Dear brother

I've acknowledge your letter upon receipt. It gave us great relief to know of your destination and that you are in good health. Our only regret is that you are not with us. Aside of that we are all in good health and that everybody is doing their part very nicely. With many thanks to the Welfare for their support that the family is able to get along. So please don't worry about home for ever since you left for the mainland I was with your family. With mother too of course and that we are doing to the best of our ability to aid <u>her</u> to her convenience. So don't worry but keep yourself in good condition

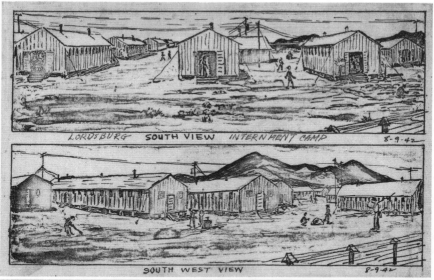

FIGURES 14.1. and 14.2. Lordsburg Internment Camp, South View, South-West View, and North-East View, August and October 1942. The bleak view of the camp at Lordsburg, New Mexico, surrounded by what George called "desolate wasteland." The North-East view was first published in *Poets behind Barbed Wire*, ed. Nakano and Nakano.

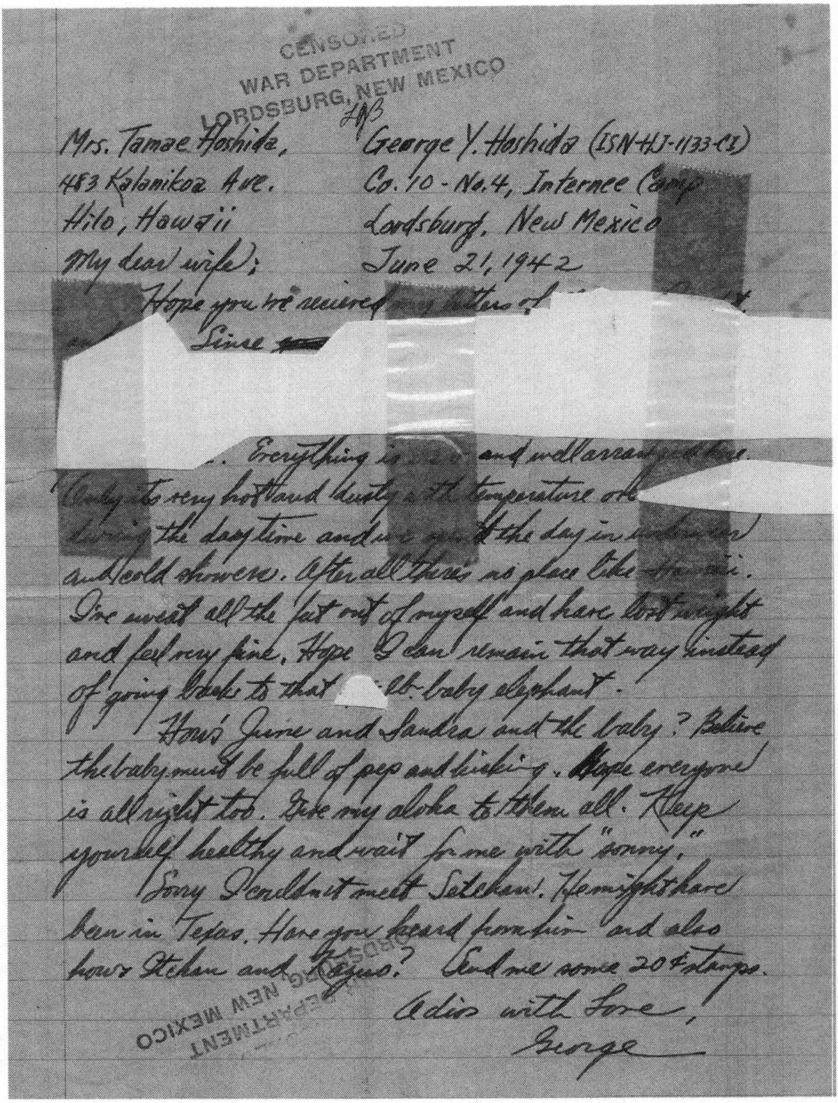

Mrs. Tamae Hoshida,   George Y. Hoshida (ISN-HJ-1133-CI)
483 Kalanikoa Ave.   Co. 10 - No. 4, Internee Camp
Hilo, Hawaii   Lordsburg, New Mexico

My dear wife;   June 21, 1942

Hope you've received ... letters of

Since

... Everything is ... and well arranged here.
Only it's very hot and dusty ... the temperature ...
during the day time and ... the day in ...
and cold showers. After all there's no place like ...
I've sweat all the fat out of myself and have lost weight
and feel very fine. Hope I can remain that way instead
of going back to that ... elt. baby elephant.

How's June and Sandra and the baby? Believe
the baby must be full of pep and kicking. Hope everyone
is all right too. Give my aloha to them all. Keep
yourself healthy and wait for me with "sonny."

Sorry I couldn't meet Satshan! He might have
been in Texas. Have you heard from him and also
how's Stchan and Kejus? And me some 20¢ stamps.

Adios with Love,
George

FIGURE 14.3. Letter from George to Tamae, June 21, 1942. This is the original of George's first letter from Lordsburg. Note the lines that have been cut out, possibly because they described the incarcerees' geographical movements. The temperature number was cut out probably as a routine precaution against numerical codes, though the "20" in "some 20¢ stamps" was left. Generally, as the Hoshidas discussed mostly family affairs, their letters were not this heavily censored.

and please <u>remember</u> this is our only prayer. Don't ever think of leaving the "Good Old U.S.A." For I guess you know that there is no other countries that is better living than the United States of America. So whatever you do please take good care of yourself. And let us pray that the war be over and that we shall all meet again. So until then.

Adios

Your brother

Raymond Hoshida

July 25, 1942

Dear daddy,

How are you? Mother, Sandra and I are in the Best of health. Grandma and uncle Takeo is staying with us. I am learning to play piano and learning to dance hula. I am waiting for you to come home to show you how I can dance. I can swim too. I go swimming with Sumi folks. We miss you very much and pray to God to let my daddy come home to us. Sandra always takes your picture and says "daddy." I am going to be in the first grade. I am going to Kapiolani School with Sumi. I will be a big girl when you come home. We all miss you. Take good care of yourself. Don't forget to come home. Goodbye.

Love,

June

July 26, 1942

{Note in George's handwriting} Rec'd 9–5–42 Ans[wered] 9–7–42

My dear husband,

I received your letter dated June 9, and was very happy to receive and learn that you reached safely. I wrote a letter to you and mailed it to Texes. I also received the letter you wrote to me from Angel Island. Didn't receive any letter from you since you folks moved to [New] Mexico. You have written for some of the boys in the camp and their families have received the letters. I am very disappointed for it looks like I am the only one who did not receive any letter from you since you went to Mexico. Please write to me first and than for the others for I am always waiting for your letter to come. If I don't receive any and other's do I get very disappointed. Don't forget to write to me whenever you have time.

We are all fine and in the best of health. I am repeating what I wrote to you last time for I don't know if you received the letter I mailed to Texes. Takeo and your mother is with me. Takeo is staying with us from May. We feel much safer with him with us so don't worry. He does my shopping, cleans the yard, watch the children and take us out whenever I want to go. Your mother helps me a lot in the housework and she even made a vegetable garden for us. Hope you were home to help us eat the vegetables. Don't worry about home for Takeo is going to stay with me till you come home. So you see we are just waiting for you to come home. He also takes care of the car so don't worry.

I am well taken cared by the welfare. I am going every month to mothers clinic and they examines me. I am just fine and waiting to see if my baby is going to be a Jr. I look very healthy and every month I am just gaining weight so you see you don't have to worry. At time of birth, the welfare is going to take care of me and let me go to the hospital. Every month the welfare is giving me money and food. All the nourishing things for Sandra, June and I. Yum! Yum! June had her glasses changed by the welfare. Don't worry about home and you just take care of yourself. Remember that after the war you are going to come back to me and the children. Whatever happens stay in the U.S. and don't move. The children, your mother, brothers, my sister, mother and the rest of the relatives are waiting for you to come home so take good care of your health.

June and Sandra is getting to be big girls. They sure miss you. June goes over to my sisters everytime and learns hula and piano. She has written a letter to you so I have it enclosed. I am going to send her to Kapiolani school for she can go to school with Sumi. She is going to stay over my sisters place after school and Takeo will go and get her so don't worry. Sandra's birthday is going to be this month and she is going to be two years old. Isn't it fast. Remember last year you were here to give her a birthday party? Time sure flies. She is starting to talk a little. She always takes your picture and says "daddy" so she still knows you. Don't worry about the children for I have them in the house and when I go or grandma goes out in the yard we take them. Sandra and June has already received their gas mask and we are very thankful for what they are doing to keep us safe. We have received word that Taeko is just fine and getting used to. She is well taken cared of so don't worry. I guess there will be a day when you and I can go over to see her.

Don't forget to write to me as soon as you can. When you need anything let us know. Take good care of yourself and don't worry about home.
Remember, we are waiting for you to come home. Write soon.

Your loving wife,

Mrs. Tamae Hoshida

Aug. 1, 1942

Dearest wife:

Haven't heard from you yet but guess will pretty soon. Hope you and the
children are all right. Believe you are getting pretty heavy by now. It's 3 months
more isn't it? Hope it'll come out all right. Be very careful and do not strain
yourself. Hope mother is with you yet. Yesterday was Sandra's birthday and I
was just wondering how much she's grown. Hope June is behaving nicely. Our
returning to Japan seems to be getting pretty sure but still is not definite yet.
I'll write again as soon as it is definite. Don't worry about me as I'll be together with Mr. Isemoto, and as soon as I can, after the war, I'll let you know about
arrangements. Perhaps you'll have to join me in Japan so be prepared for any
change. I believe everything will turn out all right. Give my aloha to all.

Love,

George

Telegram to George Hoshida

LETTER RECEIVED DON'T REPATRIATE ALL WELL =
TANAE [*sic*] HOSHIDA

Hilo, Hawaii

August 1, 1942

My dearest husband,

I received your letter dated July 13th on August 1st I am happy to know
that you are in good health, but try not to get any thinner for I prefer you as
you have been. I have answered two letters previously one to Texas and the
other to New Mexico.

As for us we are getting along moderately. The children are all healthy,
and I am expecting the newcomers sometime in October. Don't worry about
the name for the relatives will think up a good name.

I telegraphed you begging you not to leave, but if you are forced to go, then I cannot prevent you from going, but if you are able to stay back, then by all means please don't go— We are all waiting for you.

As you know Uncle Sam is taking care of me the best way he can. When I give birth, Uncle Sam will again aid me. Are you going to desert him now? You have a debt to pay, not in the sense of money but by being loyal. I know you have not done anything wrong. No country is as [lenient] as the U.S. and now as helpful. I am positive you will be giving a chance to start over.

June will be a first grader starting Sept. She has grown quite a bit. She always ask about you. Sandra is now two years old and growing too.

I wrote to Waimano home asking about Taeko. I have received word from the institution stating she is fine and that she has gained weight, but physically and mentally is the same.

Takeo and mother are still with me. Takeo is helping me quite a lot. I shall close now, but again do not worry about us. Please write soon and decide for the best. Let me know whether you have received my two letters. Take good care of yourself and I shall pray for the day when we can again be together.

Good-bye,
With love
Tamae Hoshida

P.S. Enclosed two pictures of the family.

Aug. 13, 1942

My dearest husband,

I received five letters from you the last of which was dated July 13, 1942. Today I received two letters dated June 21, and July 3rd so I received the letter you mailed on July 13, before the other two.

I am glad that you are healthy and getting along fine.

There is absolutely no worry about home. In fact we worry more about you so please take good care of yourself. The children are very healthy. June will, as I have told you before, attend school this September. I shall enter her in the Hilo Standard for she has a fine record. Sandra is now able to jab[ber] away. She is lots of fun and very cute. The baby has not yet arrived. I expect ("him or she") about the middle part of October.

The next time you write tell me about your daily life. Everytime when I receive your letter its been censored and cut off, so whatever you write please be careful.

I wonder if you have received my <u>wire</u>. Again I beg of you, please don't leave the children and me, because we are all waiting for you. Please come home after everything is over.

In your previous letter you stated that you dreamt of the family. I do the same. The funny thing about it is that whenever I dream that you were home with me I always receive your letter the following day. This has happen everytime when I receive your letter.

Takeo and your mother are still with me, so don't worry. Both grandmas are waiting for you too. All the relatives and friends are all fine. They all send you their best regards, and that to keep yourself in the best of health.

Kazuma is at Wisconsin. Kazuo and Itsue are at Ohio State.[3] This is their address.

> Itsue Hisanaga
> Talcott Hall
> Oberlin, Ohio

Setsuo is at Little Rock Arkansas.[4] His address is Corporal Setsuo Takemoto 19083457

> Co. "C" 61st Tmg. BN., 13th Regt.
> Camp Joseph T. Robinson, Arkansas
> U.S. Army

I am sending you five 20¢ stamps now but the next time I'll send you more. Well, I guess this is all for now. Please write to me soon & I shall do the same. Take very good care of yourself & be good.

> Good-Bye
> With love
> Tamae Hoshida

The thermometer registered 58 this morning. It's getting cooler steadily. It is said that it gets below zero during the winter and that it will snow sometimes. I'll have a new experience in seeing and feeling the snow. But its really hot during the day. It must be around 110 outside now at 12:50 P.M.

Received letter from wife for the first time day before yesterday since arriving in mainland June 1st. Receiving letter is quite an event now. Some who were lucky had received their first letters but many haven't yet, although packages and telegrams were received by some. The letter must go through censor three or four times before being received.

June has [turned] six on June 23rd and Sandra two on July 31st. They sure must have grown and changed since I left six months and 13 days ago.

Aug. 19, 1942

Dearest wife:

Received your letter of July 19th, day before yesterday and was sure glad to get it. Many haven't received theirs yet and a letter from home is really a great event. Glad to know that you are all doing well. I feel very much relieved to know that Takeo and mother [are] with you. I'll know that you'll be safe. Received your telegram on the 6th and have written an answer the next day but I knew that you'd be worried, so have arranged to have telegram sent you a few days ago but I believe it's not sent yet.

I might have to change it or cancel it if it costs too much as although we have an allowance of $3.00 a month from the government, we cannot use our own money which is in custody at Washington. Anyway don't worry as I have decided to stay. I have taken up art again and have made sketches along the way on train. Will have quite a collection to show you when I go home. Also am busy doing pen portraits for people here to send home.

Give my regards to all. Write often.

Love,

George.

Aug. 25. 1942

My dearest Husband,

I received your letter dated Aug. 7 today and I was very glad to know that you have changed your mind about going to Japan. I was worried because if you go to Japan you might get drafted and that will certainly mean the end of you, and living in Japan is not like living in Hawaii the Paradise Isle. No matter what happens I shall wait & wait for you here until your return, after all I love only you and too we have our own property here the home you and I strugled to build. Surely you and I can live in Hawaii like we use to after the war and its so convenient don't you think with our closest relatives near us, and besides Taeko too must not left alone. We must go and see her sometimes. Mr. Nagao will be going to Honolulu this weekend and have offered to go and see <u>Taeko</u> for us. I shall write to all about her after he comes home. I am sending you a letter from the Institution about Taeko. I'm sure you'll be satisfied after you've read this.

The Welfare takes such good care of me and the children that I simply couldn't live another day without their help. I'm very fortunate don't you think so after all they're even going to help me during delivery time. So don't worry about me but please take the best of care of yourself and just wait patiently until the war ends.

So far I have written you 4 letters with stamps enclosed. Strange that you did not receive them. If its possible why don't you enquire at your office. They probably will know something about it.

Is it true that you are allowed to receive newspapers from home? If so please let me know. How are your clothing do you need any. Let me know. If you need some money don't hesitate to ask because I'll do anything to send you some.

June will start going to school on Sept. 28. I am sending her to the Kapiolani School. She sure has grown big now. She always ask me when does daddy is coming back. I liked to see him come home quick. I told her after the war ends he'll be back so be nice girl and wait. Sandra is in perfectly good health and she so mischieveous and beginning to look like you everyday.

Your mother and my mother are anxiously waiting for your return. They said no matter what happens they'll wait for you. So please take good care of yourself and come home after the war ends.

Brother-in-law is home now. They are all happy to see him come back. I wish I have a time like them.

If your able to why don't you write to Setsuo he is in Arkansas and his address is in the previous letter.

Toshi will probably marry Robert in the near future, if she makes up her mind. She is considering the matter now. But she's certainly happy. She wish you were here to give Robert some good advice.

Please take good care of yourself and be sure to come home for I am waiting for you everyday. I will write again.

With love

Tamae Hoshida

P.S. I enclosed some stamps for you for your convenience.

Aug. 31, 1942

My dearest husband,

I was so happy to receive your letter of Aug. 19, today. It is happiest and most encouraging letter since you left. I am glad that you have decided to stay and that you are busy with your hobbies. Surely we'll have so much fun after the war, looking at your sketches and talking things over of ourselves. I hope everything will be over quickly.

I am getting heavier everyday and will soon have the blessed event. My only wish is to have a son then I know you'll be the happiest man. Sister-in-law Mrs. R. Takemoto said that she'll wire you as soon as I deliver so please don't get shocked.

Won't you write to me more about yourself, and while you are there please take very good care of yourself. Your birthday will be in October and June remembers that day very well and is already prepared to send you a present. Isn't she cute?

Yesterday the Takemotos' received a notice saying that their dog "Fly" is to volunteer in the U.S. army. They are very proud of him and feel sad even if "Fly" is only a dog after all he is treated just like one of the member of the family.[5]

I have answered all your letters everytime I received them, and have also enclosed stamps in two letters so I guess you'll receive them all very soon.

Everybody at home is fine so do not worry.

Take good care of yourself and [be] patient for you'll have a "son" soon. Best regards from all. Please write often. Always waiting for you.

With love,

Your wife

Tamae Hoshida

P.S. Enclosed you will find letter from your daughter June.

AUG. 27, 1942 (THURS.)

It was cloudy and sunless this early morning and only now the sun started to cast its pale warm rays through the break in the thinning clouds. It's 10:27 AM now and cool. I'm in undershirt and shorts although it is a bit too cool for this scanty attire,

It's about two-and-a-half months since our arrival at this camp in the middle of the scorching summer month of June. The camp was not yet finished [and we] found the latrine with only couple of bowls and a single faucet which were usable so that the 250 internees who were herded into one section of the compound had a difficult time trying to wash up the dust which covered our faces. We were the first ones to come into camp and to make this hellhole livable was a tremendous task.

The grounds were dug up and not yet leveled. Rubbish was strewn around all over. The dirt dug up dried up into fine dust and was stirred up by the whirlwinds which attacked us every few minutes. We had to cover our mouths and nostrils with wet handkerchiefs to keep the dust out of our lungs and prevent from choking.

We were given instructions from the officer in charge about assignments of barracks, distribution of supplies and requests for volunteer cooks and KPs. When each of us received quarters in the barracks, we were given individual cots. The younger ones were asked to go to the storage barrack for blankets, sheets and pillows. Others helped each other dusting up the cots, cleaning the sills and windows covered with brown dust and then sweep the mess out of the barrack. However, this was not easy, for as soon as we got some cleaning done, the whirlwind would blow through one end of the barrack to the other and cover everything with dust again. Someone had to watch the double door at the end of the barrack to close it as soon he saw the wind coming.

But when the windows and doors were closed, the above hundred degree heat would become unbearable. So it was miserable either way until the afternoon waned into dusk and the air became cooler and the wind also subsided. Then after dark, the millions of stars twinkling in the clear desert sky made this hellish abode into a beautiful dreamland. So this life wasn't all bad.

The cooks and the KPs were having their problems too in getting started. Equipment and supplies had to be brought in and preparation of food according to the menu supplied by the authorities was a slow process without organized system. However, they somehow managed to cook up something for the hungry internees. We all appreciated their efforts and although their future was uncertain, the tired internees felt real relief from the long track through this huge continent, and slept well that first night at this new camp with an assurance that their journey had ended at last.

FIGURE 14.4. "Our Barrack, Lordsburg Internment Camp, Company 10—Barrack #4," July 4, 1942. This drawing was done very shortly after George's arrival at the camp. Note the difference between this rather spare barrack and the drawing in figure 15.1, which shows the barrack after the internees had purchased and constructed various comforts.

AUGUST 29, 1942

There were 32 workmen assigned for outside duty today through the order of the Camp Commander, but it seemed quite unfair when compared to the proportion of men put out from the other compound. We've refused to work outside of our own compounds, on grounds that it should be on voluntary basis. The other camps where we were in didn't force us to work outside the enclosure where we were confined. Also the internees who came in from Missoula Internment Camp[6] said that, according to the order and understanding from the State Department under whose jurisdiction we were confined, we were under the prisoner of war regulations which forbid any outside work except on volunteer basis.

So we refused to work and as punishment we were confined in our barracks for a day. Representatives were then called to the office of the camp commander for discussion. Compromise was reached with the understanding

FIGURE 14.5. "Lordsburg New Mex. Internment Camp 1st Nite," June 18, 1942. The stars came out on the first night, after what George described as a long day of cleaning in the dusty heat. The horned toad drawing may be a later addition, but he was always curious about the unfamiliar plants and animals on the mainland.

that not more than 75 men were to work outside, and that only during the cooler morning hours.

However, for some reason, the camp commander didn't stick to the agreement and ordered more men to work outside of our enclosures and also forced us to work in the afternoon too.

Then two weeks later, the commander sent out questionnaires asking individuals whether "we would work eight hours daily if necessary inside or outside our compound as specified under the Internees' Regulations and Geneva Convention PW Regulations." Interpretations on this question varied. Since it said that "as specified under the internees' Regulations," it sounded legitimate but the preceding "would work 8 hours daily if necessary inside or outside our compound" was actually consenting to working outside 8 hours a day—meaning we would be working outside voluntarily and would fit into the commander's original wishes. So, this question was very tricky and actually no different from what the commander wanted in the first place.

The other companies said 'yes' but we in Company 10, consisting of the original Hawaiian and Alaskan internees, decided to wait for the arrival of our protecting power, the Spanish Consul in Washington, and act according to his advices. We had wired several times to have a representative from the Spanish Consulate come and were expecting his arrival soon.[7]

We wired twice again to the Spanish Consulate when we in Company 10 were segregated from the rest of the internees in Compound One and transferred to Compound Two. All but those classified as "C" (ones who were too old or sick and unfit for labor) were confined within the barracks with guards stationed outside to prevent us from going outside. All privileges such as canteen service, light at night, and going outside, except to the latrine and breathing period for 2 hours in the afternoon between 1 to 3 PM, were denied to us strikers.

The Ambassador from New Orleans finally came accompanied by a man from the State Department. The camp commander, Lt. Col. Lundy, also was present at the meeting held with our representatives. Our representatives were Mayor Kawabe of our company, Vice Mayor Kango Kawasaki, and ex-mayors of Co. 10 Sugimachi and Mihara.[8] They thrashed it out there at our office. The man from the State Department believed that we should work outside the compound and the Spanish Ambassador wasn't sure. But he advised us to work while he reported to the Consul at Washington and get the right answer. The camp Commander admitted his mistake in stating that work outside was voluntary and yet having us work without our consent. So we decided to work until proper interpretation on this issue was cleared.

We responded to the work detail called for by the commander's headquarters but it seemed that the commander was bent on retaliation for our disobedience to his command. Our men were assigned work every day for eight full hours, most of which were heavy outside pick and shovel details. Men qualified for heavy work were put under different classification from those only fit for light work (classified under "L" to do only light indoor work). However, since the order called for heavy work every day, we had to ask some of the men from "L" group to relieve the regular workers from overworking themselves at long hours of work in the blistering sun.

The work itself wasn't too bad at times but the scorching heat which went above 100 degrees was very cruel to the workers. The workers averaged over 50 years old and the majority of them, being businessmen, ministers, and school teachers, were not used to hard labor, especially in this cruel heat. We wouldn't mind and would have been willing to sacrifice ourselves if we were treated fairly in proportion to the men from the other compound. There were about 1000 men in there and we had only 191. We should, therefore, be assigned less than 20% of theirs. But as far as we could see, there didn't seem to be very many men doing outside work from there, and also their work was mainly indoor light work. They also worked only during the morning and very seldom in the afternoon, while we were forced to work the whole day. The commander definitely seemed bent on revenge and punishment on us who had disobeyed his wishes.

We filed complaint through our company representative and were relieved of the assignment on that day. But the following day saw increased assignments again, and today, 8 men more than usual—a total of 32 men in the morning and 24 in the afternoon—were drafted. Twenty-four of the workmen were for outside work.

The work in the administration compound was quite apprehensive, for the guards assigned to us regarded us as dangerous and tricky war criminals. Consequently, they were afraid and nervous themselves. They wouldn't have hesitated to shoot us down if any one of us [made] a sudden move which they may misinterpret as showing hostility to them.[9]

I went out once as overseer for a group of workmen from our company because I could talk both English and Japanese and can act as liaison when necessary. For the same reason I was elected as captain of our barrack and later given job also of assigning work detail for our company.

I went out for the first time with about 20 people for weeding assignment in the administration compound grounds. Two guards stood watch over us with bayonetted guns. One of them was a young man but was quite hostile his attitude toward us. He would shout at anyone who slackened his pace at work and commanded him to get going and menaced him with his gun. I finally decided to have a talk with him and approached him. He then moved back, and pointing his gun at me, ordered me to keep my distance. Apparently they may [have] been given orders to keep some distance from us.

I stopped then and asked him in a friendly tone why he was so hostile toward us. He answered, "I can't trust you guys and if you make any false move, I'll shoot you down!"

I answered, "I'm sorry you feel that way toward us but we are not here because did anything wrong. Actually, these people are business men, ministers, school teachers, and those in leadership positions in our community back in Hawaii, and they have no intention to cause any trouble."

"But you must have done something wrong or the military wouldn't have sent you here. Anyway, I hate you Japs! My twin brother was killed at Pearl Harbor when your people bombed the harbor!" he countered.

"I'm sorry to hear that. I really can't blame you for feeling that way. I sympathize with you. We hate the war just as much as you do. It's really tragic and sad to see so many people killed and injured in a war which we as individuals have [done nothing] to cause. We are just as much a casualty of this war as you are to have to be here in this hot sun to watch us. We only hope that this will be settled as soon as possible so that we all can go home and live peacefully again. But in the meantime let's not make things any harder for each other. We people from Hawaii are not used to this hot desert sun nor to this kind of work."

He then seemed to soften in his attitude and after a while when time for a break came, he suggested that we rest in the shade of a shed nearby instead of the hot sun. So, as days went by and the guards began to understand we were not dangerous war criminals but just as human and no different from them, they became quite friendly. However, there were changes of personnel periodically, and when new ones came in, we had to bear their hostility again until they got used to us.

SEPTEMBER 2, 1942

A hearing is being held today for the killing of two internees, Mr. Hirota Isomura and Mr. Toshio Kobata. A group of mainland internees was transferred from the Santa Fe Internment Camp on July 27th. They arrived early in the morning and since the two of them were ill and unable to walk to the camp, they were left behind at the railside to have them transported to the camp by jeep. While they were left unattended when the guard went to get a jeep, a sergeant came along. Seeing them alone he thought that they were attempting to escape. He must have approached them with drawn gun and the two becoming panicky at the sight of the gun, may have run. The sergeant then shot them down in cold blood.

Story came in later that people at a bar at the town of Lordsburg praised him as being a hero shooting down the dangerous Japs single-handed, and gathered a collection to reward his bravery. This is one of the tragedies coming from the evils of war. The sergeant was later declared innocent by the military board of inquiry and nothing was done to compensate for the tragic death of these innocent internees. Before leaving the camp, I had occasion to visit the graves of these two and felt deep sorrow at the tragic fate of these unfortunate men.[10]

The Alaskan internees who came with us to this camp and now in our company have very interesting stories of their lives to tell. When we met them at Fort Sam Houston camp, we felt them very peculiar, for they hardly spoke Japanese. Being very few in number, they usually lived by themselves among native Eskimos or with other nationalities so that having no opportunity to talk in Japanese, they had gradually forgotten their native tongue in the many years of their lives in Alaska. But gradually as they associated with us, they started to regain their ability to speak.

Some of them were married to Eskimos and many of them just single. Seems they had led very difficult lives in the frozen north but some had struck [it] rich. There was an old man by the name of Frank Yasuda who was married to an Eskimo woman and although we didn't learn much about him, we learned about thirty years later that he really had contributed tremendously to the welfare of a group of native Eskimos who were starving to death. His story came in the form of a movie made by a Japanese movie firm and the title was "The Alaska Story." It told of a young man who came to Alaska as a seaman and settled in a seaside village, making his living among the natives hunting whales. However, whaling business went on the rocks due to indiscriminate slaughter of whales by unlawful poachers. Frank volunteered to find the place to relocate and through overwhelming odds, he led the whole village of people to another settlement where they were able to find sustenance. At of the time of his confinement as internee, he must have been in his sixties and when his story came out as a heartwarming story, he was gone. But his children are still living and succeeding him in his valuable work as savior of these poor natives.[11]

SEPT. 8, 1942

Received letter from home again dated August 1st, the day she had telegraphed me not to repatriate. She had received my letter of July 13th in which I had written my plans for repatriation.[12] Since the future here in confinement was very uncertain, many of the internees had been discussing repatriation to Japan. The authorities had announced plans to exchange internees here with those Americans interned in Japan and many had expressed desire to repatriate.

Mr. Isemoto, the contractor who had come together with me, had planning to repatriate since he had some money in the bank in Japan. He said that since Japan is taking over the southeast Asia districts, he felt that he may be able to go down there to investigate about opportunities for some business ventures. However he would need someone to accompany and act as assistant and wanted me to go with him. With so many people talking about repatriation and this country of my adoption apparently not giving me any hope of a better future, I was swayed into thinking of repatriation.

So, I had written to Tamae about my thoughts. The answer was fast. A telegram came saying, "Do not repatriate. Stay where you are!" In fact I dreamed the night before the telegram arrived about her calling me on the phone. When I answered, I could see her face on the other end of the phone and she looked very much agitated and displeased. I greeted her but she would not answer and just glared at me without a word. The dream ended without her uttering a single word. It seems that I must have ESP or something, for many a time, when I receive letters from her, I would dream about her or the home and this one was really clear. Tamae also writes that that the same thing happens to her too. Buddhism speaks of seventh and eighth sense besides our regular six senses and it says that when one is deep in trance or sleep, the eighth sense sometimes is activated and such phenomena as ESP occurs. Guess that must be the answer. Anyway, this ended my plans for repatriation and Mr. Isemoto changed his plans and stayed back. It proved to be a wise decision, for after the war, we heard about the hardships these repatriates went through in the old country destroyed by the ravages of war never experienced before in Japan. Also some ablebodied men were conscripted as soon as they landed in Japan and many killed or injured at the battle front.

Two snapshots of Tamae and the two children were enclosed in her letter. It really gave me great pleasure seeing them again even in the picture. They seem to have grown quite a bit—the children in height and wife in girth. She'll be giving birth next month. Hope it will be a boy this time; if not, hope it will be an easy birth. The Welfare Department seems to be taking good of them and with Takeo and mother living [there] to help, I am very much relieved.

I came into the hospital yesterday as my neuralgia has been giving me [pain] and commuting for daily sun lamp treatment was becoming very inconvenient. I had the first attack two months when the 4th group from Hawaii arrived. I was laid up in bed for two weeks. It eased up but then came back again two weeks ago. This neuralgic pain seems to be the result of the back injury I suffered while packing cane bundles in the fields. It had been flaring out once in a while but believe due to the change in living condition and the climate here, this looked like the worst I've ever experienced. The cool autumn weather seems to affect it the most.

Sept. 2, 1942

My dear wife:

Received your letter of Jul. 28 and am very sorry to hear that my letters were late. I had written the first thing since moving in here but the conditions now make it very uncertain. But as long as we keep on writing we'll keep on receiving so keep on writing regular whether you receive them or not. Write at least once a week. Receiving letters are our greatest pleasure and it seemed a long time since I received your first letter addressed to Texas.

Hope you received my answer. Received your telegram on 6th last month but wasn't able to reply at once as I didn't have any money. So sent telegram around the middle of last month when I received my monthly allowance of $3.00. Got Takeo's letter & answered it too. Glad mother & he [are] with you. It's good of the welfare to take such good care of you. I'm very grateful. Hope it will be a Jr. too. Glad June is learning hula & Piano. Thank sister for her kindness & give my regards to her and family. Was hoping June would write so was very happy. Have her write often too. Believe 6¢ airmail will be just as fast. Will write June separate. Love, George.

Sept. 3, 1942

Miss June Hoshida,
483 Kalanikoa Ave.
Hilo, Hawaii, T.H.

Dear June:

I was very glad to receive your letter with mama's. Daddy is glad to know that you are learning to play hula and piano. Daddy will sure be happy to see you do the hula and play the piano when he goes home. Be good to Sandra and play nicely with Sumi. Obey what Grammas and Uncles and Aunties tell you. Tell Sumi, Matsu, Yuki, Haru, and Aunty, "thank you" for teaching you hula and piano and being so good to you. Obey what they tell you and be a nice girl. Glad you go swim[m]ing with Sumi. Be careful, though, and don't go in deep places. Send daddy snapshots when you can so daddy can see how big you grow. Tell mother to send telegram when baby is born and send photo of whole family and grandmas after baby comes. Study hard and be a bright girl when you go to Kapiolani School. Daddy is very healthy and drawing pictures. I will have lots of nice pictures for you to see when I go home. Write when mama writes. Love, Daddy.

SEPT. 11, 1942

Received 3 letters in a bunch today from home—two from wife and one from Takeo. Ones from wife were dated August 25th and 31st. This is the fastest I've ever received since coming to this camp. Receiving letters is really the greatest in this confined life and to receive three at one time is quite a thing. Although

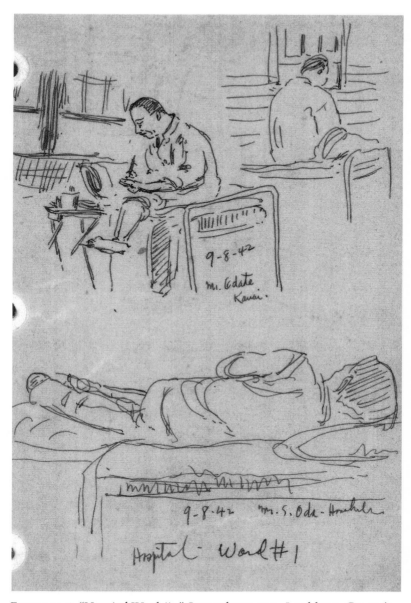

FIGURE 14.6. "Hospital Ward #1," September 8, 1942, Lordsburg. George's neuralgia, the result of a back injury he suffered packing cane in his youth, flared up in the colder weather of New Mexico, and he had to spend several weeks in the hospital and then return daily for heat treatments.

there's hardly anything different in the letters, they really give me the warmth and love I need so much in this life. However, they also make me long for home and my family more acutely.

The news brought in by the orderlies said that Port Moresby at New Guinea seems to be in danger of falling into Japanese hands. The Japanese army has crossed the mountain peaks in the northern section of the island and is within 5 miles of the port. Stalingrad in Russia is waging a fierce but losing street battle against the invading Germans and the end is reported to be within a few days. [Novorossiysk] navy port has fallen completely into German hands and [Grozny] fields are in danger. England is trying to take Madagascar from the French, and Japan has sub and air base there to fight for the French. It looks like the Allies are having a difficult time.

Sept 14. 1942

Have changed ink for my pen today. There's a little history behind it. The black ink which I had been using was purchased at Texas Sam Houston Internment Camp a couple of days after reaching there by Mr. Kagawa. He had given custody of the ink in my hands for me to help people correspond with their families. I have written a lot of letters with it for myself and others. Perhaps more for others because letters had to be written in English and practically all the people in the barrack couldn't write in English. I also had to read and interpret their letters from home. The letters to their families must have gladdened the hearts of many when they received the papers which the ink had turned into affectionate letters. These letters have traveled for thousands of miles, and if they were alive, what stories of joys, sorrows, and longings they could have revealed. A bottle of ink, just ten cents in money, but its work cannot be figured in money. They were precious acts of Karma. It has carried messages from hearts to hearts and created emotions which cannot be fathomed materially.

Wrote a letter to wife before noon in answer to her letters received on the 10th. I couldn't answer her sooner since I had already written my allowance of two letters per week to her last week. Letters are also limited to 24 lines on special forms given us by the military. So, of necessity, the messages have to be brief and it is quite difficult to express all we wish. I've written answers to her letters on this one but will have to write again to give her [my] news.

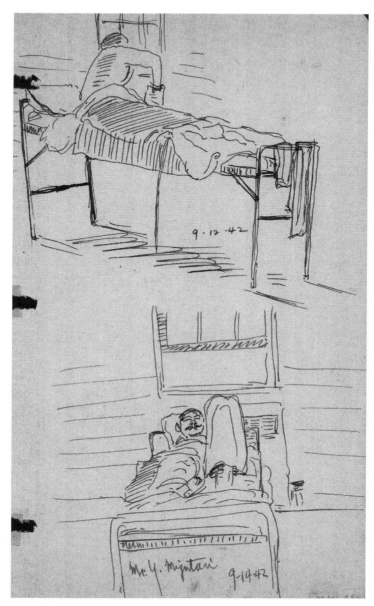

FIGURE 14.7. "Mr. Y. Mizutari," September 12 and 14, 1942. These sketches of fellow incarcerees (or perhaps both of Mizutari) resting in their cots convey the loneliness and isolation expressed in George's diary entries around these dates.

SEPTEMBER 16, 1942 (WED)

Dr. Furugochi has his hands full. He works hard from early morning through midnight. I saw him making his rounds checking on patients, treating ones in pain, even covering up one who has his blanket off and giving encouragements to others. He is a true doctor in every sense.

Patients, however, keep on increasing and there's 14 in ward 2 already. There's rumor that about 50 internees will be leaving this camp to be repatriated. Many have filed applications but the majority of them seem to have no chance on this boat. There was an article in the newspaper from Hawaii saying that 50 families of internees are to be exchanged with families of Americans interned in Japan. The evacuees in relocation centers are also given [the] chance to repatriate. Quite a number of them seem to have applied and may be leaving on this exchange ship. Arrangements for exchange are said to have encountered some difficulties at first but they have been [made] and the ship is leaving soon from New York. This ship is scheduled to rendezvous with repatriation ship from Japan somewhere near the Indian Ocean and exchange of internees done on the high seas.

I am doing some pencil drawings since few days ago and have finished seven. Have them pinned up on the wall by my side. They seem to attract attention and soldiers and officers stop by to comment favorably on them. It is pleasant to lie looking at one's work well done. Of course they cannot rate very highly as an art but for an amateur's work, they are not too bad. Hope I can keep up with the practice so that I may be able to make something of my interest. Cartooning would be a good line but guess it won't be too easy. Anyway, this is a good way to utilize my time and keep myself occupied with some productive work.

SEPT. 24, 1942

Received letter from wife today. Answered and mailed it out at once. She seems to be expecting baby earlier than scheduled. Hope it will be over quickly and safely. Mr. Nagao has visited Taeko at Waimano Home when he went out to Honolulu on a business trip recently and reported that Taeko is doing fine. It really was kind of Mr. Nagao. With Taeko at Waimano Home, it [will] be of great relief to Tamae especially now that she is faced with the birth of a new baby. Taeko was one of my biggest worries after being con-

FIGURE 14.8. "Pvt. Paul Hazelrigg" and "Brady W. Sterns, Sgt.," September 29, 1942, and August 14, 1942. Portraits of two soldiers at Lordsburg. George wrote often (not all passages included here) of drawing portraits, usually keeping copies. Another can be seen in figure 21.1.

fined away from home, but she now under the care of the government, I feel very grateful for their help. There's no hope for her recovery from that condition and her future really is dark and hopeless, but at least for the present, she seems to be under good hands.

Sandra, Tamae reports, is growing and learning to talk something new every day. Sure miss my children. How long will it be before I see them again? It would be many times more so with my wife, now separated from me and with all the struggle of supporting and taking care of the little ones. Above all she is now faced with one of the most important functions for a woman—child birth.

Lunch time now so I'll leave here.

SEPT. 25, 1942

Weather is getting cooler by the day and we are using the heater now to warm the room in the morning. The desert is greener with grasses and brushes enlivened by cool weather and occasional showers. Temperature is usually below

60 in the morning. There are some pretty wild flowers that gladden our eyes with their bright cheery colors. I should sketch them some day when I am able.

There are two new young doctors from the military now and they are very kind and considerate. The sergeants and soldiers in charge here very friendly too. Three army nurses are here but they work in the soldiers' ward and do not come into our internee wards. Three or four girls working in the supply room and other officers come to the consolidated mess hall for lunch. Being hungry for the sight of the opposite sex, they look very attractive and beautiful to our eyes.

Oct. 2, 1942

It's October already! Time sure is geared to high these days. It's almost ten months since the War started and, looking back at the events that had piled up, it seems more like ages. Wonder when it's going to end.

Things back here in the barrack appear different to me after being in the hospital for some time. It looks really shabby and cluttered up after the clean and comfortable hospital ward. The floor of our barrack [is] especially bad. Unseasoned lumber had been used and they had shrunk so that they leave wide half-inch cracks throughout the floor where cold drafts blow in.

I am in bed now although I do not feel any pain. It's just for precaution. The room heaters are working and the warm air blown by the fans feel good. The men are all engaged in some hand crafts. It changes from time to time. It keeps them pleasantly occupied and frees them, at least while they are engaged in it, from family worries. This is one experience which cannot be appreciated even if we want to at ordinary times.

The atmosphere in the camp has been greatly relieved since the transfer of the military commander and arrival of a new commander couple of months ago. It was the result of the investigation on the tense situation which led to our strike and interview with our protecting power representative. Seems the military had been checking into this and must have found the former commander at fault. So our strike after all was not in vain.

The new commander is a very gentle and warm person and understands our unfortunate position. He has been doing all he could to improve our condition so that life here has become much more bearable. A system of coupons has been adopted and each internee provided with coupons amounting to three dollars a month to be spent at the internee canteen opened in each compound. So now we are able to buy whatever simple needs we have in meeting our daily requirements. We could even buy some refreshments when we find that our immediate needs are met for the month and some coupons are left over. For the first time I enjoyed the taste of beer when a fellow inmate treated me to a bottle after sweating and working at the craft shop in the hot weather. Had never had any taste for liquor and felt only bitterness in beer but taken here in the heat of summer, it really tasted good.

Oct. 4, 1942

Dearest wife:

Received your letter of Aug. 13 together with 5 stamps yesterday. That one sure took time in coming. Anyway I was happy to receive it even if it was out of schedule. Glad to get the addresses of the niece and nephews. I'll write to them. We had [an amateur] show last night. Singing, dancing, and short plays. There are a lot of good ones and the show don't look like [amateur] and I surely enjoyed seeing & hearing them. Wish you could have seen them. I made sketches of them for my collection so you'll see it when I return home. Our daily routine is very simple. I woke up around 6 o'clock, go to toilet & take shower (we have hot & cold shower anytime). We breakfast at 7 on hotcakes, coffee, mushee and etc. and return to our barracks. Some take turns in going out to work around the camp while the majority stay back and are free to do anything. I usually have a big bunch of drawing orders and am occupied most of the time with it. Others make wooden slippers, cigaret pipes, polish stones, and play checkers, cards, and etc. We lunch at 12, supper at 5 and evenings are free or classes on language, hobby, religion are held. 10 o'clock we go in bed and dream of home. There's 3½ hrs. difference from Hawaii so you can figure out on what I'm doing any time of day. Well, happy dreams & Love, George

OCT. 7, 1942 9:25 PM

Today is exactly ten months since the war started and eight months and a day from the day I was taken for detention at the Kilauea Military Detention Camp. Since this period had been filled with so much new and extraordinary experiences, it feels like a long time and yet so short. We were presented with a case of tea sent from Japan through the International Red Cross today also. We really appreciated the present and tasted the Japanese tea which we had not had ever since we were confined. It sure tasted good and refreshing and made us feel nearer to our home. However, food seems to be scarce now. Ration we are having is very poor. Hope this is a temporary situation.

Oct. 10, 1942 (Sat) 8:35 PM

The letter that came on the 5th was written in different hand—probably by Tamae' s nephew, Masayuki. All the others had come in wife's handwriting, although I believe they had been helped out by others in composing and correcting, since she had very little schooling due to being sickly because of her injured hip during her childhood. Separation makes one worry on slightest things and this letter written by a different hand, makes me imagine things. It makes me worried a bit although there's nothing in it to make me do so. Guess that's human nature. Returning from the next compound at dusk, I thought of home on the way. Dusk, I believe, is the most depressing time of day, especially when one is away from home. My wife used to mention it in her letters and I believe that although she is used to it by now, she must have cried a lot during the early days of my internment and separation from my loved ones. She said that she used to cry at dusk when I went away for even a couple of nights on business or other trips. Guess it's because we are attached so much to each other. We've been married for over nine years now but our love has not waned yet, and I believe never will. We seem to be made for each other, and our temperament and spirits fit very well. The accident with the years of sorrow and mental sufferings must have welded our hearts tightly together. Of course we had our spats sometimes but they never lasted long and instead of forming a break, they helped to bring us together closer.

There was a radio broadcast last night by someone—I believe it was a priest—about peace. He pleaded for the immediate end to the war. He said that we should not fight with hate in our hearts and build up hate for the enemies. We should consider the fact that our ideals should not blind us to the ideals of others, and let others live in peace no matter what our differences.

I believe he has spoken with wisdom. The Allies may be against the enemy's form of government and their actions, and are fighting to awaken them to their way of government. But we must not think selfishly. Democratic form of government is no doubt very good, but it has many faults too. The Axis form of government may have their evils but they are fighting for their self-preservation also. So why can't we shelve our selfishness and meet each other on a common ground of human to human and not with our differences in race, nationality or creed. After all we are not perfect and although we may consider ourselves as right, we really cannot be so as long as we are humans with human imperfections.

Pearl Buck said that we should break down racial barriers and regard each other as fellow humans before peace can be attained. Are the Allies really conforming to this? How about Britain? Did she regard people in Asia as fellow humans? Haven't they taken over many of their countries for her selfish purpose? Is she regarding those people, who she had forced to submit to her control, as equals? If so, why are their conditions so much lower and miserable? And why did they turn around and help Japan when they were invaded by them? Not only Britain, but how about this United States? Have you read what Pearl Buck has said about the treatment the negroes are receiving in this land of liberty, equality and justice? Have you ever considered about how the negroes feel about separate waiting rooms, restaurants, train and bus seats, and many other discriminations just because they are of different color? Other minority groups have also been discriminated to varying degrees. Many of our people of Japanese origin who are actually citizens of this country through right of birth, have also been thrown into detention camps and internment camps. They are now in the process of putting all the people on the West Coast into what they call relocation camps, but actually concentration camps, regardless of whether they are aliens or citizens. Can you call this freedom, equality or justice?

Oct. 22, 1942

Received telegram from home this afternoon. "Baby girl arrived seven AM twentieth. Named Carol," it said.[13] We had been expecting today or tomorrow so it was pretty accurate. It doesn't say anything about Tamae but she's all right. I've received letter from her yesterday and she had written that she's expecting soon. We've figured on a boy but believe we don't know how to produce one, for this is the fourth girl. But since Taeko is in Waimano Home, this baby will be taking her place. Wonder when I can see her? How is Taeko doing at the home, poor child!

The telegram was sent by Brother Riichi, and it sure came fast considering the other one from wife which took 6 days, and mine sent her on August 20th had reached her Oct. 4th—15 days!

Oct. 23, 1942

Received answer from nephew Setsuo. He's a corporal at Camp J. P. Robinson in Arkansas. I had gotten his address and written to him a while ago. He seems to be getting along fine. Kazuma, Tamae's sister's son, is a sergeant, he said, and doing all right too. It's good to hear that they are doing fine in spite of their being placed in a difficult position among the soldiers of different nationalities.

Itsue, Kazuma's sister, is in Oberlin College and Kazuo, her brother, is in Columbia University. Happy to hear that they are continuing with their studies in spite of the present conditions. Kazuo had tried to get in the air force or marine, but had been refused. Guess it's quite natural for the U.S. to distrust Japanese blood. But if they should have more faith and a broader mind, it would be far better for the country, for after all, the country is made up of all different nationalities. It is only at times like this that this country can show its true worth in spite of all the mixture of different nationalities. If it has to discriminate against her people who are of the origin of the countries with whom they may be fighting, how can other people feel confident and safe from discrimination themselves when and if they were to become at odds with their own mother countries. By distrusting their own citizens just because they are of enemy blood, it will create doubts in the minds of all the people of this country, for after all, if they discriminated according to blood, there are none with true American blood, except perhaps the Indians. But these Indians too are not given equal rights as the white people who had invaded and taken over their land. If this country wishes to survive as a solid nation, they should consider this point more carefully before acting in such a hysterical manner.

Oct. 27, 1942

Received a letter dated Oct. 15th from wife yesterday. She had written it 5 days before giving birth and says that she is spending her time crocheting with

Toshi and neighbor. She sounds all right so guess giving birth wasn't very difficult. It keeps me worried, but believe I needn't.

Made a painting easel today. I copied it from one Mr. Wakasa, who is supply attendant, made himself. He is graduate of Washington School of Fine Arts and seems to be quite good at painting. The painting I made of the praying child was [asked for] by Mr. Isemoto. I did another oil painting on card board of a bust of an actress. It turned out quite well but the mouth didn't finish out very satisfactory. She came out looking like a prostitute. The color shading and features seems okay. Guess I'll be learning quite a lot here. Tamae has written that she had sent my Federal School Course. Will be able to study when it comes and it should help me in my art class.

Oct. 28, 1942 (Wed)

About 50 Japanese Prisoners of War and 60 internees from Hawaii came in this afternoon. The majority of the POWs were captured adrift in life-boats after the Battle of Midway where the Japanese navy suffered a great loss. They were the engine crew of aircraft carrier *Hiryu* sunk at Midway.[14] They were picked up completely exhausted since they were drifting without food and water for about 15 days. The group included five officers— the head a commander, the next a first lieutenant, one lieutenant and two non-com[missioned] officers. Five others were captured in the Aleutians and were members of a sub which was sunk. One was taken from a lookout boat near Ogasawara Islands off Japan.

Oct. 31, 1942

This morning I saw frost for the first time in my life. After breakfast I set out together with three of my fellow inmates for my daily walk around the compound. One of our companions, Mr. Tamura from Seattle, pointed at the porch of Barrack No. 1 and said, "There's frost this morning." Looking at the porch we saw it gleaming like silver or powdered sugar. When I scraped it with my finger, it left a mark like sugar or salt. I learned later that the temperature was 27 or 28 degrees outside. If this was true, gave me confidence that I could withstand the winter cold here, for it didn't feel any colder than at KMC Detention Camp where we were detained first at Hawaii.

The new arrivals from Hawaii were welcomed at a simple reception party last night. Now the internees from Hawaii have swelled to 246. It seems that authorities have about exhausted apprehending ones who they considered undesirable and there may not be many coming in hereafter.

Mr. Sakaguchi of *Hawaii Mainichi News* in Hilo was one of those who came in with the last group and he gave a detailed talk on the conditions at Hilo, at the party. Things seem quite settled down at present and it relieved our worrying hearts about our families.

About 2000 books were received from the Prisoner of War Protection Dept. of YMCA, and 500 of them were placed at our compound library. I went to look after supper and picked up "The Mysterious Rider" by Zane Grey, my favorite author. Found also the famous best seller of couple of years ago, "Gone with the Wind," and sat for a while reading the last part. Took home the Zane Grey book and read it in the bed until a while ago. Then started writing this diary so that I'll not miss writing about the frost and because this is the last day of the month. Next month on November 11th, it will be the Armistice Day of the last World War I. When will this war's day be?

It's 9:45 PM now and although this is Saturday and lights are allowed until 11, the men are going into their beds. Believe it's on account of the chill in the air. It won't be long before everyone will be asleep. I had better wind this up and go to sleep too.

Nov. 3, 1942

Received birthday greeting card from wife, a letter, book, and 2 "Readers Digest" from Setsuo, and a notice of subscription acceptance from "Saturday Evening Post" subscribed for me by Brother Jimmy—all yesterday. Also a notice of registered letter mail came too and I went to get the letter from the censor's office this morning. It was from Takeo. It brought me great relief reporting that both wife and baby are doing fine after birth.

A grand picnic was held by the inmates of the whole camp of 1600 internees at the Compound Three ball ground. It began with a short religious service at 9 AM and games, wrestling and contests of all kinds followed. I was given the job of one of the prompters but after serving the whole morning, I became tired and returned to my barrack to rest. I had intended to go back but felt exhausted and was afraid of my neuralgia so that I stayed back.

It's 4:30 PM now but it is still going on for I can hear people cheering once in a while.

There are news and words of evacuating some people of Japanese from Hawaii. It is reported that General Emmons, the military commander there, had announced.[15] Word has also come in, that Dr. Kuwahara, S. Arakawa, the county civil engineer, Aoki, American Savings manager, and others who are citizens of Japanese ancestry and presently confined at Sand Island, are getting ready to come over to mainland camp with their families. Since they are internees, their families seem to be the first to be evacuated. Perhaps my family too, since they are under the care of welfare, may be required to evacuate also. It will be safer in case Japan should decide to invade Hawaii, but there will be much difficulty in living in this strange environment for my family with wife and three little ones. It is difficult to predict which would be better but there's nothing we in our present position, can do but to wait and hope for the best.

Hilo, Hawaii

Oct. 21 1942

Geo. Y. Hoshida (ISN-HJ–1133-CI)
Comp. 2. Co. 5—B4—Internment Camp
Lordsburg, New Mexico

Dear Brother:

"Congratulations" You're a papa for another one in your family. You have been presented with a seven and a half pound baby—Guess what it is Boy or a Girl. "Boy?" Well youre wrong. You've earned yourself with another daughter. She's the cutest little thing you ever saw. She's only two days old and she's already sucking her tiny fingers. I forgot to tell you. She made her delivery at Matsumura Hospital, Oct. 20, 1942 about 7:30 AM, and both mama and baby are doing fine. I visit her in the morning and in the afternoon's. I take June to see her in the afternoon for she could not go in the morning as she has to attend school at the Kapiolani. Don't worry about her condition. She's doing fine. In fact she had a very easy birth. She went to the Hospital at 4:30 AM. Mr. Takemoto called for the ambulance and at 7:30 AM the Hospital notified us that it was a girl. So we told the Takemoto's and from there she satisfied the relatives. And many thanks to Mr. R. Takemoto for his kindness. He put the wire through to you. And to the Hisanaga's for giving their help.

I guess you'll like to know her name. She named her "Carol" though her middle name is not decided definately. But I think it will be, "Carol Aiko Hoshida," for she thought of that name herself. She thought it was going to be a boy so she was unexpected with a girl's name.

Mother was so sure that it was going to be a boy. So you can just imagine how she felt when it was a girl. But no matter what it was we're all happy she has delivered safely and that they're both doing nicely. Today Oct. 21, 1942 is the second day after the birth and before I left the Hospital with June, she told me the [sic] maybe there is a letter at home from you. That if there was she asked me to bring it to her in the morning. Sure enough when I got home mother told me there was a letter from you. It was [one] for me of Sept 28, and a postcard for June Sept. 11. I'm going to bring it down to her in the morning and read it to her. Guess it must have been her natural instinct that there would be a letter from you, as you see she always has a dream about you being home. And the next day she's bound to receive your letter. It always has happened that way. (over)

Well anyway I'm very glad its all over. And am glad to know you yourself is getting fine with comfort. Please study hard and make a success of it. That we shall pray when the war is over you come back to us in good health.

As for the book you requested we've sent them all with the other things. And whenever you need anything just yell and we'll send it over to you. I'll write again as soon as possible. So until then adios

Your brother,

Raymond T. Hoshida

P.S. We have subscribed the paper for you. I think you will receive accordingly. Raymond

Oct. 27, 1942

Dearest Husband

I came home yesterday from the Hospital. Please don't worry because baby and I are doing very fine. There's nothing wrong with the baby. My only regret is that I could not have presented you with a boy. But even if it's a girl I guess we have to be satisfied. I'll be waiting for you to come back and then I guess by then we can have a boy. I'll be looking forward to that day.

By the way you know something she looks exactly like you her eyes, nose, her lips. She's all over like you. I only wish you could see her. Of course my friends and relative come to see me all the time. They treated me very nicely, showering the baby with many gifts. But how I wished I had you here. Even if you were the only one to come and see me, I'd rather have you come than a million others. I never felt so lonely in all my life. Especially when seeing others husbands coming to visit their wives. My thoughts was all of you. I guess the baby was lonely too without her Daddy. She would just cry in her little crib. It seems as though she's calling for you. Oh! how I wish you could see her now. But I guess that's impossible so I'll just imagine that you're on a long trip that you're coming back soon so I'll not feel so lonely. I'll send you a snapshot of her after about a month later though I would like to send it to you sooner. But I guess its better after I regained my strength so baby and I, in fact all of us would take together. So please be patient and wait until then. Her name is Carole Aiko Hoshida.

I received two of your letters today dated Oct. 4th and 5th. I was very glad to know that you are doing fine and that you are enjoying your stay. Please keep up that spirit and not to worry about home for I am very well taking care of by my relatives and friends, especially Mr. and Mrs. Nagao. They are very nice to us. I really don't know how to thank them.

By the way I was very interested in reading your letters. I'm glad to know that you have gained weight. But please don't get fat like "Baby Elephant." Ha! Ha! Ha! Please write more about what you are doing for both our Grandma's was very glad to know what you were doing. They're all waiting for you to come back as soon as war is over. They have been always worried in what you were doing that if you were taking time to enjoy yourself. That made them happy to hear you're enjoying yourself. So please don't forget, write more about yourself. Especially what you do to amuse yourself, what recreations. I'll be waiting for your coming letter, and as for me I'll write to you as much as possible about how our baby gets along.

By the way I've sent you the packages in three times the thing you requested I hope you will receive it. Brother R. Takemoto sent the wire through for me about our baby. I hope you got the message. Well, I guess I'll wait for your letter. Until then take good care of yourself.

Your loving wife,

Tamae Hoshida

Nov. 21, 1942 (Sat)

Mr. Kanno of our barrack received letter from his wife in Hilo that she with the two children were ordered to evacuate to mainland and are preparing to do so. It didn't state whether it was compulsory or not. The order was on the tenth and I am afraid my family may have received the same order too since both families are in similar situations. Of course it will be safer, but to come over in the middle of winter right after giving birth would be very difficult for my wife and the little baby. There will also be the two other little ones to consider also. It gets me quite worried.

Nov. 3, 1942

My Dearest Husband

I received your letter of Oct 15, today It makes me very proud to know that you are an Instructor for an Art Class. Please make good success of it. I'm praying for it.

Today Brother received a letter from Setsuo, mentioning about you in his letter, he was very shock[ed] to know that you have been interned and that you were in the mainland. He stated that he would do all he can to help you get whatever things you need. Though I think he has wrote to you about it. I was really very glad to learn of his consideration. I wish when you write to him please extend my appreciation toward him although I am going to write to him too. And please write to Brother R Takemoto too for sending the wire through for me.

It's already two weeks since the baby was born and Baby and I are in very good condition so please don't worry about us. Baby's growing to be a very nice girl. I only wish you could see her now. She's sure a peppy girl. She's just like you. She must be a gas bag always giving out those gases. Just like her Daddy. As for Mama, she sure is a heavy eater. She eats and eats and still its not enough. Gee I hope I won't get too fat like you "Baby Elephant" Ho! Ho!

June and Sandra both are getting along fine. June attend the Kapiolani School every day. She is a very brilliant child. She have very good reports getting practically all 100's in her works. I'm just hoping she'll keep that up. She's keeping all her records to show you when you come back home. She also received your letter and a post card but she hasn't answered yet. She is going to write to you soon. As for Sandra, she's grown up to be a big girl.

She is sometimes a very stubborn cuss and a chatterbox as well. Oh Yes! She sure is learning to talk fast these days. We could understand her quiet clearly now. Aside of that everybody's "Okay" They all want me to extend their best regards to you and wishing you success.

I'm sending you the following items you have requested. (1) Forty-five sheets of thick white Drawing Paper; (2) Six Jar Show Card Color (3) One only Water Color with 4 Brushes inside (4) Two Dozen Drawing Nibs (5) Two pen Holder (6) Two Eraser (7) Three Bottle WaterProof Ink (8) Six Tablets Drawing Tablet

Hoping these things you shall receive in good order. I'll write to you as soon as I can. So please take good care of yourself.

Yours with

Love

Tamae

P.S. Within you will find 4 snapshots taken before birth.

Nov. 10, 1942

Dearest wife:

Received your letter of Oct. 27 on Nov. 4, just after mailing you one. These days your letters seem to come just after I mail you one and have to wait until another week before I can answer. Today is Tues. and I waited until now in hope that I might hear from you again but since I haven't, I've decided to write. Received the Course books & slippers on the 5th. There ought to be volume 6 of Illustrating course. Please look around for it & send. Also got first copy of "Sat. Ev. Post" yesterday. I'm helping arrange library books now. So you see I'm fully occupied now with all the things I like. Yet I miss you and the children very much and I keep on having dreams of you and the baby almost every night. Wish the dreams will become real soon. I can understand your being lonely, for I feel it too whenever I think of the time when the other kids were born. But since we cannot help it let's look forward to time when we can be together again. It's very windy & biting cold today but I went out for a 2-mile walk around the camp early this morning after breakfast with a couple of others. I do it every morning to keep fit. It's very good. It's 11 AM now and warm and comfortable with the heater going and the warming pad under my seat. I've been doing some drawings & also letter writing for others. I got a good desk I built myself with books, magazines, drawing materials all around me, and also paintings I did and our family photo and your snapshots on the wall in front of me to keep me company. Heard some families are coming to mainland. Let me know if you are concerned. Hope you have recovered when this reaches you. Love to all.

Yours with love,

George

Nov. 16, 1942

My Dearest Husband

I hope you received our wire and the things you've requested. I hope you're getting along fine and as healthy and strong as ever. I have not receive your letter for [quite] some times and am wondering what happened. Today we received a Post Card from you to June dated Sept 30. She was very happy when I read it for her. She giggled and laughed when I read it for her. She sure was happy to receive it. So please send as much as possible for her and she will write to you as soon as I am able to do things. I wish to notify you that in the near future I might be joining you, as I have been notified by the authority and was asked if I would like to join you, but not knowing for sure that we could be together I would like to know if you had any notice on whether we could live together in a separate place with home and expenses furnished by the Government as I am understood. If there is any arrangements made in this matter please let me know. If not please find out. Though at present in my condition now it is impossible for me to take any long trips. So I have asked to have it extend if possible. But it seems once you have a notice to go I was told its best to be prepared. So I am now trying to get things ready. Only I am worried about our home. I don't know what to do. In case I'm to join you. Some of our friends and relative [advise] not to sell that it would be easier for us to come back after the war if we had property here and can start life over again. So please let me know if its best to sell all the things we have and pay our debts or ask our relatives to take care of it and look after our interest. So please give details to whatever things best to be done in your opinion. By the way please don't get alarmed for this is just in case of emergency. That if I am to go I'll wire you message "I have decided." So you will know I'll be going. When I'm to go I'll be going together with Mrs Ochiai and many others I know, so please don't worry. But if it's possible

FIGURE 14.9. "Art Class," February 19, 1943. George had high hopes for his art class; Tamae was very proud of him. While in camp, he also took some art classes in Japanese drawing techniques and painting.

I would rather stay a little longer until Baby and I will be strong enough to take the trip. Though they told me its nothing to get alarmed in my condition. That its only best to be prepared since I had been notified. That in case I have to go, I'll be well taken care of, by doctors and nurses. So I guess its okay. Aside of that everybodys okay. Baby's [be]coming healthy and strong and doing fine. And our many friends and relatives showered her with gifts and am very thankful to them all. By the way her name is "Carole Aiko" in case our first letters never reached you. Carole still a gas bag like you. She's still throwing out those gases. Ha! Ha! Ha! As for me I am still a big eater and am getting stronger each day. Its 23 days today Nov 16, since Carole was borned. And this coming Sunday Nov. 22, will be 33 days and I guess by then I can leave my bed. So as soon as I'm able I'll take some snapshots of Mr and Mrs Geo. Y. Hoshida's newly arrived family "Carole" and families and relatives and our home and its surroundings as you have requested. So please be patient and wait a little longer. I know you want to see Carole's picture quick so I'll send you her close up so you can see her clearly. I'll send it to you as soon as possible. As for June and Sandra they are both healthy and strong. June goes to school every day, and she's doing very fine work in school. She brings back her report and she received all "100s." She's saving it for you to see when you come back home. As for Sandra she stays home and play with her things. She sometimes goes to Grandma's to play or with Mr Nagao's son, Makoto. She plays very nicely when she's let alone, but when she is bothered, she sure gets mad and very stubborn too. She sure grew up though. I'll send her closeups too. So until then, Take Good Care of Yourself. And may it be possible that we can be together again.

   Love.

   Tamae

Nov. 27, 1942

Dearest wife:

   Received your letter of Nov. 16 & also pajama & socks. Glad to hear that you are all getting along fine. Believe you've regained strength by now but be careful. I've been expecting your letter and wasn't surprised about your notice to move. The first group, I hear had reached here & had settled down in relocation center at Arkansas. We are planning to send petition now to have us join our families as soon as they arrive but believe will be delayed until facilities are made available. So if you come you'll probably have to live by yourselves for a while but [I] believe [it] won't be very long. Since Hawaii is in the front line of war I believe it will be much safer to come over than to stay and since the war might be long it might be better for us. Of course you'll miss the conveniences of home but we'll be all together and will be able to get along fine after we adjust ourselves to this life. The winter will be quite hard but believe it won't be so bad with heaters. Better not sell house & furniture if relatives can help us look after them. Rent or have Takeo take care. Will go back after the war. Bring simple carpenter tools: Hammer, small saw, small plane, files, stone, sandpapers, etc. Also plenty of warm clothes & baby blankets to use on way. Of course if you had decided to stay it might be all right as we cannot tell about future. Sell something & bring some money if coming. Good luck & Love, Your husband.

Dec. 7, 1942 (Mon.)

I've been laid up with flu for the past week but it wasn't too bad for I've almost recovered from it now. I've rested my art class for the two nights but expect to be back on Friday. Got some T-squares and rulers from the War Prisoner Aid but they won't be of any use without drawing boards. Anyway it was good of them to send us something at least.

It's exactly one year today since the war between Japan and U.S. opened up at Pearl Harbor. US officially announced their total damages suffered that first day at Pearl Harbor. It included 9 battleships and others totaling 18 damaged or sunk together with 177 aircrafts destroyed. US had suffered quite a beating this past year but Nimitz in Hawaii, commanding Pacific Fleet, expressed confidence that US will ultimately win.[16] But today, it surely looks bad in both in Africa and South Pacific.

I received word from wife that she had received notice from the authorities to evacuate. She said that it wasn't compulsory but she is preparing for it in case she should receive order to go. Today, Mr. Arita received letter from his wife and in it she mentioned also that Tamae will be coming over if order comes. So she must be coming over after all. Believe it will be all right as she must have regained strength by now. It would be safer here [than] there since our home is so near the airfield. Her letter which came last was dated Nov. 16th and I should be hearing again from her with more information soon.

Dec. 26 1942 (Sat)

Yesterday was Christmas and I certainly missed my family. Millions of people are being missed this Christmas and we certainly cannot say that this was a Merry Christmas. Though separated, we are still alive but there are thousands and perhaps millions in this world who are permanently separated never to meet again in this life due to this tragic war. War is cruel but it is inevitable in this human world. Perhaps it is natural when viewed from the Law of the Universe but it certainly is breaking the hearts of millions and bringing sorrows and miseries to all. Are these sorrows and miseries intended to wake up the humans into seeking ways for permanent peace? It doesn't look like it.

Dec. 31, 1942 (Thurs) 10,40 PM

An hour and 20 minutes more and 1942 will end, heralding 1943! I've never dreamed of greeting a New Year in an internment camp. Last year I greeted it with my family, although it was black-out and anxiety of the outcome of the war during the year to come was clutching at our hearts. Now the year is about to go and this great upheaval in this world had brought tremendous changes. Never was there an event so great that influenced so many people. It has left practically no one untouched. It was unthinkable that the country which had been my home for practically all my life would turn me into their enemy. Sometimes I cannot believe that this is real and feel as though I am in a horrible nightmare. But this is real!

Wonder how my wife and children are spending their last night of this year now? Are they still in Hawaii or are they here in mainland? Mail has stopped since her last letter of Nov. 16th. In it she had written that she had received notice of evacuation. Many other families of internees had received similar notices. However, evacuation wasn't compulsory and she had written that she would wire in case she was coming. But personal wires had been forbidden and consequently there could be no radiogram. Registered letters which were coming fast are no longer coming because all mail had been ordered censored at New York. Guess this is one of the privations which we'll have to bear as internees of war.

Well, it's 11 o'clock now and only an hour remains before this year is gone. There's 30 members in this barrack which is Barrack 4, Co. 5, Compound 2, Lordsburg Internment Camp. Wonder how it feels to greet the New Year here?

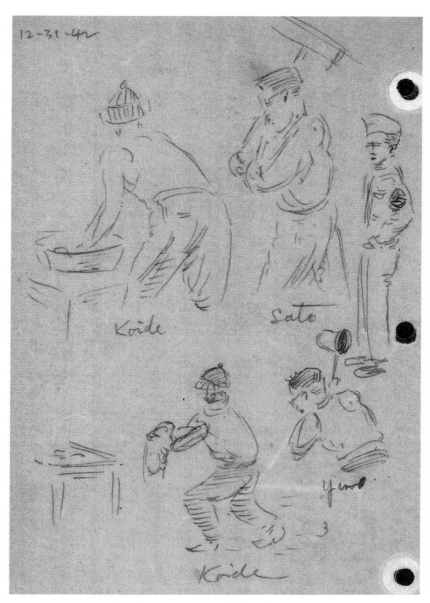

Figure 14.10. Pounding mochi for the New Year, December 31, 1942, perhaps under the watchful eye of a guard. Mr. Koide, identified in the upper left and at bottom, was one of George's particular friends; they went to Jerome and Gila River together. Mrs. Koide went to Jerome with Tamae.

We pounded mochi (Japanese rice cake) for us to greet the New Year in our customary Japanese fashion. Will be having Zoni (mochi and vegetable soup) too. It is quite difficult to be having them outside now. So in a way it is better here than outside.

Things are getting scarce now. This country which seemed so prosperous and overflowing with abundance, has come to suffer acutely for lack of food and materials. She had been caught unprepared. Who's to blame? Greek and Rome fell when they reached what seemed their height in prosperity. Is history repeating here in America too? One should not forget that material wealth alone is not true wealth. Spiritual wealth is really necessary for a nation to stand truly strong and firm. Wasn't America actually failing in its concept of true wealth through their illusion of thinking material wealth as true wealth?

NOTES

1. Nephews and a niece, referred to with the affectionate suffix -*chan*. See note 3, this chapter.

2. This censored line, judging from the text that follows, explains the job offer from another incarceree who was planning to "repatriate" to Japan. See George's diary entry of September 8, 1942.

"Repatriation" was a government program through which Japanese Americans could apply to be sent to Japan permanently. As *Personal Justice Denied*, the report of the Congressional Commission on the Wartime Relocation and Internment of Civilians, pointed out, very few people applied in 1942, when Japanese sympathizers would logically have immediately requested it (251–52). Over the next couple of years, as disillusionment and despair grew, the growing number of requests for repatriation alarmed the WRA. (There was a separate provision for renunciation of citizenship, which Roosevelt signed into effect in 1944.) Ultimately, however, only about 8,000 people went, and of these, many later returned (this was more easily accomplished by those who had been minors at the time, typically native-born US citizens taken by a repatriating parent).

Contemporary analyses of the disparate motivations for repatriation requests appear in the second volume of the publication of the government sociological study of the WRA camps: Thomas and Nishimoto, *The Spoilage*. For more, see, for example, Lyon, *Prisons and Patriots*.

3. As the address shows, Kazuo and Itsue Hisanaga, Tamae's sister's children, were actually at Oberlin College (Kazuo later did graduate work at Columbia University). They were part of the effort of the president of Oberlin College, E. H.

Wilkins, to enroll deserving Japanese American students who, as a result of the incarceration, had had to leave their West Coast colleges. At the time of Pearl Harbor, Itsue (known as Sue) and Kazuo (known as Casey) were attending Pomona College in California. Pomona's president, E. Wilson Lyon, and Wilkins made a quick transfer agreement, and the students were sent east by train only days before mass incarceration in April 1942. Oberlin enrolled over twenty Japanese Americans in 1942. Kenji Okuda, a young man from the Granada camp, eventually became student president, and many of the students traveled and spoke locally to raise public awareness of the incarceration. (Ochoa, "Another Day of Infamy"; Austin, *From Concentration Camp to Campus*, 58, 88; Franks, *Crossing Sidelines, Crossing Cultures*, 93.)

Kazuma, who was in the army in the 100th Battalion, was at Camp McCoy in Wisconsin. Like his siblings, he had attended Pomona, where he played football and baseball, and graduated in 1941. (Hisanaga, "Dedication Ceremony Remarks by Kazuma Hisanaga.") See chapter 17, note 3, for more information about the 100th Battalion.

4. Setsuo (Richard) Takemoto, Riichi's son, went into the Military Intelligence Service (MIS) and served in the China-Burma-India theater. At this time, he was getting his basic training in Arkansas before going in July 1943 to MIS Language School training at Camp Savage in Minnesota, which trained 6,000 men during World War II. The most famous MIS veteran was perhaps Setsuo's fellow Hawaiian, Senator Spark Matsunaga, who trained at Fort Snelling, Minnesota. Due to the classified nature of their work, MIS veterans received far less recognition than their comrades in the all-Japanese American army units. (Miyasaki, ed., *Japanese Eyes, American Heart*, 428; "Setsuo Richard Takemoto"; *The MISLS Album 1946*, 126.)

For more information on the Japanese Americans in MIS, see Azuma, "Brokering Race, Culture, and Citizenship." Azuma provides a powerful discussion of the problematic nature of overglorifying Nisei service as representative of a colorblind America or as proof of loyalty, citing as one such text the official army history by McNaughton, *Nisei Linguists*).

5. Fly, a German shepherd, was the beloved pet of the Takemotos and by extension the Hoshidas, who lived down the street. About 20,000 dogs were procured by the volunteer Dogs for Defense organization (which had a Hawai'i branch) or directly by the army for the program popularly known as the "K-9" Corps. Of these, about 10,000 made it through training and worked as sentry, sled and pack, messenger, mine detector, and scouting animals. At the end of the war, at least some dogs in the Marines were euthanized because the military believed them to be unfit to return home; upon the protests of individual military personnel, the military established a program to detrain the dogs and "rehabilitate" them for

civilian life, and offered them back to their original owners. As far as the Hoshidas remember, Fly never came home, but they do not know why; he might have died, or failed at rehabilitation, or the Takemotos could have declined to have him back, though this last seems unlikely. (Waller, *Dogs and National Defense*, 9, 14, 46, 49; Putney, *Always Faithful*, x, 208.)

6. An INS facility in Missoula, Montana, that held Japanese and Italian nationals until it was turned over to the army in 1944.

7. One wire read, "WE WIRED TO YOU TWICE URGENT STOP CONDITIONS GET-TING SERIOUS SINCE THEN STOP ALL JAPANESE INTERNEES CONFINED IN BARRACKS UNDER SPECIAL GUARD WE REQUEST TO SEND YOUR REPRESENTATIVE AT ONCE PLEASE ANSWER." (The document is held in the National Archives; reprinted in Kashima, *Judgment without Trial*, 200; and Culley, "Trouble at the Lordsburg Internment Camp," 230.)

8. Sotaro Kawabe from Alaska, Yaimichi Sugimachi, who was the Company 9 mayor, and Genji Mihara from Seattle, the Company 11 mayor. (Kashima, *Judgment without Trial*, 197.)

9. This complicated dispute over the incarcerees' rights lasted throughout the second half of 1942, encompassing the fatal incident described in the next diary entry. Company 10, in particular, resisted what they considered violations of the Geneva Convention and were confined to barracks, for some periods without even the two-hour rest period described by George. The three company mayors were arrested. The meeting with the Spanish "Ambassador" (actually consul) and State Department officials occurred on August 9 or 10 and ended the strike (also releasing the mayors). The incarcerees agreed to work unless they had health problems, but as George's account shows, they still felt that their work was unfair. It was not until December that the report of the consul and State Department came, outlining the type of work that they should do and excluding work that did not directly benefit them, such as cleaning the military mess halls and latrines. The problem of allowable and forced labor was a significant one in the incarceration as a whole, with different rules and pay scales for aliens and citizens (who were not protected by the Geneva Conventions). (See Culley, "Trouble at the Lordsburg Internment Camp"; and Kashima, *Judgment without Trial*, 196–203.)

10. The deaths at Lordsburg form one of the infamous stories of the incarceration, due to the celebratory acclaim that the shooter received (as George describes). The two men were supposed to be allowed by the armed guard to walk to camp, resting as needed, not left alone to wait for a jeep as George writes. PFC Clarence Burleson shot them under heavily debated circumstances and was cleared by a military court-martial. As there were no other witnesses and no autopsy was permitted, Burleson's testimony that the two men had started running for the fence

went largely undisputed, though friends had testified that they could not run and most certainly would not have been able to climb a fence to try to run away. One incarceree testified that he felt that this shooting was closely related to the strike and tense disputation that George describes in the previous entry, as their arrival had coincided with the strike. Senmatsu Ishizaki said, "I don't believe the two were shot for trying to run away, because they were striking here and had the internees shut up in the barracks for more than 10 days, and it was done just for an example. I think that is why the shooting was done. They were not the kind of men who would run away." (Kashima, *Judgment without Trial*, 187–90, 283n26.) Given George's involvement in the strike, it seems probable that he would have mentioned this view if he had shared it. Kashima and Culley both give detailed accounts.

11. George's summation of Frank Yasuda's story is fairly accurate. The Point Barrow community, suffering from disease and the decrease of whaling and other hunting, needed to relocate, and Yasuda led the community to Beaver, over 400 miles inland to the southeast and across the Brooks Range, where they adjusted to an entirely new way of life. Accounts differ on whether he led the trek, led several convoys, or merely sent word, but undoubtedly his action helped to save the community. (See Inouye, "Yasuda, Frank," 422.) A fictionalized account of Yasuda's life can be found in Jiro Nitta, *An Alaskan Tale* (Lanham, MD: University Press of America, 1990).

12. See George's letter of August 1, 1942, in chapter 14.

13. It took a while for the confusion over spelling to be sorted out, but the baby was named Carole.

14. The famous June 1942 battle between the United States and Japan at Midway Atoll, 1,300 miles west of Hawai'i, resulting in a decisive victory for the U.S. Navy. The *Hiryu* was one of the four Japanese carriers sunk.

15. General Delos Emmons replaced Major General Walter Short as the military commander of Hawai'i. He was known for opposing mass Japanese American incarceration in Hawai'i, saving the bulk of the population from sharing George's fate.

16. Admiral (later Fleet Admiral) Chester W. Nimitz, commander in chief of the U.S. Pacific Fleet. He replaced Admiral Kimmel in Hawai'i after Pearl Harbor and then commanded all Allied units in the Pacific from 1942 until the end of the war.

CHAPTER FIFTEEN

A New Year in the Internment Camp

JAN. 1, 1943 (FRI) 9.00 PM

So this is 1943! We've been hoping that we could be celebrating New Year back at our homes but this large scale war is not so simple as that. It has revealed itself as an honest-to-goodness huge World War. But hope it will be settled during this year.

We stayed up until after 12 o'clock last night and greeted the New Year in our barrack with a can each of crab, salmon, pineapple, some yokan and shoyu sauce.[1] Hata contributed the cans of crab and salmon, Mr. Y. Mizutari the can of pineapple, and I donated the yokan which Mr. Maehara, who got it from Shiroyama of Hilo, gave to me. It was a simple celebration but we all enjoyed it and wished each other "Happy New Year" when the watch indicated the birth of a new year.

I woke up around 5:30 this morning and after taking a nice hot shower, dressed and went to receive blessings and pray for health and good fortune to one and all at the compound recreation hall where preparations were made

DOI: 10.5876/9781607323440.c015

for the New Year service. After the service I made a sketch of the service platform. Returning from there, I went around to Barrack 8 grounds where some people had made a miniature of Atsuta Jinsha shrine.[2] I made a sketch of that too and returned to my barrack with my hands numbed by the cold morning air. The thermometer at the Barrack 3 porch indicated 28 degrees. Frost covered everything as usual and the moon and stars were still up high shining brightly. But the eastern sky showed signs of dawn. Dawn breaks around 8 AM and sunrise a little later.

The main event of this day came around in the afternoon with "Shishi Mai" (lion dance) winding its way together with other dancing groups and performers parading through the compound. The parade is a customary ritual in Japan and it is supposed to chase away evil spirits and bring in good luck. It consisted of a "Tengu" (a long-nose heavenly being) in the lead with two prancing "Shishi" (lions) doing the main dance. The lions were cleverly made with fierce heads and painted drapes simulating the lion's bodies. Each lion was manipulated by two men. They pranced, snapped and writhed in step with drums and flutes played by other costumed men numbering about a dozen. Three men attired in dancing girl costumes together with three others in male costumes gave a very good performance in the open ground before our barrack. The other members consisted of a clown, a flute player, two drummers, a tsutsumi (small drum played on the shoulder and beat by hand) and a Karasu Tengu (heavenly being with a crow's head) taking up the rear end.[3]

They sure made a fine show going from barrack to barrack in turn. We made a collection of a penny each to tip them. I really enjoyed this novel exhibition. It was the first one that I've seen, although I've heard about these ceremonial dances being done as usual thing back in Japan. Capt. Stull and a young lieutenant came to witness this exhibition and they seemed to enjoy its novelty too.

All in all, today was a very memorable day and it couldn't have been better in this internment life. But I missed my family—my wife and the kids—very much. Wonder how they are faring right now. 10:00 PM—time to go to bed.

JAN. 3, 1943 (SUN) 8:35 PM

Rev. Tanaka stopped me this morning on the way to mess hall and announced news that I've been waiting for—that 420 evacuees from Hawaii had reached the Jerome Relocation Center in Denson, Arkansas.[4] It was heard announced in news broadcast over the radio by someone in his barrack. The news spread in no time and from the fact that it had not been denied even tonight, it seems to be true.

Reelection for Co. 5 officers were held to select barrack captains, mayor and vice-mayor. We held our election of our Barrack 4 last night and I was reelected captain again. To be a barrack captain is sometimes very disheartening when people start to complain. There were many hectic times trying to run things smoothly under the narrow-minded camp commander with his unreasonable demands which stirred the tempers of people within the barracks. At times I tried to resign from my position when the going got rough. During the strike, tempers got short and there were arguments within the barrack. One man who was quite prominent in the Japanese society at Hilo, started to argue about outside work assignment. He was one of those who tried to get away from active work with loud talks. I tried to reason and settle the argument but then he started to shout profanity at me using his advantage of age and prestige. But other older people, seeing his unreasonable attitude, sided with me and finally talked him into submission. We have now become a big harmonious family. This was quite remarkable when considering the fact that the majority of them had been leaders in their respective communities before being interned and they were not used to being led.

(The Hawaiian evacuees, including my wife and children, going through on the Southern Pacific rail line en route to Arkansas, must have been passing nearby while I was writing the above diary. They reached Jerome on the 5th at night—I heard later.)[5]

Jan. 12, 1943 (Tues)

Got a telegram from wife yesterday, dated Jan. 8th. It said, "Arrived safely Jerome Relocation Center 39—3-D Denson, Arkansas. Everybody fine. Tamae Hoshida." It relieved me a great deal. Several others got theirs also and we were sure now of their arrival. Rev. Takesono received his too and asked me to write for him another one to have his wife apply for family reunion. Hope I too can join them soon.

There's rumor that this camp will be taken over as training camp for draftees and that we are to be moved to family camps and other places. Guess there seem to be some changes [in the next] couple of months. Hope we can go to the family camp.[6]

From

Hoshida, Geo. Y. (ISN-HJ–1133-CI)

Comp. 2—Co. 5—B4, Internment Camp

Lordsburg, New Mexico

Jan. 11, 1943

To

Mrs. Tamae Hoshida,

39—3-D

Jerome Relocation Center,

Denson, Arkansas

Dearest Wife:

Received your telegram of Jan. 8 and was very happy and relieved to know that you have arrived safely and fine. I've sent a telegram on Jan. 6th and hope you've received it by now. I've applied for family reunion myself but wired you to apply also just to make sure. It might not be necessary but it's better to make sure. I hope you have done so through people in charge of your center. I've heard that the family camp is to be completed sometime this month in Texas and hope that we'll be able to be together soon. Hope the weather is not too cold and hard to you and the children. It must be hard to look after the 3 kids by yourself in this strange surroundings but do your best & take good care of yourself. Hope the baby is getting along all right. I'm looking forward to the day when I can see her and all of you. I received letter from Takeo, dated Dec. 20th when you received notice. I sent answer. I'm grateful for the relatives' help. Guess it's just as well that we sell the house. I'll be hearing about it when I [am] together with you. Hope this letter reach you in time. Take care & give my regards to others. Love, George.

JAN. 23, 1943 (SAT) 7:25 PM

Wonder how wife and the children are getting along? The weather there in the damper air of the Mississippi basin must be much severer than here. Coming from the temperate climate of Hawaii, it must be quite hard for them. Believe she will be getting help from those together with her but especially at night with those three little ones. Carole is only three months old and it would be a real problem to take care of all her needs in new environment.

I read in the Dec. 22nd issue of Tribune Herald sent to [me] that our house is now being occupied by a fellow named Nada, an employee of American Factors. It seems so unreal that the house we've struggled to acquire should no longer be called our home. It feels as though a bond which has been binding us to Hawaii has snapped. Perhaps we may never return there again.

We've dreamed of the future but this condition and radical changes were undreamed of. But guess this is life and we'll have to make the best of it. It must have been heart-breaking for my wife to leave that home which we've loved and where we had planned so much for the future together.

Then there's Taeko to consider. The crystallization of our love, born perfect but crippled so tragically by that horrible accident. I cannot think of her without tears blurring my sight and my heart aching for her. Believe she'll have to stay there for the rest of her life, for if she should live crippled as she is, it would be quite impossible to take care of her together with our other children. Life seems so cruel to have such a thing happen to an innocent child who cannot even realize what had happened to her. But what will happen to her in case the war comes to Hawaii again and destruction runs wild? I shudder to think. But there's nothing we can do about it. Only the future will tell.

Wind still is moaning on the barrack roof. What lonely and depressing sound! Guess it will blow through the whole night. Time 8:05.

A Mrs. Sato from Jerome has been here to visit her husband for about ten days now and she has been seeing and talking to people with families in Jerome. We met at the censor's office and were able to talk with her to our hearts' content. She was a very attractive woman of about 42 or 43 but looked much younger. She spoke to us frankly and sympathetically and gave us full detail on the conditions and structure of the camp. Facilities are very well arranged and attention given to all possible comforts and welfare of the evacuees. They have not started gardening yet and the main work at present was woodcutting to provide wood for the room heaters in the barracks. They have a good hospital with doctors and orderlies. Patients are being cared for very well. Even milk for the babies have attendants in each block to sterilize the bottles and fill them with milk and formulas. I've been worried about our baby but this news relieved me a great deal.

I gave Mrs. Sato a snapshot of myself to be relayed to my wife. Believe Tamae will be happy to have it and also hear about my interview with her. Wrote a letter last night about it and sent it this morning. Haven't received any from her yet but hope it will come soon.

Mr. Mizutari, the Japanese teacher from Kaumana, is reading a novel to some people, as he had been doing usually at night for some time. I read to them sometimes too. It helps them to pass time pleasantly and forget about their worries. Mr. Hata and Mr. Shindo are playing "Go" and Mr. Takata and Mr. Uyeda are watching.[7] Behind me Mr. Arita, Mr. Kagawa and Mr. Fujita are talking about fishing. One of the heaters is on. The fan sounds like the sound of ship's engine and the waves beating against the side. They bring back memories of the torturous journey aboard the ship which took us from Hawaii to this land. It's 8:38 now. Had been writing for 38 minutes.

Feb. 1, 1943

Wife

Hope you received my 2 previous letters & packages. I haven't heard from you yet but hope you are getting along all right. I've been very much worried about you & the baby but today I was very fortunate to be able to meet Mrs. Sato from your center. I believe she will have given my message to you by the time this letter reaches you. I heard all about how things are arranged & done at your place & was very much relieved. I believe it must have been very hard for you at first & is still not easy to take care of the children but hope you have become quite used to the life by now. Anyway keep your chin up & try the best you can. I received cards & letter from Hisanaga, Hisako & your brother R. I was very glad to hear from them but couldn't write yet as I've written my limit of cards & letters. I wrote to your brother thanking him. When writing next, address it as follows: Geo. Y. Hoshida (ISN-HJ-1133-CI) K2—Co. 5—B4, Lordsburg Internment Camp, P.O. Box 20, General P.O. New York, N.Y. & write "Internee of War Mail—Free" on right top of envelope. Needs no stamps. Love George.

FEBRUARY 9, (MON) 9 PM

Letters from Jerome Relocation Center are arriving but none from wife yet. Believe she and the children must be all right but it keeps me in suspense. Not

FIGURE 15.1. Incarcerees playing Go and cards, October 7, 1942. Card games were a way of amusing themselves in the evening. Below is a sketch of George's Lordsburg barrack, fixed up with all the incarcerees' carpentry work and catalog purchases.

being a very good letter writer, together with the care for the little ones, must be keeping her from writing.

Letters to Ando and Arita have come. Ando's letter was dated Jan. 9th, exactly a month ago, and in it she mentioned that my wife is having a difficult time with the baby. She must have become used to the life by now since that was during the first days when their baggage wasn't received yet and getting adjusted must have been very difficult. [. . .]

Last Friday, Feb. 6th, was my anniversary of internment. It was exactly one year ago that date that I was taken into detention at the Kilauea Military Camp. When I think back at that date, the days and months of radical changes flood back into my mind and get me sentimental. It still feels like a nightmare and sometimes I cannot believe that this is actually happening. Yet this is real and the future is very dark and uncertain, especially now that my family is here and there's no home in Hawaii. But there's nothing much that I can do except to wait and hope for the best. Only time will tell.

NOTES

1. Yokan is a gelatinous dessert made from sweetened red (azuki) bean paste. Shoyu is the Japanese word for soy sauce.

2. The Atsuta Shrine in Nagoya, Japan, is a famous shrine of the Shinto religion. Many of its buildings were destroyed by fire in the bombings of World War II and later rebuilt. Shintoism was viewed by U.S. authorities as the most suspect of the various religions practiced by Japanese Americans because it was perceived as a religion of "emperor worship."

3. Tengu are magical spirits common to Japanese folklore, interpreted slightly differently in various religions of Japan.

4. The Jerome camp, officially Jerome Relocation Center, was one of the ten WRA camps and was built on a swampy site near the Mississippi River. The Hawaiian population made up about 10 percent of the total camp population. A study that focuses on Jerome and the nearby Rohwer camp is Howard, *Concentration Camps on the Home Front*.

5. Added in the 1970s.

6. A large number of references to the "family camp" follow, sometimes by name. The camp in question was the INS facility at Crystal City, Texas, and the Hoshidas and other Japanese Americans, particularly those from Hawai'i, petitioned the administration unceasingly to be allowed to reunite. Some families did ultimately reunite there; it also housed German and Italian nationals.

7. Go is a board game of strategy popular in east Asia. Because the board and pieces are very simple, this was easy to construct and transport in the camps.

CHAPTER SIXTEEN

{Tamae's Journey}

Life for Tamae also settled into routine, with Yoshio's brother Takeo and his mother helping out with the work around the house. As she gained weight steadily from the life growing within her, it became increasingly difficult for her to attend to the many chores of a household with two little children. But she was relieved of most of the work with Takeo attending to all the outside errands while mother-in-law handled the inside chores. Her mother came over often to help out looking after the children. Yoshio's mother even started a vegetable garden behind the house and soon harvested enough to give away to Riichi's and [the] neighbors, [the] Nagaos. There was also no alarming news about Japanese disturbing the peace of these islands. The war seemed to be moving toward Southwest Pacific against the Japanese and in Europe with Germany and Italy.

Then came a day when Yoshio wrote with thoughts about repatriation to Japan, for he saw little future back in Hawaii after the war. He said that many were contemplating repatriation, and Mr. Isemoto the contractor from Hilo had asked him to accompany him and try their fortune there.

DOI: 10.5876/9781607323440.c016

This came as a shock to Tamae, for she feared that she may not see him again if he should go over into such places where future fate was not very certain yet.

When Tamae relayed this to her brother and sister's family, they were indignant and alarmed and advised her to send him a telegram to discourage him before it was too late. Her sister Yoshino then drafted out the message and had it sent out to Yoshio at once. A month later an answer arrived through mail to assure them that he had changed his mind and will remain and return to Hawaii when the war was over. He had sent a telegram also, but it arrived a month after the letter. Looked like a record in slowness. So this was settled to their satisfaction.

However, there was other disturbing talk going around about people being evacuated to mainland or gathered into concentration camps in Island of Molokai.[1] Brother Riichi brought home news which confirmed some of them. It was especially for families of those who were interned in the mainland. It became true when some of the families received notice that they must be prepared to evacuate within a few months. Tamae was apprehensive also since she was under the care of the Welfare Department and it seemed that those under its care were the first to receive notice. So she was prepared but quite shocked when she actually received notice herself. She was in a quandary since it might mean unpredictable difficulties for her with two little ones and another expected within a few months.

She talked to brother Riichi for advice and he contacted people in charge through various channels but realized that it was extremely difficult to change a general order to suit individual cases. He advised Tamae to start preparations in case there was no way that it could be changed. Others who had received orders were preparing for evacuation. So Tamae resigned herself to start preparation by sewing warm clothing and doing whatever she could to meet this situation.

There were problems of the disposition of household goods and, more importantly, about the house itself. But since there was no notice of any definite date, it was very difficult to decide. The approaching time for the birth of their new baby added to her worries. But this important event arrived in the midst of this confusion.

Labor started early on the morning of October 20th. Around 4:30 AM Brother Riichi called the ambulance and had her taken to the Matsumura

Hospital next to their last home at Kilauea Avenue. Since it was prearranged, she was admitted at once and taken into the labor room soon after her arrival at the hospital. Delivery was easy and their new fourth daughter arrived at 7:30 AM.

They had been expecting a son this time, but it seems they were destined to have all daughters. She named her Carol Aiko but later added an "e" after the first name, and their last daughter to be was registered as Carole Aiko (Aiko meaning Love Child) Hoshida. She was the heaviest of all four girls and tipped the scale at seven-and-a-half pounds. She was healthy and normal as any baby could be. Tamae also came through the delivery without any difficulties in spite of her deformed hip.

Although Tamae was greatly relieved that this important task was accomplished successfully, she felt extreme loneliness and longing for her husband. He had been always at her side when she had the other children. But this time, she felt envious of other mothers having their husbands visiting them. However, this was an abnormal time, and she must bear it and be strong for the sake of their children and Yoshio. Perhaps when this was all over, this experience may come to mean something of value to her.

Her recovery went normally without any complications and the doctor ordered her release about a week later, on the 26th. Homecoming was good, but she felt loneliness assail her again when she was alone. How she longed for the presence of her dear husband—his words of joy and endearment, and his gentle intimate touches.

Days went on uneventfully except for the added care for the new baby, Carole. Feeling of approaching time for evacuation of the families of internees was sensed increasingly. However, Tamae was kept in bed to recuperate from her childbirth. The normal practice of being in bed for thirty-three days was enforced on her by the two grandmothers who knew nothing of modern practices of getting out of bed within a week. Tamae worried about her preparations for evacuation, but she felt she had to observe the old tradition also for fear that violation of it might bring irreparable damage to her health. Thus a month of uneasy rest prevented her from doing anything to relieve her anxiety about evacuation preparation.

Finally, when the days of confinement were over, she hurried into the sewing room to resume preparations for warm clothing for the camps in the mainland. If they should be ordered to depart soon, they would be arriving at the camps in the middle of the mainland winter, which to ones from the temperate climate of Hawaii would be awesome. It would really be an overwhelming ordeal for Tamae and the three little ones who had never experienced such climate.

Brother Riichi looked into all channels to see whether their departure, if inevitable, could at least be delayed until the baby and mother could bear better the strain of travel and the severe mainland winter. But his efforts were in vain, for the order came for their departure within three days, on the 21st of December.

Since the house and everything in it, except clothing and some necessary items for the trip and living at the camps, had to be disposed of within the three days before departure, it really was a hectic and nightmarish task. Although Riichi and others helped all they could for the preparation, there were some things which required Tamae's personal attention. The sale of the house was complicated due to it being under the jurisdiction of the Enemy Alien Property Authorities. There was so much red tape attached to the process of its disposal that Tamae had to go repeatedly to the office of the Authority. They had purchased the house from Contractor Isemoto for $3000 and that was all they could sell for. What remained was the difference between it and balance of the loan principal. It amounted to only $800. Then together with the sale of household appliances, furniture and other major goods, the total realization came to about $1,300. Tamae decided to take $500 from it and left the remainder in custody of her brother Riichi to draw from it when necessary.

The things to be sent through freight were packed in plyboard boxes and crates which the authorities furnished. She retained her sewing machine since it would be sorely needed to make whatever clothing was necessary.

Any one of the grandmothers would have willingly accompanied her and the children, but due to their advanced age and difficult circumstances, they had to abandon the idea. Parting was sad indeed and all shed tears at this turn of events. June and Sandra, quite oblivious to the meaning of this parting, ran around gleefully at the assembly of close relatives and friends and played until the army truck arrived to pick them up.

The ride was short, and in about ten minutes they were at the wharf. The interisland ship lay docked, waiting to ferry a large number of families on their initial trip to Honolulu. Tamae and her children were given a small

Mama Sewing   *Jerome R.C.*

3-4-44   4:20 PM

FIGURE 16.1. "Mama Sewing," March 4, 1944. Tamae had wisely packed her sewing machine and was able to make the family's clothing while incarcerated in the Jerome camp. She was an extremely accomplished seamstress, according to her daughters, and often made their clothes after the return to Hawai'i as well.

room with four bunk beds. There was a porthole, but it was blacked out, and the cabin was lighted dimly by a little light fixture in the ceiling. Carole was fussy, and Tamae had to fix a bottle with canned milk and hot water, which she brought in a thermos. When she fed Carole, she quieted down. But the other two became restless, and it became a difficult task to confine them in the stuffy room as ordered by the guards.

Transportation of the evacuees seemed to have been completed by mid-afternoon, and at about four o'clock the ship moved off the pier. Restrictions were relaxed, and the passengers were allowed some freedom. They talked about the letters they received from their husbands in the camps and their hopes of joining them soon. A couple of them were older Issei women, and they mentioned about being helped by Yoshio in their correspondence.

Tamae had been planning to visit Taeko at the Waimano Home if possible. Fortunately, her wish was granted, and the following morning one of the personnel from the State Department called on her and took her in a car to the Home. The supervisor greeted them warmly and led Tamae into a lounge next to the front office. There Tamae found a lone child sitting on the carpet, her head bowed down with a thumb in her mouth. Tamae didn't recognize her at first, for her head was shaved and she had a gray hospital gown draped on her. "Taeko! It's Mama. Don't you know me?" she repeated and gathered her in her arms. Taeko must have recognized her voice at that, and perhaps the familiar scent and warmth of her mother's body sounded something which had been missing ever since being taken from her home several months ago. She suddenly hugged Tamae's neck and showered her with kisses. Tears flowed down Tamae's cheeks as she hugged this pitiful child. Why was life so cruel as to treat an innocent soul so mercilessly? If it wasn't for the war, we could still have had her at home and given her love and care even though she was so tragically crippled. But now we were all homeless and on the way to an unknown fate in the far off unfamiliar land.

After two days and nights at the Immigration Station, the day of departure to the mainland arrived. Christmas eve and the day were spent at the station with hardly a trace of holiday spirit. They were transported to the pier where a huge passenger ship, painted completely in black, awaited them. At the pier there was a crowd of several hundred people who they found were families from this island. Another group consisted of men and, from their appearances, Tamae gathered that they were the husbands of families being evacuated.

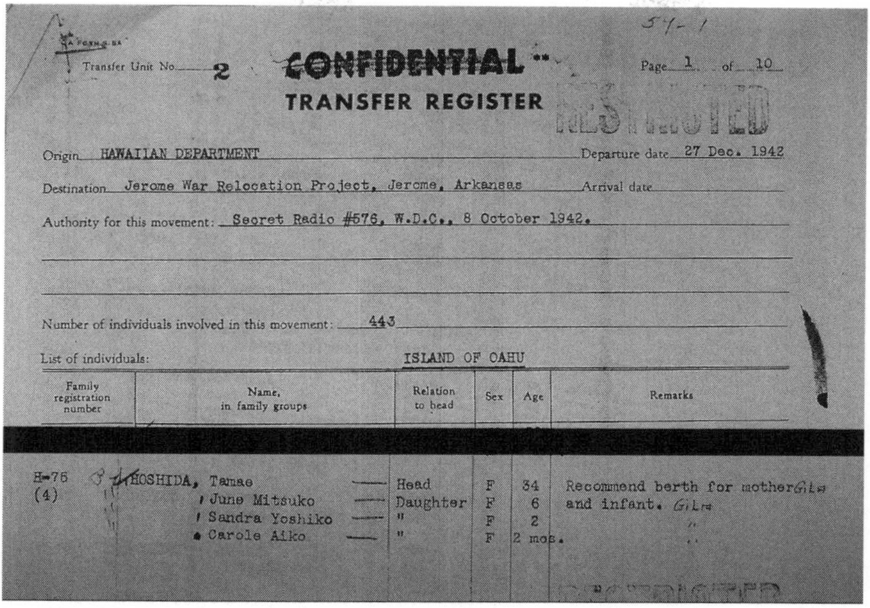

FIGURE 16.2. The original transfer list for Tamae and the girls, shipped from Hawai'i to San Francisco and overland to Jerome. Her brother Riichi Takemoto had tried to get her an extension, since Carole was so young and Tamae was barely out of childbed, but he failed. Carole was the youngest baby on the transfer.

The voyage lasted for about five days. There was a convoy of several ships which guarded this passenger ship. Fear of submarine attack was ever-present, but fortunately they were able to reach the mainland coast without any incidents. Tamae was miserable for the first two days, but with her body getting used to the movement of the ship, she managed to get up and attend to the needs of the family. The size of the ship prevented undue rolling and dipping, and the trip was relatively calm. Carole was almost never in their cabin since several of the women came around to take her around.

At early dawn on the sixth day—it was the New Year's Day—word came around that they were approaching San Francisco. Tamae hastily changed her family into appropriate dresses and decided to go up on deck with others to watch their approach to the mainland for the first time in their life.

The day was bright and clear with the rising sun gleaming just above the eastern skyline. Then, there in the distance, she caught sight of the famous

Golden Gate Bridge which spanned the entrance to the San Francisco Bay, gleaming in gold from the reflection of the sun! For several moments they all stood enchanted and spellbound. But they were soon awakened from this trance by the announcement by the chief of guards ordering them to clear the decks and return to their quarters to be ready to disembark.

Disembarking from the ship was another nightmare for Tamae again since everybody was preoccupied with their own problems and no one could come to Tamae's assistance. Carrying Carole with baggage in her arms, while trying to manage Sandra hanging on to her and fussing and June grumbling about the share of handbags she had to tote, was an extreme torture in the crowded passages and stairs of the ship.

A long line of cars was waiting for them on the siding of the railroad some distance from the pier where again they were lined up for name-calling and assignment to various cars. The final march to the car was led by some military personnel. Tamae found to her great relief that it was a pullman coach. Some women within the coach assigned their berths according to their names.

There was a stern-faced nurse in attendance to care for the little children's needs. The main work was to provide the little ones with milk bottles. Since it was some distance to the diner where the milk was formulated, it was not very easy, especially when the train was running. So she was quite grumpy whenever there was an order for milk. Many of the mothers didn't understand English, and when there was any problem, it was difficult to communicate. Tamae understood the difficulty, and when she had the opportunity she offered to interpret and also assist her with the milk. The nurse appreciated her help, and her antagonistic attitude, which apparently came from having to serve people of enemy nationality, softened and she became sincerely friendly and helpful thereafter. This made the long trip easier to bear.

The trip on the train was long—3 days and 4 nights—across mountain ranges, through endless deserts, large farmlands, rugged landscapes, and finally into green lush forestland and farms in between. The long trip finally came to an end on the fifth day at about eight o'clock in the evening. The train stopped at a siding where they were greeted by a huge bonfire and many people from the camp waiting for them. When they disembarked, the people came forward to help them with their handbags and the children. They were then again called out by the State Department personnel so that they could be led to their barracks.

The track to their barracks was quite difficult due to the muddy road which threatened to rob them of their shoes. People here all wore rubber boots, and it was only through their kind assistance that they were finally able to get through to the assembly point within two blocks.

There they were again called and led to their barracks. Tamae was given Barrack 03 Apartment D. The barracks were partitioned into five or six apartments, and Tamae's family was given a medium-size apartment. The block number was 39, and the Hawaiian people were given this and Block 40, which were located at one edge of this huge relocation camp.

However, what greeted them within the apartment was of no comfort, for it was just a bleak room with cracks between the boards of the walls and the floor leaking cold damp wind and chills which crept into their bodies through their inadequate clothing. There was a wood-burning room heater located on one side near the entrance, but no fire which could give them warmth. They had been given instructions to get their own firewood, which was piled high in the center of their block.

Tamae stood in the middle of the apartment—helpless with three fussy children shivering in the miserable room. She had been given instructions to go to a barrack at the corner of the block for blankets, sheets, pillows, and pillowcases as well as brooms and other necessary articles to get the barrack ready for occupancy. The cots were there with mattresses for the four of them, but what should she do first with no one to keep watch of the children? She had to depend on June for this, but being late and sleepy, she didn't look like she could be of any help. She would also have to get the heater started to fight the chill which made them miserable. But how was she to get the heater started?

While she was standing there helpless, she heard a knock on the door. There was a man standing there who had befriended the children and her during the voyage on the ship. His name was Mr. Ideta, and he had come here with his only daughter. They had come to Honolulu only a few months before the war from Japan and hence arrested on suspicion that he might be undesirable for the security of this country. His wife was still in Japan waiting for him to settle down in the city. His daughter was in her early twenties, and he himself was in his forties. His native prefecture was Kumamoto—same as Yoshio's birthplace. This fact had led them to become friends, and he had been very helpful during the trip.

"I was worried about you and the children and thought you might need some help in getting started. My daughter is taking care of things at our apartment only a couple of doors down in this same barrack," the man said. "I believe you should get your heater started so that you can get rid of your chills. I'll get some wood. Some kindling and scraps of coal to get it started are in that little box by the heater. Then after we get the heater started, I'll help you get the blankets and other supplies to get you settled here. You just sit on the cot and keep your children company. Perhaps you can get your children to sleep on the cots too and cover them with some clothing. They seem real sleepy and fussy."

This unexpected help was heaven-sent for Tamae. She thanked him and felt tears of gratitude and relief welling in her eyes. Ever since Yoshio had been taken, she found times when there didn't seem to be any God or Buddha in this world. But there always came help to save her at the last moment when everything seemed hopeless. This was one of those times when help came at just the right time.

Jan. 14, 1943

My dear husband,

Received your telegram after I sent to you. I was so glad that you wired to me.

We left Hawaii Dec. 24th and stayed Honolulu three days. We reached to mainland on New Years days. We rode on train 3 days & 4 nights. We certainly had a long trip and was very tired. Especially the children they were tired & besides they had trainsick. June had stomachache on the boat & on the train. I certainly had a hard time with the children. We reached this camp in the evening about 8 o'clock. It was very cold and was rainy day so the road was very muddy and we could hardly work. But I was [accompanied by] many friends and they all help me so I was lucky. Even now everybody pitty and treat me so good they help me carry things. We have to go and get our own woods for the fire so that's the time I certainly have a hard time and some times it make me cry by thinking of you. And wish that you were with me. I wish we could be together soon. As you have told me to apply for the family reunion. So I did before you telegram. They are trying to let the family together, but before we'll be together we have to fill the applications. So if you can do please do it too. I am trying my best to do fast so we can

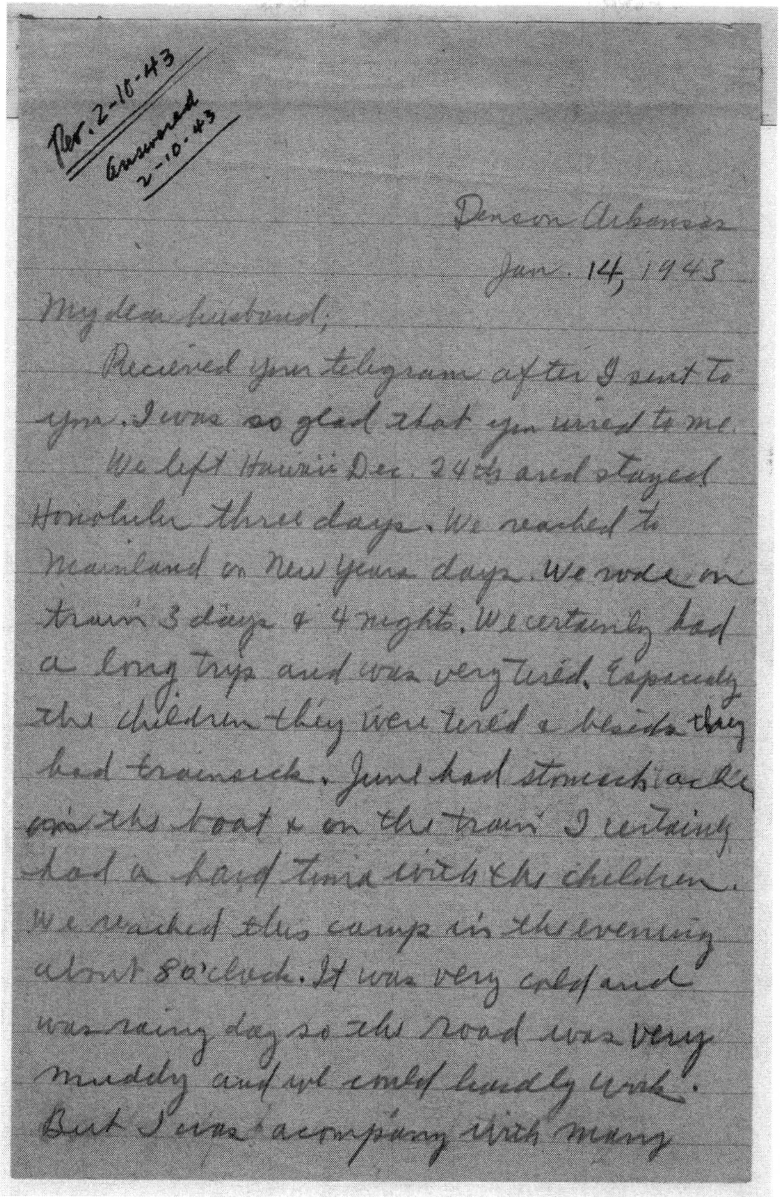

Denson Arkansas
Jan. 14, 1943

My dear husband;

Received your telegram after I sent to
you. I was so glad that you wired to me.
We left Hawaii Dec. 24th and stayed
Honolulu three days. We reached to
mainland on New Years days. We rode on
train 3 days & 4 nights. We certainly had
a long trip and was very tired. Especially
the children they were tired & besides they
had trainsick. June had stomach ache
on the boat & on the train. I certainly
had a hard time with the children.
We reached this camp in the evening
about 8 o'clock. It was very cold and
was raining day so the road was very
muddy and we could hardly walk.
But I was acompany with many

FIGURE 16.3. Letter from Tamae to George, January 14, 1943. Tamae wrote
most of her letters from Jerome; earlier letters from Hawai'i were often
penned by relatives.

be together quickly the children always mention about you and ask me why daddy is not here. I have to tell them that daddy is coming soon. I guess they misses you a lot. Baby Carole is very strong and healthy so don't worry. I am trying my best not to let them catch cold or any other sick. They certainly making me worry. If you were with us I don't have to worry so much. Before we left Hawaii they told me that we can be together right away but since we are not together yet, I hope we can be together soon.

I think you have received a letter from Takeo by this time. By mentioning how I did with my property. I sold all the things before I came here I certainly had a hard time to sell the property but after all I had a good buyer so not so bad. It was Mrs. Ushigima of Kukuan I guess you knew this person. I will tell you the prices after I'll be together with you. I won't mention now. Everything was sold in good prices so don't worry.[2]

Before I came to mainland I had a chance to meet Taeko at Waimano Home. She certainly grown big. She have recognized my voice. I told her this is mama, and she smiled at me and hold my hands she certainly made me cry I really had a hard departing. It makes me cry if I think about Taeko and you. I wish you could see her once. I could not explain you how I felt on that day. But she is well taking care so I don't have to worry about her but after all she is far away from us and don't know when we can meet her again. So no matter what happens please be together and lets go back to Hawaii after everything is over because all the relatives and friends are waiting for us.

This camp is very big place. I met lots of my old friends in this camp. I also met my schoolmate her name is Yuriko Nagasako. She is married to Mr Kobayashi. They were very nice people. She comes over the house and do my washing and take me to the store, and the husband made a nice chair for us.

When you write to Setsuo please tell him that I am in this camp and also give him my address so he can come and visit us it is not far away from here. He might be surprised when he [hears] this. I hope I can meet him before I be together with you. Please write to all the relatives of Hawaii whenever you can and mention that I am alright.

I have so many things to write but I'll write again so please take good care of yourself. I hope we can be together soon.

Love,

Tamae

Document 1. Col. Bendetsen to Lt. Col. George W. Bicknell

January 2, 1943

From Karl R. Bendetsen, Colonel, G.S.C. Assistant Chief of Staff, Civil Affairs Division

To Lieutenant Colonel George W. Bicknell
A.C. of S., G-2
Hawaiian Department
Honolulu

. . . The second evacuee party arrived aboard the Lurline yesterday morning and the ship docked about 2:00 P.M. The party had a good crossing, were well treated and seemed fairly happy. [. . .]

The party was disembarked on the San Francisco side (Pier 32), and was then embarked aboard the Army Queen, an ATS harbor tug, which stood by to take them over to the Oakland side where a train was ready. They reached the Oakland side between 4:45 and 5:00 P.M. Because the routing to Arkansas was via Santa Fe, there was diner trouble and the Port of Embarkation had some difficulty in procuring diners for the first leg of the run. The Southern Pacific finally agreed to loan two diners and these were due to arrive at the Oakland mole [*sic*] at 5:00 P.M. The Southern Pacific slipped on the agreement and the diners didn't show until nearly 8:00 P.M. However, there was orange juice and milk available and this helped a great deal for the younger ones, who would otherwise have had a rather long stretch of it without food—their last feeding having been just before 2:00 P.M.

Document 2. Memorandum for Col. Bendetsen

MEMORANDUM FOR: Colonel Karl R. Bendetsen
SUBJECT: Evacuee Transfer Unit No. 2 from Honolulu, T.H. to San Francisco.

From 1st Lieutenant Walter Prock to Col. Karl Bendetsen
January 20, 1943

[. . .] Insofar as the trip to Jerome is concerned, the entire trip was made without incident and the two officers in charge were most accommodating and helpful to Captain Freund and myself. Upon our arrival in Jerome, even though it was at night, sufficient facilities were provided for the handling of all passengers and their baggage. On arrival, the evacuees were immediately taken in trucks to their barracks which had been prepared and were waiting for them.

NOTES

1. Many federal officials wanted all Japanese Americans in Hawai'i incarcerated, which General Emmons resisted. Government documents show that there was a large amount of discussion of the specific possibility of putting all Japanese Americans on Molokai, an island of about 260 square miles. One memo from President Roosevelt in February 1942 to the secretary of the navy, William Knox, began, "Like you, I have long felt that most of the Japanese should be removed from Oahu to one of the other Islands." It ended by encouraging Knox to "agree" with Stimson (meaning Henry Stimson, the secretary of war) on a system and to "then go ahead and do it." (Taylor, "Report from Jerome Relocation Center.")

The many twists and turns of the federal government's consideration of the Hawai'i situation can be found in Robinson, *By Order of the President*. For more on the internal Hawai'i situation as well as the federal level, see Okihiro, *Cane Fires*. Odo, *No Sword to Bury*, provides the perspective of young Japanese Americans in Hawai'i at the time. Weglyn's *Years of Infamy*, 174–75, reprints two government memoranda on Hawai'i.

2. Earlier in this chapter, George details some of the sales. In his claim filed with the Department of Justice under the Japanese-American Evacuation Claims Act of 1948, he asked for compensation in the amount of $9,632.50. This included the loss of value on the hasty sale of their home and household effects, the cost of clothing for the journey, and George's lost salary. He was awarded $275.00 in 1952. (Hoshida Collection, JANM.) This was typical for the claims, which were subject to severe questioning, a heavy burden of proof, and slow bureaucracy. Most applicants were compensated for only a fraction of their losses.

CHAPTER SEVENTEEN

{Waiting for Reunion}

Tamae Hoshida
39-4-E
Jerome Relocation Center
Denson, Arkansas

Jan. 31, 1943

My dearest Husband:

Received your letter and the nice gift which you had sent for us. We are
very happy to have such pretty wooden slippers. We are making very good
use now because this place is very rainy and muddy. Its very hard to walk
with shoes so with the wooden slippers it is very easy to walk. Most every
family received the wooden slippers from their husbands. June was very
glad when she got the slippers. She told me to thank you.

June is going to school from Monday Feb. 1, she couldn't go for about
two weeks because she was sick. She had a cold but now she is getting very
strong so don't worry. She has grown very big girl. I think when you see

her you'll be surprised. She is very tall for her age. Everybody thinks that she is older than her age. I am glad that she is big and strong. Sandra and baby is healthy too so don't worry. I'll try my best to take good care of them.

I did applied for family reunion already so I guess we can be together soon. We had a meeting last week and heard that the families with the small children will join the family first. I guess [we] can be together soon. I hope I do quickly because am having very hard time with the three little children. It is very hard to stay without the husband because you cannot depend on some one else all the time. We have to do most of the things such as carrying the woods for the fire to burn in the evenings and so forth, I wish I can be together with you soon.

By the way did you received all things which I have sent to you from Hawaii. If you did please let me know. When you write to your brother Takeo please give my love to him. He was very nice to me when I was with him. I certainly miss him and Mother. I wish we can go back to Hawaii again. There's no place like Hawaii. I certainly miss Hawaii. So when everything is over lets go back to Hawaii again. Don't forget. We must think about our daughter Taeko too. She is waiting for us. When I think about her I always cry. Its very hard to explain in here how I feel toward her. I guess you do the same. Her birthday was yesterday but I couldn't bake cake or do anything for her for I am far away from her. Some days when I go back I'll do for her.

Last week we had snow fall in Arkansas. It was very cold and was very pretty. The children enjoyed to walk on the snow and play. But after snow melts its terrible the road is muddy and its very dirty. I have to carry Sandra on my back to go back and forth and to Mess Hall for Kau Kau.[1]

Will write again so please take good care of yourself and hope we'll be together soon. Like we sure to be in Hawaii. Good-Bye

Love,

Tamae

Feb. 10, 1943

Wife:

Received your letter of Jan. 14th today &was very much relieved that you are all right. I was worried as your letter was late, & had just written a letter this morning. I get it back from our office & am rewriting it. I sent the warming pad today with cord & some candies for the children. The warming is old & might cause trouble so use only when you are around. Heat the bed before the children go in. If you use directly on the childrens' body, they'll feel cold after you take it away. We here are doing all we can to speed reunion. I sent petitions twice myself, & yesterday, all of us from Hawaii with families in Jerome, signed together petitions to be sent to 4 places. So believe we'll have results. There's rumors that we'll be reunited next month. Hope so. I sent 3 letters before this and a package of wooden slippers, also message thru Mrs. Sato. Hope you received them. Glad to know that many are helping you. Please extend my thanks to them, especially to Mr & Mrs Kobayashi. Meet Mrs. Yoshiko Fukuyama, 31—4-E. She is Mr. Mizutani's daughter. I'm glad you met Taeko. We'll see her again when we go back. Everybody's fine here. Had snow yesterday morning. Nice day today. Will write to Hawaii soon as I can. Do your best. Keep healthy & your chin up. Hope we'll be together soon.

Love,

George

FEB. 18, 1943 (THURS) 8:18 PM

Five or six people came from Jerome for a visit. They were Arita's son Yoshihiko, Mrs. Chiko Odate and daughter, Mrs. Minoru Nakano and son, and Mrs. Sueoka, all of them members of Hawaiian internees' families. I was able to meet Arita's son Monday morning as soon as he arrived, and got news of my family.

Toshihiko brought with him cards from my children to me. They were Valentine cards with lollypop attached to them. June had a message on it in long hand. She had been writing previously in print but she must be taught script in school. Tamae had written from Hawaii remarking about her good marks. She must have good intelligence—taking after her pop? She, however, is a real tomboy and rough, but hope she'll get to be more feminine as she grows older.

An incident arose yesterday which almost proved very serious. The outside detail under Anderson, building road outside of the fence above the hospital, was the scene of it. About 30 men, 8 from our Co. Five and the rest from

Compound Three, were there in the morning. But since the bulldozer there broke down, and there being not much work to do, the guards advised them to quit work and return to their respective compounds. That was before ten and earlier than usual.

There must have been a mistaken or false report on this, for the commander heard about it as being a strike. Consequently, under this false impression, the commander became furious and ordered stricter enforcement of work when the men returned to work in the afternoon.

The workmen were doing their work conscientiously, following the bulldozer closely. Then a Capt. Jack Sufford of the M.P. Detachment came riding a bicycle. He seemed very much agitated. He located the foreman, Kawashima, from Compound Three who was assigned during the afternoon to prevent any trouble as there was some news of misunderstanding. After accusing the workers of not working properly, the captain pulled his revolver and shot at Kawashima's feet. Kawashima was astonished at this unexpected and wholly unjustified action. He wanted to ask the captain for the reason of this outburst, but since he couldn't understand English very well, he could only guess. Others who were there and could understand English said that the captain had threatened them as to what would happen if they did not work properly.

The work however, had been done very well. The bulldozer was digging in front while the men followed it closely heaping up the soil to form the road bed, and no more could be done. Apparently the head guard on the guard tower must have twisted his report through the telephone to headquarters, and the captain, suspecting some serious rebellion on the part of our workmen, had come rushing up intent on immediate discipline of them. In his haste and excitement, he had not taken the trouble to investigate before taking action. So, after cooling down a bit, he must have realized his mistake, for the workmen said that he appeared a bit sheepish, when he left.

Kawashima picked up the bullet which luckily missed his feet, and also the cap as evidence. Then they kept on working until time and returned to their compounds.

It must have been a misconception on the part of the captain of the guard. But for an officer of his rank to make such a blunder was inexcusable. The officers of the two compounds met and investigated but found no fault on the part of our men. The trouble seemed to lie in the fact that the guards for the morning shift must have handed in a false report to cover up their returning earlier than usual. The tower guard in the tower during the afternoon also must have received order to be alert about any suspicious actions and had read some imaginary suspicious actions in our men.[2]

Until this was settled we decided not to send any workmen out of the compound for outside detail. The governors, vice-governors, secretaries and detail chiefs of the two compounds met with the camp commander this morning, and the incident was thrashed out. As a result, the commander realized and admitted his mistake. He discharged Capt. Sufford from his position and the guards were given strict orders to prevent recurrence of such incidents. The present commander seems to be a very understanding man, unlike the first. If it [had been] Col. Lundy this would have ended in another strike, for the action of Capt. Sufford was a duplication of the first commander.

We internees cannot be forced into unreasonable submission. All we ask is understanding and fair play. We wish to be treated like fellow humans not like common criminals, for we are not criminals. The only reason for our being here is because the higher authorities do not understand our true nature. We are not ones to do anything subversive. Uncle Sam may think otherwise, but the fact that there had not been a single case here or in Hawaii with concrete evidence of any shady deeds should be proof enough.

Feb. 7, 1943

My dearest Husband:

Received your letter of Jan. 24th on Feb. 5th and I was very glad to know that you are healthy.

The children and I are doing fine so don't worry. I am trying my best to take good care of them until I'll be together with you. I am wishing everyday when I can be together I hope the camp will complete soon. The children is just wondering why we cannot be together. I have very hard time to explain them why we cannot be together. June always mentions about you and ask me when she can go to your place. She always say that when she goes to your place she liked to tak[e] lots of present for you. We can visit you anytime but it cost me a lot and besides its too far away so its very hard to me to make my mind up and besides the children is so small. The people who has their husbands in Louisiana have already visited their husbands. Those people who met their husband is really happy I [suppose]. I guess somedays we can be visit or be together so I am waiting for the happy days to come.

This morning Setsuo came over my place. I was so glad when he came. I almost didn't recognized him. He has changed. He looks like his father but his face changes. He brought lots of present for the children and for myself. He even told me to give some money to spend but I told him instead of giving me the cash I wanted to buy a suitcase and some other things so he is going to send me later. I was very glad that he came over to see all of us. He told me that he is coming again. He stayed until noon, but next time he is going to stay over night. I hope he do that so we can have a long talk so when you write to my brother will you tell him that Setsuo has visited us and also thank them because they were very nice to me when I was home. Please write to brother Jim too and also to my sister. She was very nice to me too. I don't know how to repay them. I hope we can when we go back to Hawaii after the war ends.

I didn't let you know what I did with the property. I guess [you] already know by this time through Takeo. I will tell you everything when I'll be together. It is very hard to explain in the letter. so please do not feel bad about it.

Do you remember this people Mr. Masumoto, Mr. Yoshiyama, and Dr. Kuwahora. There people are very nice too me. Especially Mr. Masumoto. She always helps me do things. Do you know Mrs. Odachi? Her husband is at your place. I think you are staying with him if you do please thank him because his family is very nice to me. They always help me carry the woods wash the clothes and watch the children. She treats me just like her daughter, that's why I am not having so hard time so don't worry.

There's another bunch people came here again yesterday. So now its overcrowded. These people are all from Honolulu. They are all nice people too.

Will write again so please take good care of yourself. Write to me often. I'll do the same.

With love

Tamae

P.S. I am sending you the news of the camp.

Feb. 10, 1943

My dearest Husband

Yesterday we were called at the Bl. 41 Mess Hall to hear Mrs. Sato's interesting news of your camp. She has visited your camp few weeks ago and have returned home two or three days ago and spoke about the people in the camp. She spoke what you people do in there and how nice heating you people are having. It was very interesting talk. When I heard everything what Mrs. Sato said about the camp it certainly made me happy and glad. After everything is over she calls the name for the gift what husband has sent to us. I was the first one she called. I was wondering what she will give it to me. When she said, "This is from your husband" and gave me your happy looking snapshot with million dollar smiles. It made me very happy and glad to see your smiling face and because you haven't change a bit you looks just like before and looks much better and handsome, so I don't have to worry so much. I showed you picture to many other ladies. They all said I am lucky to see your happy looking face. I showed to June and Sandra and they were very happy and glad. They always wish if you were with them so we are all waiting for the happy reunion day. I guess it won't be very long.

I have small children and cannot work so the government is giving us the money to spend for the daily using. They have giving me $8.75 already so please do not worry about the children and myself.

I am trying my best to take good care of the children so don't worry and besides I am very strong and not like before. Since I came here I have very good spirits so don't worry and take good care of yourself and wait for the happy days to come. [. . .]

Your loving wife

Tamae

P.S. Did you received my snapshots which I have sent to you from Hawaii? It was taken on 33 days after I had Carole. If you did please let me know. Don't worry about baby Carole she is very strong and healthy.

Feb. 20, 1943

My dearest Husband,

Today Arita's boy came over and told me everything what you have told him. I was very glad when he told me not to worry about you because you are healthy. I guess you heard everything from him too. I have many things to tell you but I'll keep till we get together. I hope we can be together soon.

There's another lady had visit your place Miss Nakano and I think you are already met her. I gave her our family pictures to give you and hope that you got them. It was Carole's pictures, that were taken after the 33 days after she was born. That was sent to you once but didn't go to your place. They sent it back with the letter together. I guess something was wrong with the letter. I hope you enjoy to see Carole's pictures.

Carole is very fortunate baby, because everybody likes her and love her and carry her all the time and besides she is the youngest baby in the camp. Wherever I go I have someone to take care her and even the little one[s] love her and try to carry her. She is certainly lucky girl. She has grown quite big now and fat too. I took her to the clinic last month and weigh her. She had 13 lbs. that was only three months old. I think she have more now. She can talk and laugh now so everybody having fun with her. Sandra and June is very healthy too, so do not worry. At first I hard very hard time with Sandra but now she is very use to it so not so bad. She started to play with the little girls. She seems to me that she likes grown up girls. They all like her and treat her very kind. They carry her all over the camp. After all I am fortunate to have a little ones because the people is so nice to me so you don't have to worry about the children and myself. I try my best to take good care of the children.

I think you have heard about the news paper subscription from Mrs. Nakano. But am writing you again that was sending by your brother (Takeo) since last Oct. 13th so please write to your brother and ask him if you want to continue and thank him for doing things for you and for me.

Please thank to Mr. Odachi because his family is very nice to me. They always wash the clothes and watch the baby and so forth. Tell him the reason and also thank to Mr. Arita, Mr. [?] because his Mrs. is very nice to me she always give me a good massage.

I will write again so until then please take good care of yourself and hope that we can be together soon.

With love,

Tamae

By the way what kind of petition form paper you have sent to me. If its necessary to sign please sent it back to me I am willing to do it.

Mar. 8, 1943

Wife:

Received your letter of Feb. 20th but couldn't answer as I've already written 2 letters, 1 to you & another to Setsuo. Today is Monday, so I can write.

I didn't get the snapshots from Miss Nakano. Guess they didn't allow her to give them to me direct. If she had returned it to you send it by mail to me again. I'm anxious to see the baby. Glad she's so healthy. She must be real cute. Wonder when I'll be able to see her & hold her in my arms. Reunion is about to start but it seems that we from Hawaii are left out or left to the last. We wrote to Commander of Hawaii asking him to carry out his promise of reunion. So guess we'll have to wait until then. That petition you asked about was petition of reunion in Hawaii but since you are here it doesn't matter I think you people had better write to Hawaiian War Dept. & other authorities about reunion too, or we from Hawaii will be left out. We here sending all we can but it will be more effective if done from your side too. Better wake up & do your best. Tell this to your leader. Hope it's warmer your place. It's spring here now & very pleasant. I'm very healthy too. Give my regards to all & keep healthy. Yours with love, George.

Feb. 26, 1943

My dearest Husband,

Received your letter of Feb. 10th and Feb. 18th and was very glad to know that you are healthy and also glad to know that you have received my letters and the news of the center.

This morning Miss Nakano returned from New Mexico and told me that you are healthy and so forth. I was sorry that you didn't get the pictures which I sent. It was Carole picture and our home picture, I am sending it back with this letter so I hope you received all this time.

I received all the things you have sent to me so do not worry. The warming pad is working alright, and I am making very good use for the children and for myself. June and Sandra were very glad when I gave them the candies. They enjoyed it very much. It is very hard to buy those candies here. Setsuo brought me a box of Butterfinger and some other things. He is very nice to the children and to myself. He wrote to me that he is coming over next month again. I am very proud to have a nephew in the army.

Please do not worry about the children and I, for we are very healthy and doing very fine. I am doing my best to take good care of them so don't worry.

June is attending school everyday and studying very hard. She is very good in everything. She seems to me that she is very good in writing and drawing, just like daddy. She always drew a pretty picture at school and have a good mark on it. She is very proud now because she can write in long hand. I think she is writing you a letter. You'll be surprised when you received her letter.

Sandra is sure grown big. When you see her you'll surprised. She can speak pretty good English now. I am glad that she speaks good English.

I received a letter from your brother, my brother, and Haru. They are all healthy and strong too. They wrote to me that they miss us very much and told me to come back when everything is over for they are waiting. So we have to go back to Hawaii when everything is over.

The people of mainland donated a money and gave all the people from Hawaii. I had $19.00. It certainly helps the children and myself. The Welfare is giving us too. I am having $8.75 every month. It certainly helps me a lot. So please do not worry about the children and myself.

Will write you again so please take good care and let's wait for the happy reunion day. I wish this happy day will come soon.

Your loving wife,
Tamae

P.S. I am sending you the "Communique." It's the news of this camp. I hope you enjoy read them.

MARCH 16 [6], 1943 (TUES) 8:30 PM

Mr. Kinzaemon Odachi of our barrack, whose bed is next to mine, is critically ill in hospital, hovering between life and death. He had high blood pressure last year and the doctors had been advising him to go into the hospital. But he had refused, for he must have felt that it would be better if he didn't. I guess it was because he is a minister of Tenrikyo, one of the Japanese Shinto religions, which preached cure through faith in their god.

He was apparently healthy and had been going on light outside detail. Then last week before lunch, I saw him vomiting into a bucket in the room. I thought it was only some stomach trouble but had the doctor called. Dr. Uyehara came and after examining him, ordered him to be taken to the hospital at once. Then yesterday we received word that he was quite critical. We decided to petition the commander to have the authorities help with the transportation for the family to come and visit him. We didn't get the answer until late today. So in the meantime, we decided to wire the family ourselves this morning. The telegram, however, came back refused, saying that only the husband can wire his family. It really was ridiculous to expect the half-conscious man to do so. But fortunately, a wire was sent from the hospital officials since the doctors had decided that he was critical. A second message was sent in the afternoon, I heard later, as it looked like the end was not too far away.

I was called on the phone by the doctors for consultation and went to the hospital. When I arrived there, the doctors were just finishing taking blood from the patient to relieve excessive pressure. His illness was not just high blood pressure but also kidney trouble, uremia, and other complications. So, they had hesitated to take out blood but decided to do so, so that they may prolong his life at least until his family arrived. He had lapsed into a coma but when I saw him, the relief from pressure must have revived him, for he was apparently conscious. However, he didn't seem to recognize me. He was in such a weakened condition that he couldn't talk either. His eyes were glazed and it was apparent that his condition was very serious.

The doctor asked me to have some people take turns to watch over the patient. So I took the first watch for the afternoon and phoned our barrack to have someone come up to relieve me in the evening. The doctor said that he was hopeless and might be gone any time. I overheard Dr. Bond whispering to Dr. Furugouchi that it might be tomorrow.

Human life is very unpredictable—here today, gone tomorrow. He seemed so full of life only a few days ago and it is very hard to think that he might be gone tomorrow. He is about 53 years old, small and frail—practically skin and bone, but he has a very strong will. To think that he should end his life after a year in this internment life, without even seeing his family who had evacuated so far from Hawaii just to join him, is a real tragedy.

It wrings my heart to think about his family. I had been helping with his correspondence ever since our detention at the Kilauea Camp. His wife had written about her hardships back in Hawaii after he was arrested. She was left after his arrest with four children to fend on her own with just a small assistance from the Welfare Dept. And now after arriving at the Jerome Relocation Center she had been happy with the expectation of getting together with her husband in the near future. She had been dreaming about the happy moment when she could see him again. But all that would remain just a dream and with these shocking tidings, her life and those of her children will be plunged

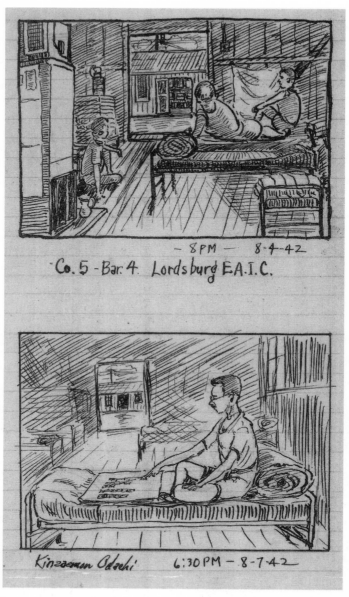

FIGURE 17.1. Another barrack view and a portrait of Kinzaemon Odachi, George's fellow Hawaiian, August 1942. George cared for Mr. Odachi throughout his long illness in the camps, while Mrs. Odachi helped Tamae in Jerome.

into a tragic nightmare. It would be more pitiful if she were to be too late to see him alive.

I had the opportunity of going out of the camp and see[ing] the town of Lordsburg for the first time. It was the morning of the same day that Mr. Odachi was taken to the hospital—Friday, March 12th. It was an outside detail to load sand on truck at the army depot in the back streets of the town.

The town of Lordsburg is about four or five miles from camp. There's about a mile-and-a-half or two miles of paved road to the main highway runs parallel to the Southern Pacific Rail line. Turning west for another two or three miles along billboard-lined highway, we came to the entrance of the town. There were many motels, some shabby but others classy, advertising air-conditioned rooms. They looked empty, and well may they be in these times of rationed tires and gasoline.

The main street consisted mainly of gas stations, cafes, hotels, motels and a few stores, on the left side, and railroad station and yard to the right. It was a pretty town as far as the main street was concerned—perhaps I felt it so on account of being hungry for the sight of outside world.

Reaching almost to the end of the town, we turned into open ground which looked like the army depot. There weren't very many presentable cottages and most of the houses were shabby and dusty. There were several Mexican adobe huts about which I've read in western novels. A street running west stopped at a dead end at the edge of the desert safe brushes and a row of odd-shaped huts. There were some Mexican women walking or standing around in the front of their huts and they reminded me of the Portuguese and Hawaiians back home.

Mar. 7, 1943 (Sun) 10:40 AM

While rearranging my bookshelf this morning, I came across my diary in Japanese which I've written in only once after coming here, but had forgotten. I had been keeping up my diary in English but had not thought about writing ever since that one entry. So I decided to do it again in Japanese. (This, therefore, was actually written in Japanese and I am translating it in English now after 33 years. I had been drafting out this MS of my life for the last four years and am now on those internment days and had been copying the diary which I kept then. Today is June 19, 1976, Sat. 11:10 AM)

I had kept diary before the war mainly in Japanese but since being interned and correspondence had to be done in English, I had been keeping my diary in English also. Not being very good at Japanese, although passable, it has become worse by this negligence. Guess I had better do some writing in Japanese so that I won't forget my mother tongue.

March 4, 1943

George Y. Hoshida (ISN-HJ-1133-CI)
Comp'D 2—Co—5—B4
Lordsburg, New Mexico

My dearest Husband;

Received your letter of Feb. 22nd yesterday and glad to know that you are healthy as usual. We are all healthy too so don't worry. Children and I are waiting everyday for the family reunion day. I hope this happy day will come soon. Over here is still cold. When we mop the porch the water forms into ice and in the ditches it forms ice too. Tonight its so cold that we could hardly walk outside so children and I didn't bathe. We just wipe our face and hands. I hardly bathe the baby. Whenever I do Mrs. Odachi always helps me. She tells me do this and that she is just like my own mother. She is very kind to me so please thank Mr. Odachi and tell him the reasons.

Setsuo came over last week Saturday and stayed over night with us. He said he is coming this weekend again. I wish he stayed this place all the time. He is very nice to the children and to me. Whenever you write to him please thank him for been very nice to us. Takeshi wrote to me from Honolulu. He left Hilo when I was home. I thought he went some other place to work but he is still at Honolulu. I wish you will write to him too. This is his address. (Mokuleia Airport, Honolulu.)

June wrote a letter to you and she also send you a picture. She is learning how to draw the picture at school she wrote the letter in long hand. She is getting smart now. I hope you enjoy read them. She is pretty smart in long hand and at school she says she is the smartest of all. Aren't you proud of it.

I am sending you another news its about this center. I hope you enjoy read them.

Please give my best regards to Mr. Odate and please tell him to take care of his body and get well soon.

I am very glad to know that you are the teacher of Art. I hope you do
your best to teach all the people. Is Mr. Kanno learning from you? Mrs. Kanno told me so. She was very glad because he is learning from you. I hope you
do your best to teach him and please give my best regards to him and all.

Please do not worry about the children. I do my best to take good care of
them. I will write again so please take good care of yourself until we meet
again. Good-Night—9:15

Your loving wife,

Tamae

March 6, 1943

My dearest Husband,

I am hereby writing to you about the matter of reunion. I thought it
would be a grand idea if there is any possibility of your being release to our
center, instead of going to the internee's camp. So with the help of Setsuo,
I sent a letter to the Commanding General, asking for your release and
waiting for the result. Think things twice whatever you do, and don't listen to
rumors.

Everybody is fine so do not worry. Please take care of yourself. Will write
again.

Setsuo is coming today. I think he is going to stay over night with me.

Your loving wife,

Tamae

Mar. 15, 1943

Wife:

Received your letters of Mar. 4th & Mar. 6. Glad to hear that you are getting along fine. I'm very grateful for Mrs. Odachi's help. Please thank her for
me. I'm glad Setsuo is coming over often and helping you. I got June's letter
too and am very glad and proud that she is so bright. Hope she doesn't get
stubborn these days. Watch out for Sandra too. Keep them cheerful & watch
their temper. I rather you didn't try for my release. I might get paroled but
I do not like the idea of being paroled under suspicion. I would rather wait
until the war is over go out without feeling that somebody is suspicious of
my actions. I have been honest & law-abiding & believe, as good a resident of
U.S. as anybody can be & I do not want any suspicious eyes trailing after me

& watch out every action I make. Then we do not know how long this war will last & in case the relocation center will be [dissolved], we'll have a very hard time making a living at this unfamiliar place & then we'll have a very hard time getting back to Hawaii too. I appreciate your effort but there's lots of things we've got to think of before taking such action. Hereafter let me know first before you do anything. It's better that we discuss this over after we get together at the Reunion Camp. But don't worry. Believe everything will come out all right. Love George.

March 26, 1943

Dear Uncle George—

At the present time I'm with aunty and will remain here for a few more days. Just this morning aunty received your letters of March 15th and 16th. She's a busy woman so she has asked me to write you this letter.

And here's a bit of good news. Carole, who was confined in the hospital for a minor ailment, is now back with aunty. She's fine and I believe the baby has put on some weight. I really believe that she looks like you, and that's no fibbing. The baby behaves well and the hospital has done wonders for Carole.

As for writing to the different authorities—As I got it from Aunty she has written missives to Washington D.C., Pennsylvania and to the Hawaiian Dep't. Commander. These letters dealt with the topic of your release and consequently of your reunion with your family. Judging from the answers received from Washington & Pennsylvania the matter of your parole, release or family re-union rests on the shoulders of the commander, Hawaiian department, since you fall within the jurisdiction of that department. So far no answer has come from Hawaii. I believe that nothing can be done until the letter from Hawaii arrives.

Aunty wrote those letters, without your knowledge, because she understood that by her efforts your release could be had. She asked for a family reunion, which naturally comes foremost to all other topics. Her pleas were that of an American citizen and I'm certain that she will be given every consideration possible. You can be sure that she's trying her best. Since you did not ask for repatriation, and I pray to God that you'll never do, you'll have a chance to be with your family.

I believe a Mrs. Odachi is now there and probably you have met and talked to her. I'm sure she can give you all details on your family.

June & Sandra are fine. June goes to school daily and Sandra stays home. Both are growing up fast and you'll have a time to recognize them.

I do hope that you are fine and getting along okay. As for me I have no complaints to make. I'm fine & healthy. In case you want to write to me the address is on the envelope.

Aloha,

Kazuma [Hisanaga]

P.S. Aunty has written to the Waimano Home. Aunty says that she has signed the family reunion papers and that the center will take care of the details.

March 25, 1943

Dearest Husband;

Received your letter of Mar. 8 and the card of Mar. 10, on Tuesday Mar. 22 and was very glad to know that you are healthy. I also received the package which content chair, candies and the slippers. I was very glad that you have sent us the nice chair for we need it very much. Did you made the chair or bought if you did made it why, you are very good carpenter. You can be a good business man too, when we go back to Hawaii.

I also received your telegram and was very glad to know that I can join you soon. As you have said to be ready to move soon, but where do we going? Please let me know. I didn't have any notice yet. I like to know for sure so until then I won't be prepared for go.

Kazuma came over today from Mississippi. He is going to stay with us until Sunday. I was very glad that he came over. He is same as before. He hasn't changed a bit only he is thinner than before. He brought a big box candies for the children. When you write to sister's home please tell them that Kazuma has visited us.

The "Life" magazine is still coming, so you better write to the publisher and find out. Tell them to send it to your place or either my place. Did you received the news of this center which I have sent to you. Please let me know. Over here is still cold. It seems to me no summer here, still windy and rain and cold.

Carole had a cold and she was in the hospital little over week. But she is Ok now so do not worry. The other two is very healthy so don't worry. By

[the] way, did you met Mrs. Odachi? I guess you did by this time and heard everything from her. How is Mr. Odachi getting along? Is he in serious condition? Please give my regards to him and tell him to take good care of himself.

You certainly had a good dream about Carole. Don't worry you'll be carrying her pretty soon. She have already made 5 months she is beginning to turn [over] so I have to be very careful she might turn over the bed. Don't worry, I'll do my best to take good care of her. She has grown quite big now. She is not very fat but just right. Not like "Baby elephant" Ha! Ha!

Next month is our wedding anniversary. Its going to be 10 years so am going to send you a flower so when you receive them please keep it good. That flower has a great meaning. Will write again so please keep yourself healthy. Until we meet again.

With love,
Tamae

Mar. 17, 1943 (Wed) 9:30 PM

Mr. Odachi's condition seemed to have improved but the doctors say that there is slim chance of his recovering. I went to see him again this evening. He opened his eyes when I went and as I spoke to him, he seemed to recognize me and laughed. He surely is a spunky old man and seems to take this serious illness in his stride to be able to laugh this way. People had been taking turns in looking after him ever since his hospitalization. Today Mr. Kanno reports he took almost a cup of milk and seemed to have gained some strength. If there's even a small chance, I hope that he'll recover, or at least last until his wife can see him.

Mar. 23, 1943 (Tues) 8:15 PM

Yesterday morning at 6 AM while it was still dark, we saw the first group of 94 internees off to Crystal City Family Camp where they are to join their families. Then this morning at 5 AM, we saw off the single people to Santa Fe Internment Camp located in the suburb of this state's capitol. We are now all to be detached from the jurisdiction of the War Department and go under that of the Justice Department.

We, with our families in Jerome, will most likely go to Crystal too but there are other rumors that we may be moved to some other location. Anyway there is no definite information and we are kept in suspense.

We felt uneasy and didn't want to be caught unprepared. So, we started packing ourselves too. I packed most of my belongings into the duffel bag but there are still many things left over, a large increase of odds and ends during the nine months here. I had a lot of magazines, books, and other similar materials to the trunk but still have enough to fill another boxful.

Mrs. Odachi's telegram came yesterday and she arrived this morning with two of her children—the oldest daughter Michiko, and youngest and only son Michio. I wasn't there at the hospital to meet her but Mr. Tamura who works there regularly as hospital KP, said that she visited her husband with the two children but left after about twenty minutes. No one was allowed to talk to her today but hope we can tomorrow. I'll go over tomorrow morning and try to get in touch with her. It really is a pity that she should meet her husband under these tragic circumstances after over a year of heartbreaking separation. It is also a bad time too for we cannot care for him if we are to be moved now. All of the patients, except four of the most serious, are to be moved and it really would be sad for those who will be left behind.

MAR. 30, 1943 (TUES) 7 PM

Mr. Odachi is much better and [I] believe [he] may recover if further complications do not develop. Mrs. Odachi left for Jerome on the 28th.

On the first day of her visit with Mr. Odachi, she broke down and wept. It is natural, as she had been separated from him for over a year and to meet him again under these circumstances was so tragic. The two children with her seeing her weeping, cried together with her and the attendants had a difficult time to soothe them. But the next morning, when I went to take my turn in nursing him and also meet them, they had recovered their composure and acted normally. She seemed very happy to meet me when I introduced myself.

The authorities there, although rejecting our request for assistance, must have accepted appeals from the leaders of evacuees there and approved financing the trip for her and her two children. She had requested for a loan from my wife but since the expenses were furnished, it wasn't necessary. It was fortunate that things came out favorably. Her stay here was limited to three days but I made arrangements to have it extended for a few days more. So she was able to be with her husband until the 28th. But her visits to her husband, like all others now, were limited to two hours a day.

Before she left, I decided to arrange for a collection to her to help her with some spending money, and with the help of several others, went around the internees from Hawaii. The amount collected was beyond our expectation. I had expected about $10 or $15 since this was the end of the month and with expectation of being moved soon, it has hastened us into spending the $3.00 monthly allowance coupons as they were of no value at other camps. But the collection came up to $38.56. The people of Barrack 5 donated the most, amounting over $16.00. Our barrack could give only $3.50 since we were all broke. I put out 85¢ out of about $1.00 of coupon I had left.

I then had the coupon redeemed at the canteen and made into check. But when the check came back, it came with additional $10.00. I couldn't figure it out but upon inquiry at the canteen, found that Mr. Odachi's fellow people of Kagoshima Prefecture in Japan had made collections too and added on to ours. I was very happy indeed and took it to the hospital on the 28th, when she was to visit her husband for the last time, to present it to her. There were other presents for the children of some cookies and fruits from some people. When I presented them to her, she was so overcome with emotions that she could hardly express her gratitude.

APR. 6, 1943 (TUES) 7:50 PM

A fierce sand storm raged for several hours today until about an hour ago. We shut ourselves inside the barracks but the fine sand seeped in through the cracks at the window casings and covered everything in the room.

Mr. Miwa quit as compound detail chief and now I was given that job in addition to my duties as company detail chief and barrack captain. Seems there's no one appropriate to handle it. It calls for added work but since it may not be for long, I'll try my best to handle them. Anyway, all the jobs combined actually don't amount to much when compared with work in ordinary life. It will also keep me occupied and prevent my being idle. It won't be good to acquire the habit of idleness. When peace comes, we will have to resume regular work to make a living for ourselves.

There were news of names of Nisei boys from Hawaii who had volunteered and were accepted into the new combat unit of American-Japanese now being organized. Tamae's brother Jimmie's son Tsuneo's name was among them also. Now one each of Tamae's brothers' and sister's boys are in the army. Setsuo Takemoto son of Tamae's eldest brother Riichi, Kazuma Hisanaga, Tamae's sister Yoshino's son, and now Tsuneo Takemoto, Brother Jimmie's son. It will be quite hard for Jimmie since Tsuneo is the only son among four children.³ But it can't be helped but since this is war and everyone will have to do what he can for his country. As American Citizens, it is their duty to fight even their ancestral country. Hope they will show that they do have the stuff in them and that Japanese blood is good blood and not a traitor's blood.

The 100th Infantry newly formed exclusively of Japanese-Americans and now at Camp Shelby, Mississippi, seems to prove the good characteristics of the Japanese blood. The commander of the infantry stated that the 100th, when compared with other battalions stationed there, can be considered the best. The recruits in the infantry are industrious, studious, and not reluctant to do hard work, and above all, good Americans. This new combat team, I believe, will prove it beyond any questions.

Loyalty is for one's country and if he is a citizen of America, his loyalty belongs to America even if his blood is Japanese. If he is not loyal to America he is a traitor. Even we who are not citizens of U.S. but living here in American soil, Japan does not expect us to fight the war for her. In spite of the fact that Uncle Sam suspects us of spying and intentions of subversive activities, I have not seen or heard of any Japanese residents doing or intending to do such things in the whole 30 years of my residence in Hawaii. Even here in this camp where all the suspects are collected, I do not suspect or hear of anyone who had done such things or intends to do them, although there are many who had lost hope or are intending to repatriate to Japan. I do not believe also that U.S. has any concrete proof of anyone who had done any subversive actions. I believe it should prove beyond any doubt that Japan does not depend on us residents to do her spying or fighting for her.

Of course as legal subjects of Japan, we have our obligations to her to [some] extent and most of us here may have at one time or other, entertained military personnel who came on training ships from Japan, and even donated something toward war efforts in China and Manchuria. However, as residents of this country with obligations toward her, it will be against our moral and ethical concepts to do anything harmful to this country.

There are many thoughts which I would like to bring out but I will not be able to express them adequately in words. However, my concept of a perfect world when summed up into a few words will be: "If all the people of this world will discard their nationalistic selfishness and regard each other on the basis of fellow humans, I believe that this world will be a far better place to live in." Wonder whether that time will ever come.

April 11, 1943

Dearest Husband;

Received your letter of Apr. 1st last Saturday morning while was doing my washing. I was so happy when the letter came I just stop my washing and ran home to get the letter. It made me happy to learn that we can be together soon. I hope we can be together this month. The children are so anxious to see you. Every morning when they got up, they said today we are going to daddy's place. How [pitiful] to me the children act that way. Especially Sandra she always mention about you, and said that she is going to ride on train and go to daddy, because we always here train passes here. I hope this happy days will come soon.

June received your letter too. She was so happy when you wrote to her. She couldn't write now, because she is busy learning "hula" She is going to dance this 15th. She can hula very good. I wish you could see her dance. When she'll be together she can dance for you. Baby Carole is almost 6 months. She is quite big baby now she is fat and good looking like daddy. Ha! Ha! She is taking SMA milk. It is very good milk. It contains all kinds of vitamins. I don't nurse my own milk very much. Carole can talk quite a bit now and she can turn over too, so I cannot leave her alone while I go out or do my laundry. But I don't have to worry over her cause I have some one to take care her. She is very popular baby. I am very proud of her. I always keep her neat and clean so everybody likes her.

This place is getting very hot since this month. I don't like the climate over here. I rather go back to Hawaii and live like before. Sometimes it's very hot and sometimes rain, tonight its very windy but not so cold. The temperature goes up to 85°.

I'm glad to know Mr. Odachi is getting better. I hope he'll be well soon so he can join his families. Is he still in the Hospital? Please give my best regards to him and tell him not to worry about his families. I heard from Mrs. Odachi everything. I guess you did too. She is very nice lady. Did you thank her for helping me?

Everybody is healthy so don't worry. Will write again so until then take good care of yourself and wait for the happy day to come.

Your loving wife,

Tamae

April 19, 1943

My dearest Husband,

I was very happy to received your letter of Apr. 6 last Saturday morning. I also glad to know that you have received the news which I sent you. I have already mailed many times. Did you received only one? Please let me know.

Last week Thursday evening they had En-ge-Kai⁴ at the Mess Hall and had all [kinds] of dance and songs. June hula very nicely and was pretty too. She can hula pretty good. She didn't practice so long but she did very nicely. I wish you could see her hula. Everybody praised her so she was very happy. I made her hula skirt with the red crepe paper with yellow blouse and orange leis. Am still keeping the skirts and leis, so when we'll be together she can hula and show you. I think we are going to have May 1st program like we used to have in Hilo. Miss Yamane of Hilo is the May queen. I think this will be swell.

June, Sandra and Carole is very healthy so don't worry. Carole is getting rascal and she can talk too. She can turn over herself, [I] almost drop her from the bed. But don't worry I didn't. I'll be very careful from now. Sandra always mention about you. She says that you are coming with the train to see her. She tells this every day. Isn't she cute? June too says this. They all wanted to see you very much. They ask me why we cannot go and visit you. The people in Louisiana always have a chance to meet. I wish I can let my children visit you or be together soon.

I heard Tsuneo is in mainland now. I do not know what State. I hope I can meet him too. I wrote to Jimmy long time but they didn't write to me. Are you writing to them? Even my other brother doesn't write to me I don't know what have happen. Takeshi wrote to me few days ago. He wants you to write to him. His address is Mokuleia, Airport, Oahu so please write to him whenever you have a chance. Haru always write to me and ask us to come back after everything is over so don't forget to go back to Hawaii. I always wanted to go back to Hawaii. I wish I can go back now.

I've already bought all kinds of carpenter tools for you. I even bought a leader jacket and some other things as a present. I'll take this thing when I go to the camp. Do you have enough underwear? Please let me know. When we go to the camp we cannot buy all kinds of things, because we cannot [hold] more than $130.00 cash so am buying somethings I need when we'll be together.

I've sent some flowers for you. I wonder if you have received them, please let me know. If you did please keep them nicely. Some is giving to me and some is made by order. Don't think I made them. I couldn't do it because I'm busy doing my house work.

I am very glad to know that Mr. Odachi is getting better. Please give my best regards and tell him to take good care of himself. Mrs. Odachi didn't received any check yet.

Well, so long take good care of yourself until we meet.

Good-night, (10:30)

Your loving wife,

Tamae

Apr. 21, 1943

Dearest wife:

I was thrilled to receive the flowers day before yesterday. I arranged them on the table and they sure brightened up this place. I announced that this was our tenth anniversary and everybody teased and congratulated me. They really are beautiful. I gave the ones from Mrs. Tanaka to the one addressed. The desert flowers are blooming now and I'm making a collection of them. I paint each of them with water color first and then press them between the book. I have about 15 of them now and hope to have plenty more before we leave here. Believe you'll enjoy seeing them. They are pretty. I got your letter of 11th today and sure was happy since I didn't get any last week. I'm glad that everyone's fine. Carole was exactly 6 mo. yesterday. Guess she'll be crawling when we get together. Believe it will be in June. Heard that the first 40 families from Hawaii are there now but since

FIGURE 17.2. "Lordsburg I. Camp, Ametuer [sic] Show, Compound 2," October 3, 1942. This is George's drawing of an amateur talent show, or "engeikai," at Lordsburg. Tamae wrote from Jerome about their engeikai, in which June danced the hula.

the camp construction will not be finished until end of next month, we'll have to wait. I'm making rice ladle now to be ready. Glad you got carpenter tools. Hope you are getting saw files, wood file, plane and ordinary files too. Received Mrs. Odachi's letter too. He's getting better every day but believe will take time. We still take turns & nurse him. Have received news you sent. Keep healthy & write once a week. I'll be thinking of you on 23rd. Love, George.

May 2, 1943

My dearest husband;

I am very glad that you have received the flowers which I have sent for you & also glad to know that you liked them. Do you know the meaning of the "Tulip flowers" and the Rose? They have a great meaning I'll tell you when I'll be together so please keep them nicely. Gee! I liked to see the flowers you keeping now. I hope I can see them soon. Please keep all the things you making for us. I guess we can be together soon. If you have any notice please let me know.

I've already bought saw file and ordinary files. I am trying to buy wood file, brace and some other things. I've bought 1¼ in. chisel and square for you.

Yesterday Setsuo visited us and stayed over night and went back today. He brought some candies for the children and the money sent through his father and from Mr. Yamanaka I received $10.00. It was given to the children so whenever you write home please thank my brother and sister-in-law and to Mr. Yamanaka. Tell them that children and I was so happy to have nice gift. I think Setsuo is transferred to Texas in July so you might have a chance to meet him. Kazuma also wrote to me and said that he might go to Texas.

How's the weather at your place? Over here the heat is just terrible. And its very funny place too sometimes its very hot and sometimes very cold. So everybody is catching cold. My children have too. Sandra is pretty bad but don't worry she stays with me. She'll be alright pretty soon. I am giving my children vitamin so don't worry. Carole is very big now, and cute too. She can talk and play with the toys and red papers and cloth. She is fat like daddy (a Baby elephant). But I am not so fat as before. I'm just right now and I look younger everybody thinks that I am only 27 years old. They don't believe that I'm 4 children['s] mother. I am glad that I look younger. Don't you think so? Ha! Ha!

Please let me know the things you want for yourself so I can buy. Not the carpenter tools some other things. Do you have enough pants to wear? If not I'm going to write home and ask them to send for you. I have all the things kept at sister's home. She is keeping most of my things. So please let me know quickly.

This will be all for this time will write again please take good care of yourself and give my aloha to all. Its 11:00 clock now.

Good-night,

Your loving Wife

Tamae

May 14, 1943

My dearest Husband,

Received your letter of May 3, today and was very happy to know that you are healthy always. We are all healthy so don't worry.

June received your card and she was so happy when I read it to her. She is trying to answer soon but will del[a]y because I was [too] busy to help her write. She can write in long hand now. You'll be surprised to see her grades, she have very good grades. She is very smart in drawing like you. She must be a daddy['s] girl. I hope she'll be a bright girl. You know dear, she helps me do things nowadays. She can mop the floor, sweep the floor and she also help wash the milk bottles. When the baby cries she takes care too. It's a great help for me now I'm glad I have all girls they can do lots of things when they grow up. Don't you think so?

I received a letter from Waimano home last week. It says that Taeko is doing very fine so I don't have to worry so much. I'm glad she is having very good care at the Waimano Home, so don't worry about her. We can see her when we go back to Hawaii.

Don't worry about the money we have in Hawaii. I don't touch anymore. I just received $150.00 last week, am keeping some to take over to the camp, so do not worry. I spent few dollars for your tools and I bought some dress goods for the children and for myself and I also bought (Miso) dry strings to take over. They are so expensive. Everybody buying so I did too. Please do not worry about the money.

I am glad that you are learning how to play guitar. I hope you'll be smart by the time we'll be together. Please learn good so you can teach June and Sandra. I'm learning how to makes dolls. I've already made one. I'll show you when I'll be together. Theres so many things I liked to learn, but I cannot because my baby is so young. I'll learn them when I go to the camp.

Don't worry about Carole I'll take good care of her. She is nice and fat and she's cute too. Everybody likes her. I'm glad I have a cute baby. I wish you can see her now. She is going to be 7 months old. She can sit up and play with the toys now. Gee! I wish I can send her picture to you. If [only] I can draw her picture OK but too bad I cannot.

I guess you know Tsuruko Koide (Shigeoka's daughter). She is not at this block she is at the block 38 same place with Mrs. Arita. But its near to us. She wanted to live with us when we go to the family camp. Mrs. Kanno wants to live near with us so remember when you go there first tell the people or the boss of the camp.[5]

Your brother Tak[e]o wrote to me last time and ask about you. He told me that you didn't write to them for a long time. Why don't you write to them sometimes. Please write when you have a time. Also to Hisanaga and

Takemotos. My big brother and sister-in-law sent $5.00 to the children as a gift, so when you write to them please thank them for they are very nice to us. Mr. Yamanaka also send us $5.00. He was very nice to us when we were in Hawaii.

I heard my mother always goes to Hisanagas to sleep since I came here. She misses us very much. I heard she cries all the time by mentioning about the children. I wish I can see her and your mother. We all miss the two grandmas very much. When I think about them, it make me cry too. Sandra always mention about your mother. She use[d] to love your mother when she came with us. I think she misses a lot.

Well its almost 11: o'clock so I'll stop writing. I have to sleep by now because I have to wake up early, our breakfast is at 6:30 so good-nite and sweet dreams. Hope we can meet soon. Please take yourself.

Your loving wife,

Tamae.

June 11, 1943 (Fri)

We've been expecting to move for some time and at last the time has arrived. We are to move to Santa Fe this Monday, 14th, early in the morning. Today we packed our belongings and sent them out to Barrack 70 to have them sent out ahead of us tomorrow or day after. So the barrack tonight is empty and bleak. It makes us feel sort of melancholy and also sentimental to think that we will be bidding farewell to what was our home for a year. Although confined like prisoners, this after all is part of our life and we have become attached to it in some sense.

Mr. Odachi in the hospital is well enough to be moved too but he will be sent by pullman together with number of other disabled patients accompanied by eight orderlies in attendance. So, I was greatly relieved, for I had been worried about him being left behind in case not able to travel.

I've produced quite a few things at the shop. First a folding baby walker which I copied from the Sears catalog. Then a kiddie car for Sandra designed after Bambi from the Disney cartoon and a couple of folding chairs for June and wife. I also made a jewel box for Tamae and by using a warped piece of scrap oak wood picked up from the rubbish dump as cover with a box of the same material, it came out quite well. The rubbish dump provided rich source of materials from packing cases. I also made three folding chairs for others and finally an attachment I devised for the baby walker to convert it into a stroller when going for a walk with the baby.

Those who had gone ahead to Santa Fe had written to us with more details about the camp. They say Santa Fe is still quite cold due to its higher elevation. So I have kept some warm clothing with me to take along. Mr. Kaneda, who had gone with the single group about two-and-a-half months ago, is waiting us to rejoin him there. Some from Co. 5 who had gone ahead had volunteered for road work in Idaho. So, we'll be missing them. However, the Hawaiian internees who had left the islands on the first and second ships and were interned at Livingston[6] are also expected to join us at Santa Fe too. If so we will be able to see our old friends from whom we had separated at Kilauea and Sand Island. It should be an enjoyable reunion with many experiences to relate to each other.

NOTES

1. Kau kau is a Hawaiian pidgin word used to mean food or eating.

2. This shooting incident is probably one of the ones mentioned in the complaint by the Japanese government transmitted by the Spanish Embassy in 1944. In addition to the two killings, three other shootings were mentioned, including a similar incident of a captain shooting a revolver to "urge internees to hasten their work," but the dates given are April to June 1943. The memo also addressed the Manzanar camp shootings in late 1942. ("Memorandum, The Spanish Embassy to the Department of State"; see also Culley, "Trouble at the Lordsburg Internment Camp," 240–41.)

3. Tsuneo Takemoto served in the 442nd Regimental Combat Team and received the Distinguished Service Cross for leading two charges directly into enemy fire in France; he also received two Purple Hearts and a Bronze Star. His father's cousin, Kenneth Kaname Takemoto, recollected that Tsuneo had a reputation for being fearless. (Takemoto, *Nisei Memories*, 29.) Tsuneo's oral history videos are available online at GoforBroke.org (registration required). His DSC citation is reprinted in Sterner, *Go for Broke*, 182–83.

There are many histories and memoirs/oral histories of the veterans of the all-Japanese American 442nd RCT and the 100th Battalion, primarily composed of men from Hawai'i and later merged into the 442nd. See, for example, Asahina, *Just Americans*; and Miyasaki, ed., *Japanese Eyes, American Heart*.

4. A talent show, what George refers to earlier as an "amateur show." These were very popular in the camps. See Waseda, "Extraordinary Circumstances, Exceptional Practices."

5. The Koides and Kannos were good friends to the Hoshidas on both sides and remained so after the war; George mentions Kiyoichi Koide and Tomizo Kanno at various points in the narrative, and they appear in his drawings (see figures 14.10 and 21.1).

6. Camp Livingston, Louisiana. Like the other military camps, this held prisoners of war as well as some of the Japanese American incarcerees. The Japanese POW Kazuo Sakamaki was moved here at one point (see chapter 13, note 2).

CHAPTER EIGHTEEN

{Tamae and the Children in Jerome}

The days following their arrival here were filled with unfamiliar tasks to make this miserable place livable. As people slowly settled down to routine, Tamae found many helpers because of the fact that her husband was not there to do as other families with men. The Odachis were especially helpful in taking care of the baby and Sandra, who tended to hang on to her mother's skirts and whimper and fuss whenever things did not agree with her. In fact, since Carole was the youngest baby in the block and so adorable, many women without little children came around to pick her up and take her away to cuddle. Sometimes Mrs. Odachi, being so devoted to Carole, would show her jealousy when other women took her away. Although longing for her mate, Tamae felt the warmth of people's kindness, filling her heart with gratitude. Thus the misery, the chills, and hardships in this hellhole became bearable as days passed.

The day following their arrival at the camp, Tamae received an unexpected visitor. She was her childhood pal at Piihau where she had lived at the time of father's death. Her name was Yuriko, and she had married and

FIGURE 18.1. "Jerome R. C.," February 5, 1944. This small sketch of Jerome was made not long after George's arrival at the camp. Like George, Tamae had arrived at the camp in wintertime, and the unfamiliar landscape and climate were among the many hardships for the incarcerees.

moved to the mainland many years ago. Tamae had almost lost track of her. She had settled in central California with her husband George Kobayashi and had been engaged in fruit farming but had been evacuated to this far-off camp several months ago. They heard about the evacuation of Hawaii people but never dreamed that Tamae would be part of them. However, through some source she heard of her and had hastened to meet her. In fact they lived only a couple of blocks away. Tamae was overwhelmed at this unexpected meeting with her long-lost friend, and they hugged each other in joyful embrace. Tamae forgot for some moments her miserable condition while they recalled the many events they had gone through in those years past.

Yuriko came often after that to help Tamae with many of her chores. She came along with her husband George. He helped her by making chairs and utility table for Tamae's use and was helpful in whatever way he could. Thus through the many kindnesses people came to show her, Tamae was able to manage in spite of the difficult conditions prevalent in the camp.

This camp was built in swampland which had been of no use for other purposes. The authorities had drained the swamp to build barracks out of raw lumber cut out of the trees in the swamp. Since this lumber was not properly seasoned before construction was started, the lumber shrank as it dried, and large cracks formed between the boards to let in freezing wind into the barren rooms of the barracks. The pathways between the barracks were still wet and muddy and made walking very difficult. Since ordinary shoes would be stuck in the mud, Tamae followed the examples of other inmates and purchased rubber boots for herself and the two children.

Located centrally were laundry, showers, and latrines under one roof to accommodate all the block population. Having a pile of diapers to wash, Tamae had to carry her washing to the laundry every morning and carry them back again through the mud to the barrack to have them dry inside with some cords strung across the room. Due to the dampness of the swampland, the wet laundry would not dry properly and Tamae had to buy extra diapers to last for two or three days. Then there was the problem of going through the mud again when the gong for mess rang out three times a day. Carrying Carole in her arms and leading along Sandra, who rebelled against walking through the mud, was another problem which had to be met each time they went to the mess. Then in the late afternoon she had to find her chance among the crowding women and children going to bathe. Getting the children through the shower and washing them required some time and effort also. So although these tasks were only routine easy duties at home, here it became miserable work, especially during the early days of their arrival here in the middle of freezing winter. It rained, snowed, and stormed quite often here, and many a time Tamae had to go to the mess hall by herself and carry the food home to feed the children. It was a difficult and miserable task going through the driving storm, and even with rain coat and boots, she and the food became wet and soggy by the time she fought her way through the spattering rain and mud. This was something she never experienced in Hawaii where the climate was mild and warm almost the year through. She often wondered why she must suffer such miseries.

Even with the kind help of many people who came to her aid whenever possible, she envied the families who had the hands of men taking care of the

1-14-44
8 A.M.

Mama Feeding Carole

Figure 18.2. "Mama Feeding Carole," January 14, 1944. Managing the care of three children was no easy task for Tamae in Jerome. Washing diapers and laundry and gathering wood were particularly difficult.

heavier work of the family. She longed for Yoshio and cried herself to sleep during the nights when things became too difficult. Being handicapped with the injured hip which left her permanently crippled, the burden of caring and worrying over her three little ones became a truly monstrous torture at times.

Added to all these difficulties, illnesses among the children overcame Tamae with further burden. First it was the eldest, June. She complained of stiffness in the legs and tiredness. Tamae took her to the doctor at the hospital which, fortunately, was not too far from their block. The doctor examined her and diagnosed it as beriberi, coming from improper food with lack of proper vitamins. The doctor gave her an injection and advised for her to be hospitalized for a few days for proper treatment.

Tamae went with the hospital attendant to the women's ward. There was no special children's section, and June was placed with some women patients. However, to get her established there was another story, for June balked when she found that she was to be left there by herself. When placed in a crib, June refused to let go of Tamae's hands and cried: "I don't want to stay here! I want to go home! Mami! Mami! Don't leave me!"

Tamae's heart ached with pity for her, but she had to be left there if she was to be cured. So she stayed with her for some time until she soothed down. She had left the other two children with Mrs. Odachi, and she had to get back to them. So finally she left with June's cry following her through the hospital corridors. She found the cry throbbing within herself even after returning home.

Next was Carole with continuous diarrhea. Tamae took her to the doctor, but the doctor just advised her to take her home and give her rice gruel with Japanese pickled prunes. The feeding had no beneficial effect and in the end blood started to show in her stool. A friend advised her to take her to another doctor and ask for help. So she packed her in blanket and took her to the other doctor, a Dr. Tanaka who was originally from Island of Kauai in Hawaii. Dr. Tanaka was very sympathetic when Tamae narrated the worries and efforts she had gone through. He promised her that he would do all in his power to help the poor suffering child and found room in the ward to keep Carole and watch over her. Carole had also developed an ear infection, and pus oozed out of one of the ears. This too he treated until both illnesses were completely cured. Leaving the children at the hospital with their cries trailing behind and haunting her was a real heart-rending experience which she felt would be with her for her lifetime. At such times she felt the absence of Yoshio's presence most acutely. Uncertainty of reunion compounded the miseries and sufferings she already had to endure physically.[1]

However, there were some joys which came her way unexpectedly. Tamae's nephew, Setsuo, eldest son of Riichi, was in training for duty in the Pacific Front and was nearby at a Little Rock, Arkansas military base. He wrote to Tamae and then came over for weekend visits. Kazuma, Tamae's sister's son, was attending Pomona College in Southern California, but he also volunteered for service and was at Camp Shelby in Mississippi, nearby. He came for visits also so that Tamae and the children could enjoy his company as well as some presents he brought with him. Thus the monotony and sufferings Tamae encountered in this miserable life were somewhat relieved.

As time passed, Tamae, together with other people from Hawaii in their center, settled down into routine life and resigned themselves to persevere without much hope for reunion in the immediate future. Conditions in the camp also improved as summer heat dried up the mud in the camp, and people worked toward making themselves at home in this God-forsaken camp. Gravel was laid to pave the muddy footpaths and ease their difficulties in moving around in the camp. Strangers from different islands living together became friends who could discuss their problems and ease their pains in their hearts. They even started to think about entertainments, and programs were set up for amusements from time to time.

However, summer heat was severe and together with the high humidity in this swampy land, it tortured them mercilessly. There was malaria with mosquitoes which laid low some victims. Dr. Kuwahara's son was one of them, and although he survived, it affected him and left its mark on him for some time. Fortunately none in Tamae's family got the sickness. But chiggers attacked them, and itches and rashes tortured them like most of the people there.

DOCUMENT 3. TAMAE'S PETITION FOR REUNION AND OFFICIAL RESPONSE

Jerome Relocation Center
Denson, Arkansas

March 2, 1943

[Sent in triplicate typescript to:]
Mr. Edward J. Ennis, Director

Alien Enemy Control Unit
Department of Justice
Washington, D.C.

Lt. Gen. Delos C. Emmons
The Commanding General
Hawaiian Department
Fort Shafter, Honolulu, T.H.

Mr. W. F. Kelly
Immigration and Naturalization Service
Philadelphia, Penn.

Re: George Yoshio Hoshida
ISN-HJ-1133CI
Lordsburgh, New Mexico, U.S.A.

I here-with present my plea to you for your justified action and every considerations humanely possible given to me, my children, and to my husband. Kindly review his case and with your recommendation parole him to W.R.A. center here.

My husband whose age is 37 36 and was an employee as a salesman for the Hilo Electric Light Co., at Hilo, Hawaii, Territory of Hawaii, at the time of his detention a year ago. Since May of that year it is believed he was definitely to be interned and sent to the mainland, the United States of America.

I am now 34 years of age, having four children, all girls. The eldest, age nine, who several years ago by cause of an auto accident is crippled and at present victim of mental derangement, inmate of the Waimano Home, Honolulu, T.H. I am here with the other three children. The eldest six years old, followed by another two years old, and the youngest at present four months old. The reasons for my being here are as follows:

I was upon three separate occasions induced upon to evacuate by army officials in Hawaii, that evacuating to the United States Mainland would mean to eventually be with my husband, which precisely interested me. However it may have been a compulsory order because my children and I were under the care of Public Welfare for financial support since my husband was detained. While at Hilo I had other support, both moral and physical. Together with some financial aid my mother-in-law assisted me for the care of my children, relieving me of great burden upon my crippled physical condition. The following will explain my physical condition.

Early in my childhood, accidentally my hip-bone was fractured, resulting in the improper development of one of my lower limbs. I am unable to walk properly, but by limping manage to get around now that I am here at an unusual place. The climate is extremely cold for me and my children, and we alternately have become ill ever since arriving here nearly two months ago, and have not as yet fully recovered. I am forced to limp back and forth from the mess hall three times a day from my barrack with my children. The words "Oh, Lord help me," was so frequently repeated by me I naturally resorted [sic] for aid thinking if my husband was only here to help me, but in vain, and yet have braced up myself again and again with courage and attempt to try my best to readjust and go on to nurse, feed, bathe, launder for all three. Of course I am neglecting myself completely and feel at times I am terribly broken up. Nevertheless before being completely wrecked, both morally and mentally I was enlightened by a hope that came to my mind to ask someone to write this letter as I described, and because a ray of hope I had left within me that kept up my courage. It was an opportunity to live together with my husband who is healthy and strong to assist me, as I have in the past completely depended upon him or his relatives back at home.

It is with my greatest wish and effort in making this statement of facts. To plead before you to kindly reconsider the case of George Yoshio Hoshida, my husband, who had been loyal to the United States, has been Y.B.A. leader advocating and advising to observe and to become law abiding U.S. citizens, and to become Boy Scouts of America, etc. Therefore please review his case and if possible parole him to this W.R.A. center at the earliest possible date in order that I may acquire my husband's aid, and live together to alleviate both moral and mental state of mind, and relieve my crippled physical condition. I pray you will allow me and my children to live like any American citizen is entitled to. I will swear before the Lord, that my husband is innocent from all activities detrimental to the interest of the United States of America, and I can testify that he is against the repatriation plan because he wants to raise his family here in the United States of America which is my country and my children's future home. Hoping that every impartial action and consideration [may] be given me, I pray,

I am sincerely yours,

[Tamae Hoshida]

Territory of Hawaii
Office of the Military Governor
Iolani Palace
Honolulu, T.H.

14 May 1943

SUBJECT: Request of Internee, George Y. Hoshida, ISN-HJ-1133-CI, for Parole and Reunion with his Family on the Mainland.

TO: Alien Division, Office of The Provost Marshal General, Army Service Forces, War Department, Washington, D.C.

1. In letter of this office dated January 22, 1943, supplementing letter of January 8, 1943, The Commanding General, Hawaiian Department, recommended to you that George Y. Hoshida, ISN-HJ-1133-CI, be paroled from internment and that he is permitted to join his family in such war relocation center on the Mainland as you might designate.

2. The Commanding General, Hawaiian Department, desires to be informed of the action taken in this case upon the recommendations so made, and resubmits the above mentioned recommendations at this time.

3. If you feel that it would not be practicable to parole internee for reunion with his family in a war relocation center, The Commanding General, Hawaiian Department, further recommends that internee be permitted to join his family at such family internment camp on the Mainland as you may designate.

4. Copies of letters from George Y. Hoshida, ISN-HJ1133-CI, dated March 6, 1943, to The Commanding General, Hawaiian Department; of Mrs. Tamae Hoshida, dated March 2, 1943, to The Commanding General, Hawaiian Department, and to Mr. Edward J. Ennis, Director,

Alien Enemy Control Unit, Department of Justice, Washington, D.C.;
and of Alien Division, Office of the Provost Marshal General, Army
Service Forces, War Department—14 May 1943

The replies of this office thereto are being inclosed for your
reference.

WM. R.C. MORRISON
Colonel, J.A.G.D.
Executive

DOCUMENT 4. LETTER FROM EDWARD ENNIS, DEPARTMENT OF JUSTICE

Department of Justice 146-13-2-21-627
Alien Enemy Control Unit
Washington

October 26, 1943

Colonel I. B. Summers
Director, Prisoner of War Division
War Department
Washington, D.C.

Re: George Yoshio Hoshida

Dear Sir:

I am referring to you for your appropriate consideration, a letter
from Mrs. Tamae Hoshida, the wife of the above-named alien enemy
internee, requesting that the arrangements for her husband's parole
to rejoin her at the Jerome Relocation Center be expedited.

Our records show that on April 3, 1943, this Unit concurred with the
decision of the War Department that the subject should be paroled to
a War Relocation Center. In a letter addressed to this Unit on October
1, 1943, Mrs. Hoshida stated that she was crippled and unable to give
proper care to her three small children, and inquired whether an inter-
im parole might be possible until the arrangements could be completed for the regular parole of Mr. Hoshida. Since the circumstances
mentioned in my present enclosure and the previous communication
seem to indicate hardship, it is felt that this case should be given whatever preference is possible.

Mrs. Hoshida has been advised of the reference.

Very truly yours,
Edward J. Ennis
Director

Document 5. "Hawaiian Evacuees," a Report from Paul A. Taylor, Project Director

Excerpts from a report from Jerome Relocation Center, Denson Arkansas, sent to Dillon S. Myer, Director WRA, from Paul A. Taylor, Project Director.

From the covering letter dated February 28, 1943
"Generally speaking, the remarks that have been made in Staff Meetings concerning the evacuees from Hawaii are much less favorable than this report would indicate."

From the report entitled "Hawaiian Evacuees":

The 810 Hawaiian evacuees at this center have not presented any particular problem to date. With a few general exceptions they have conformed with the general behavior pattern which we have come to accept as typical of the other residents. But there is reason to believe that they have been cooperative because of fear and because they want to keep on the good side of everybody.

The other residents have accepted the Hawaiian group in good grace, in spite of such repeated complaints as "They don't talk English like we do" and "They're all pro-Japanese." The women wear typical kimonos and more colorful dress in general. Most of the men wear army overcoats. On warm days they have already begun to indulge in what we have been told is the Hawaiian custom of going barefooted.

The first of three contingents, numbering 107, arrived November 23. The second group of 443 arrived January 5 and the last 260 February 6. [. . .]

These people were received at the center in the usual fashion, with the notable exception that immediate steps were taken to provide proper clothing for this climate, through grants and regular orders. Other blocks went out of their way on several occasions to extend hospitality. [. . .] A campaign within the center, in which the administration had no part, raised more than $1,000 which was distributed as emergency funds to Hawaiian arrivals. Most of this money went to individual families—where there were many children and no father or where evacuation had left the family destitute.

NOTE

1. Although George does not state it here, Carole's illness was very severe, and according to the stories she heard from her parents, she nearly died from this dysentery.

CHAPTER NINETEEN

At Santa Fe Detention Station

JUN. 18, 1943 (FRI)

This is Santa Fe Detention Station, as it is called, but actually an internment camp, or more properly, a concentration camp. I am in Barrack 58 together with 61 other internees. On Monday morning June 14, 350 of us marched out of Lordsburg Camp at early dawn. It was 6 o'clock, and at 7:45, we boarded the special train to Santa Fe.

When the train pulled out, we had a last look at the camp in the distance, so lonely and forlorn when viewed from this distance. It stood in the middle of the desert surrounded by mountain ranges on all sides. A feeling of attachment and nostalgia assailed us, for although this was actually a prison to us, it had grown in our hearts as a place of many memories, both unpleasant and pleasant, for the past one year.

The trip was long and tiresome and we reached Santa Fe sometime between nine and ten o'clock at night of the same day. Curious Santa Fe residents greeted us at the station. But we were packed into trucks and buses at once, before they could quite make up their minds how to receive us. We

DOI: 10.5876/9781607323440.c019

FIGURE 19.1. Santa Fe, October 15, 1943. Santa Fe was a dreary place for these men hoping to rejoin their families. "This camp, so far, is the worst equipt camp of all we've gone through," wrote George. His drawing shows how tightly packed the barracks were.

were taken up the slope of a mountain which reared high above the city across a valley.

The barracks to which we were assigned were new ones built recently to accommodate us and were built at the foot of slope in the valley. The older barracks, which were remnants of internment camp from World War I where German internees were confined, were above us on the slope. We found out next morning that although the barracks there were old, they commanded a beautiful view of the city, and we enjoyed the refreshing view when we were called to breakfast at the only mess hall located on top of the hill.

About twenty internees from Lordsburg, including myself, in the first truck, were herded into Barrack 58. There we were pleasantly surprised to be greeted by people from Hawaii who were interned at Livingston Camp at Louisiana and had preceded us to this camp only a week ago. They said that internees with families here in mainland now and some old and sickly people were transferred here. Others were taken to Missoula, Montana. We had thought that these people were already in Crystal City with their families and were really surprised to find them here. We of Block 58 were KPs at hall yesterday, and with 350 increase in inmates from Lordsburg, we are serving all the 1600 people arriving here.[1]

JUNE 23, 1943 (WED) 7 PM

Early this morning, about 2:30 AM, we were awakened by the loud clang of mess hall dinner bell followed by the blast from the steam laundry whistle. Someone shouted, "Fire!" and another said, "It's the mess hall!!"

I jumped out of the bed and through the window to the north, I saw the glow of fire. I ran to the front door with the other inmates and saw the roof of the mess hall on the top of the slope, licked by fierce flame. There was no wind but since we had been warned of the low supply of water, I feared that this fire would be very difficult to extinguish.

Many were already running up to help. I returned to my bed to pull on my pants and shirt, and with a pair of gloves and hat, I followed the crowd at a brisk pace. To run in this high altitude with its rarefied air would mean exhaustion, and even walking got me out of breath from excitement.

Nearing the fire, I noticed that the wind was blowing toward the hospital. Then it reminded me of Mr. Odachi in the hospital and I turned my steps toward it. Men were helping the people living near the mess hall carry out their belongings to safety. The firemen with their engines had arrived but they seemed slow in getting started. Other cars were rushing into the camp from town and the foreground was crowded with people, some helping and others just watching.

When I reached the hospital, the orderlies were moving out the patients from the hospital building. Other patients were evacuated to the separate TB ward situated to the south. But it didn't look very safe there too if this building was to catch fire. So talking over with the other men, we decided to take Mr. Odachi down to our barrack.

After wrapping him up in clothing and blanket, I carried him out on my back. To avoid exciting him, I chose a route away from the scene of the fire and came out to the open ground leading down to the lower compound. The fire had already spread to the lower building adjacent to the mess hall. It housed the library, recreation hall and the tailor shop. The recreation hall, where movies and other activities were held, seemed to be burning but the barracks in the foreground hid it from clear view. The open ground here was covered now and the fire engine still was not in action. Perhaps there was no water to operate it.

I carried Mr. Odachi down to our barrack and laid him in my bed. Then I went back to the hospital for his bed pan. The fire kept on burning fiercely. I stood watching for a few moments but fearing that Mr. Odachi might be needing assistance, I returned to our barrack. There I had to help him with the bed pan. After helping the patient, I went out again but saw that the fire had subsided somewhat. Walking up, I saw that the other buildings were now out of danger. The burning buildings had collapsed to the ground and fires were smoldering low.

I took out my sketch book and drew the scene from several directions to add to my collection. When I finally returned to my barrack, most of the people were back in their beds. Finding an empty bed left by Mr. Kinoshita who had gone to hospital orderly duty, I crawled in for a few winks. I felt tired but sleep wouldn't come until dawn lighted the windows. Some men then came to take Mr. Odachi back to the hospital. I got up too and followed them up to the hospital.

The burnt-out ruin was still smoldering and the firemen were busy dousing it with streams of water from the fire hose. Many inmates were searching among the ruins for something and finding some cans of milk and eggs, they were feasting. I joined in and found a couple of eggs too. A man went around the barracks with the announcement that breakfast was being prepared at the state prison in town and it will be ready around eight. Until then, everyone was advised to remain in their barracks and not go up until the bell rang in order to avoid confusion. We were all hungry and the breakfast bell seemed very slow in ringing. But it finally rang around 8:30. We lined up to receive the ration of a cup of coffee, one bun and an egg at impromptu serving tables line up at the open ground above our compound. It wasn't quite enough to fill our stomachs left empty from the excitement of the fire. But lunch and supper were better considering the lack of facilities. The army field kitchen from Albuquerque is to be brought over tomorrow morning.[2]

June 25, 1943 (Fri)

With the only mess hall burnt down, we are in a fine pickle. The internees had increased to 1899 with the arrival of the remaining internees from Lordsburg and some from Sharp Park.[3] The food is being prepared at the state prison at present until a temporary kitchen can be set up in the garage. They are working on it now. Meanwhile, meals are served at the ground between the Liaison Office and Barrack 13 at the upper compound. We line up in half-a-dozen lines with steel plates and cups salvaged from the fire. Breakfast consisted of bread, coffee or milk and egg. Lunch was again bread, with piece of abalone, canned fruit and coffee or milk; supper, stew, bread and coffee. The meals weren't too good even when the mess hall was there but it's barely enough to keep us from hunger. I've got indigestion and am taking baking soda but my stomach doesn't feel right. The construction of a new mess hall is to start as soon as possible. They have two planned and internees are now drafted to clear the burnt debris.

This camp, so far, is the worst equipped camp of all we've gone through. Hope it'll be improved. The food is bad; barracks overcrowded; insufficient water supply; defective toilet and poor sanitation with flies all over the place from the sewage plant next to the camp in the valley.[4]

Serving eats outdoor
7-15-43

Santa Fe N. S.

Looking down town   Dusk & light shower
7-17-43

FIGURE 19.2. "Serving Eats Outdoor," July 15, 1943, at the Santa Fe camp after a fire burned down the only mess hall. Below is a view of the town.

JULY 26, 1943 (MON) 7:00 PM

The Spanish Ambassador of San Francisco visited us in the early part of this month to investigate the conditions of our camp. He represents Japanese interests here and held interviews with the internees on various complaints and requests. We from Hawaii asked his assistance in speeding up our family reunion. He promised to help and also appeared optimistic about it. The result of his efforts has materialized and about 30 are to go to Crystal City after August 1st. It looks like Hawaiian internees but names have not been announced yet.

In this connection over half of us Hawaiians waiting for reunion received answers to a joint petition sent on the 21st last month to Mr. Ennis of the Dept. of Justice. The answer stated that we are to be paroled to the relocation centers provided it was satisfactory to the Relocation Authorities; and that we will be notified as soon as they consented to it. We discussed it and decided to petition Mr. Ennis to permit us to go to the family camp instead of being paroled to the relocation center. For us from Hawaii, it would be better in many ways. We drafted the petition and submitted it for mailing last Saturday. Believe it was sent out today.

There has been a change in the policy of the Relocation Authorities and they have now drafted out a plan to segregate the disloyal from the loyal within the centers through questionnaires. The disloyal are to be sent to the Tule Lake Relocation Center.[5] The people asking for repatriation to Japan will be sent first and then others after being given individual hearings. Believe we will be sent there in case we are paroled to the center. Either way we will be better off in the family camp. Even if we are to be regarded as loyal and kept in the regular relocation center, we may be sent outside to live if the centers should be closed after most of the people are relocated. To make a living with the family in this unfamiliar environment will be very difficult for us from Hawaii.

Also, judging from what it is costing our family living there, we'll not be able to live there even if we are to be kept until the end of war, for it is actually costing my family about $100 a month. Tamae had brought with her about $525 when she came here in January and a couple of months ago she had $150 sent over from the reserve in Hawaii of about $800 from the sale of our house and furnishings. In a recent letter she wrote that she already has already spent most of it, and would like to have more sent over. It seems that she has already spent about half of what she realized from the sale of our possessions. Believe she needs the money to live normally with others. But I cannot understand it since she is getting food and shelter and also some clothing allowances from the W.R.A. Guess it's too easy to spend with the high cost of things, and things necessary are limitless.

I realize that too, for today we were allowed to withdraw $30 from our account in custody of the authorities here. My money in custody was $33 and some odd cents which I brought over from Hawaii. I drew out the $30 today and already spent about $5.00—$1.25 paid back to Mr. Kagawa borrowed from him to pay for the group photo we took couple of weeks ago; $3.00 for a knap-sack and cord I've ordered to prepare packing for reunion; and $1.00 for some delicacy to take to the children. If I didn't have that money, I could have managed somehow but with money in my pocket, it became too easy to spend. I guess it's the same with Tamae, for Mrs. Odachi with four children, is getting along somehow with only the money of 10¢ an hour she is earning at work at the mess hall. Of course I cannot blame my wife only, for I've helped spend some of the money by asking her to purchase a guitar, some tools and other things. Guess that's how money goes. But we cannot be spending at that rate, for we now have only $600 left in Hawaii, which at the rate of $100 a month will last only 6 months. Believe if we can go to the family camp, since people there mostly are in the same economic position, we may not need to spend as much as in the relocation center with people having more money to spend.

Hoshida, George Yoshio
BK-58 Santa Fe Detention Station
Santa Fe, N.M.

Aug. 11, 1943

Mrs. Tamae Hoshida
39—9-F Jerome R.C.
Denson, Arkansas.

Dearest wife:

I haven't received letter from you this week but I received word from Mrs. Arita in regard to parole. I would like to explain to you why I prefer family camp instead of parole. I believe you know that the W.R.A. are planning to keep only Tule Lake as Relocation Center and the other centers are to be closed in time. That means that the people in centers like yours will have to move out to earn their living as soon as possible. Did you stop to think what would happen to us in that case? We are from Hawaii and don't know anything about mainland. Also I'm not a citizen and do not have as good a chance as the citizens. On top of that I do not believe that I can do any steady work. I didn't let you know because you might worry, but my back had been bothering me all along since coming to mainland. Soon after reaching Lordsburg, I had an attack of neuralgia and couldn't walk & was in bed for about a month. I got better but when I started doing some office work & sat for half a day in the office, it came back again & I had to go to hospital for a month again. It got better but as soon as I try to do work for long, I feel the pain & have to lay down & rest. So you can see that I can neither do work standing or sitting unless I can rest when I want. Now I hope you understand that if I should be paroled to your center, you'll not even receive any clothing allowances and when we are let out of the center, we'll starve unless I can work & I don't think I can work. So there's no choice except Tule Lake or family camp. Which do you prefer? Tule Lake have better climate but family camp have better facilities. I'm quite sure we can go there by Oct. for Mr. Kelly promised us first chance. Of course it's up to the authorities if it's parole, we can't help it but make the most of it. Don't believe in rumors unless you know it's true. I believe centers are the worst factory of rumors.

Love,

George.

AUG. 31, 1943 (TUES) 9:16 PM

The last date on my diary is June 30th—over a month ago. I've been so busy during that time that my heart wasn't on any writing or desk work. I haven't touched a paint brush either after arriving here, except once. The art class was started but dropped after only one lesson on account of lack of place to hold classes. There have been several changes too with people coming in and going out.

Mr. Odachi became worse again and blood had to be taken out to relieve his high blood pressure. He was, therefore, transferred to a private room for special care. It became necessary also to have nightly attendants to take care of him. People at first were willing to help but with such long term illness, their enthusiasm has faded away, and it has become very difficult to recruit people to volunteer.

Mr. Jenson, the head of this camp, has arranged for Mr. Odachi's parole to his family as soon as he becomes well enough to make the trip. An attendant will have to go with him and I may volunteer. Then also I may be able to obtain temporary parole and go to the center earlier than others.

Oct. 5, 1943 8:00 PM

Letters came in reporting malaria in Jerome Center. That camp was actually built on the mud of the swamp land by draining some water. But it really was a very unhealthy place, I believe selected by some people who regarded people of Japanese blood without much compassion. This malaria will be a very serious thing, for there's deficiency of quinine supply now since Japan took over Java where most of the quinine came from before the war. Hope it can be controlled before it becomes too bad. Mr. Kurita's child is in hospital from that disease and today, he asked me to write a petition for temporary parole to Mr. Ennis.

Oct. 22, 1943 (Fri) 9:05 PM

Mr. Odachi finally passed away last night about 7:25 PM after seven months of illness. He seemed quite all right when I was with him a few days ago, although he was attacked by convulsions and was in a coma for about a day. I was searching for a special night orderly for him and had finally found one volunteer. Mr. Odachi had been scheduled for parole as soon as he was able to travel to his family in Jerome and it is truly unfortunate and sad that he was not able to make it. I feel very close to him although I had not known him before the war. Coming to mainland together and sleeping next to each other at Lordsburg in the same barrack had brought us very close. We often talked about our past and although our religion was different, I found in him a very warm and sincere personality which attracted me to him. He had asked me to write to his family the first time when we were confined at the Kilauea Military Camp and through correspondence, I became familiar with the difficulties and sufferings his family was going through after his separation from [them].

10-8-42 - 9:30PM

Tahata

T. Kanawo
Playing Chess

Odachi

Hata

FIGURE 19.3. Kinzaemon Odachi, lower left, who passed away at the Santa Fe camp. He was only months away from finally reuniting with his family at Jerome. "If the authorities had been really sincere about it, they could have carried out their promises a long time ago," George wrote in a rare outburst of bitterness after Odachi's death.

Wire was sent to his family and answer came this afternoon. It said that Mrs. Odachi was not able to come and requested that the ashes be sent to her. It must be on account of their financial difficulty, for she had no savings and was supporting her family of five working at the mess hall on a meager wage of $16 a month. A trip here would be a real hardship.

Mr. Okazaki, also a Tenrikyo minister interned here, I found, is a relative of Mr. Odachi and he had been looking after him too. He and the ministers of their religion came to me to discuss about the preparations for the funeral. We had planned at first with Mrs. Odachi's presence in mind and her answer caused changes in our plans. We decided to hold the funeral earlier and set the time for 2 PM tomorrow. The funeral will be performed under their Tenrikyo religious ceremony and I am to attend to other details.

The body is to be sent by rail to his family in Jerome right after the funeral services. It would give the family at least a chance to see his face. It is fortunate that it could be so, for the army does not pay such expenses but this Justice Dept. under which we are now, will do so. (The body, however, was cremated and ashes sent to the family due to the difficulty and time it would take to transport the body.)[6]

Oct. 23, 1943

Dearest wife:

Received your letter of Oct. 19th and was glad to know that you are all healthy. I'm lively as ever and the cold weather seems all right for my back. I got the overcoat and other things you've sent me and am making good use of them. Hope you received my package. Sorry I couldn't send anything for Carole. Today is my birthday but it wasn't a very happy day, for we had the services for Mrs. Odachi's husband. Ashes will be sent as soon as ready. I'm very sorry for Mrs. Odachi. Try your best to console her and help them as much as you can. If there's anything I can make or do for them let me know. I believe you didn't understand the meaning of my letter of 15th about reunion. I'm doing all I can to speed my parole but what I want to have understanding with you is this: There is a possibility that we from Hawaii may be granted reunion soon and in case the order comes for us to go to family camp, would you want me to refuse and wait for parole here instead of going there first and be together and wait for parole after that? There are quite a few who don't mind parole but are planning to go to family camp if they should receive chance to go there. If you and I should refuse, we'll be the only ones left behind. Would you refuse to go even then. Remember this is in case the order to family camp should come before my parole order, for it might happen so. I'm saying this because I want to be together with you and the children as soon as possible, in any way possible, not because I do not want parole. So let me know if you still want to wait for parole even if you will have to stay behind after every one else have gone to family camp. Remember that we have just as much chance [of] parole from there as from here. Also why are you wasting time petitioning Mr. Ennis when the right place is WRA headquarters? It's up to Mr. Myer to accept me now. Petition there.

Love,
George

Oct. 29, 1943 (Fri.) 8:30 PM

It snowed on the lower slopes of the mountain range today and it was very chilly in the basement shop. Believe it will start snowing here soon too. The leaves on the trees have all turned golden except the evergreens, and leaves are falling. It's real autumn now. I would like to do a painting but have very little time since I am busy making trunks and chairs to order.

I read the letter Mrs. Odachi had written to Mr. Okazaki. It showed blotches of tears and I couldn't read it without tears welling out of my eyes, myself. They had come to mainland with the promise from the Hawaiian Authorities that they would be reunited with their husband and father immediately on arrival. But the promise had not been fulfilled and only excuses had been given to all the pleadings from the family. If the authorities had been really sincere about it, they could have carried out their promises a long time ago.

Of course, being enemy aliens, we cannot expect favors. But the children being American citizens through right of birth, for a democratic nation with ideals of justice and equality to all, this apparent lack of human compassion and consideration does not speak very well of this country's future stability. No matter what the circumstances, the true test of any individual or a nation is their actions during times of stress such as this.

Hoshida, George Yoshio
BK-58 S.F. Detention Station
Santa Fe, N.M.

Nov. 20, 1943

Mrs. Tamae Hoshida
39–09-F Jerome R.C.
Denson, Arkansas

Dearest wife:

Received your letter of Nov. 16 and was sorry to hear that June and Sandra
was sick but am glad they are over it and also relieved to hear that Carole
is getting better. The main thing is to keep healthy so try not to worry too
much, for I believe everything will turn out all right. It's all in the way you
take things. To be separated is heartbreaking but if you think that you
are getting valuable experience in taking care of things by yourself, it is a
wonderful opportunity. It is only by hardships that you can really develop the
best in yourself. If you brood about this hardship you'll gain nothing and the
result will be only misery and misfortune. Many people cannot be together
until the war ends and in fact thousands of people cannot meet again. If we
think of it we shouldn't complain about being separated so long as we can
keep ourselves healthy. You speak of not petitioning in groups, but we should
do it in group once in a while for it has more force. Of course it is necessary
to do separately too. Anyway it's better for everybody to join their families at
the same time if possible, for everybody wants to reunite as soon as possible.
I would like to have it that way too if possible, for I wouldn't feel good to go
only by myself. The others will be feeling just as bad as you feel when other
husbands return while I don't. I am doing all I can to help others. I wrote
many petitions for the Hawaii people and even when I do my own petitions
I don't feel right unless I write for others too, for most of them cannot do
by themselves. Please do all you can to help others too. Don't do anything
selfish. Be good to everybody and above all don't feel bad toward people
repatriating, for they have their own reasons for doing so. It is important
that you keep your soul pure. Any bad thoughts will darken it. Don't order
presents for children. I ordered them.

Lovingly yours,
George.

The diary at the internment camp ends here [on November 18], and the next entry is at the Jerome Relocation Center in Arkansas. Yoshio was paroled from the internment camp at Santa Fe and released on Dec. 4th, 1943 (Sat) together with 7 other parolees. They were taken by army truck to board a bus at Santa Fe City bound for Albuquerque where they were to take the train for the trip to Little Rock, Arkansas. All except one of the parolees were going to Jerome. The other one was destined to Rohwer,[7] which was not too far from Jerome and also in Arkansas. Although Yoshio had some entries in Arkansas, it contained little detail. So, we will resume narration the same as before these entries in the diary were taken up.

NOTES

1. The Santa Fe camp, which has already been mentioned several times as the origin or destination of other incarcerees in transit, was an INS-run camp that held, at its height, about 2,000 incarcerees of various origin, including Japanese Latin Americans. Many men here were awaiting reunion with their families, like George, which led to protests and the imprisonment of 360 incarcerees in the stockade in 1944, long after George's departure. (Kashima, *Judgment without Trial*, 118.)

2. The fire at Santa Fe is also mentioned in Yasutaro Soga's memoir; he says that the fire was probably electrical and that nobody was injured. (Soga, *Life behind Barbed Wire*, 129.)

3. Sharp Park, near San Francisco, was one of the internment camps used to hold aliens arrested directly after Pearl Harbor, and held aliens of all ethnicities, including Japanese Peruvians, for the duration of the war.

4. Conditions got worse, Soga wrote, after a massive landslide on June 28, which made the unsanitary conditions even more dangerous. (Soga, *Life behind Barbed Wire*, 130.)

5. The questionnaire to which George is referring contains the infamous "loyalty oath." On this questionnaire, which asked for basic identification information and any Japanese connections and language ability, questions 27 and 28 asked, "Are you willing to serve in the armed forces of the United States on combat duty, wherever ordered?" and "Will you swear unqualified allegiance to the United States of America and faithfully defend the United States from any or all attack by foreign or domestic forces, and forswear any form of allegiance or obedience to the Japanese emperor, or any other foreign government, power, or organization?"

Given the lack of information and context given to the incarcerees, especially the Issei who were not eligible for American citizenship, these questions produced much anxiety and confusion and elicited extremely varied responses. The stigma-tization of those who answered "no-no" was dramatized powerfully by the writer John Okada in his famous novel *No-No Boy* (1950). Tule Lake, the camp where these "incorrigibles" were segregated, experienced a great deal of unrest and unfavorable publicity.

Tamae answered 'yes' to both questions. George, being in different custody at the time, was probably never given the questionnaire; it is not in his records. Most histories of the incarceration treat the vexed history of the loyalty question-naire at least in part; for more focused studies, see, for example, Muller, *American Inquisition*; and Lyon, *Prisons and Patriots*.

6. Mr. Odachi's death was felt keenly among the group from Hawai'i, not only because of personal mourning but because it highlighted the long wait for family reunion; it is also mentioned in other published letters. (See Honda, ed., *Family Torn Apart*, 142.)

7. Rohwer incarceration camp, one of the WRA camps called "Relocation Centers." The Hoshidas misspell this in various ways, but I have corrected them throughout for clarity. This paragraph is clearly a 1970s addendum.

CHAPTER TWENTY

Parole and Reunion with Family at Jerome Relocation Center

{TAMAE'S POINT OF VIEW}

Then in November Yoshio wrote that there seemed to be hope of parole to the relocation center in the near future. In fact, many of the Alaskan and mainland internees were being released to their families in the centers. He mentioned in a later letter that there was a list of parolees in which a couple of Hawaiian internees were included together with a group of Alaskan people, and Yoshio was one of them. It seemed that their dream was finally becoming real.

December came, and the long wait was finally rewarded with a telegram from Yoshio. It said "PAROLED LEAVING HERE 4TH 3 PM BE SEEING YOU ALL MONDAY LOVE." Monday would be the 6th. Was this true? It felt like a dream but the telegram which came was real. The telegram came on the evening of the 4th. So Yoshio must be starting the journey from Santa Fe and be on the train from Albuquerque. Tamae's heart beat faster whenever she imagined the heavenly moment she would be greeting him here at the door. She prayed that nothing would happen on the way to delay his arrival.

DOI: 10.5876/9781607323440.c020

Then a second telegram arrived from Amarillo, Texas. It was a bit of a letdown saying, "DELAYED AT AMARILLO LEAVING HERE SUNDAY 815 PM BELIEVE WILL REACH JEROME AFTER MIDNIGHT MONDAY NOTIFY MRS NAKANO." But it was just a delay and nothing to be alarmed [about]. Also his mentioning Mrs. Nakano meant that Mr. Nakano, whose family was in their block and coming from Kauai, must be with him. Tamae hurried to give the message to the Nakanos in the next barrack behind theirs. Mrs. Nakano was expecting her husband also and although the delay was a disappointment, Mrs. Nakano was grateful that Yoshio was together with him.

The children were all excited and kept asking Tamae when their father was coming home. Carole, being born without her father's presence, seemed oblivious to the excitement which was building up each moment. However, Tamae had been showing them Yoshio's pictures often and having them recognize him as their Daddy. Sandra, now nearly three-and-a-half years old, may not remember her father, for she was not quite two when he was taken. But since Tamae had been pointing at his pictures often and mentioning "Daddy," she must have felt closeness to him as though he was living with them. When Tamae asked her about him, she would say, "Daddy, Santa Fe."

Monday dawned bright and chilly. It was winter now, and Tamae remembered clearly the day they arrived here that dreary cold winter night, disappointed that her husband was not here to greet them. Tamae never felt so miserable and disheartened as that night which was exactly eleven months ago. But now the months of perseverance were about to be rewarded. Yoshio was coming home!

She had gone to the beautician to have her hair done and tried on her make-up to see that she would be at her best when she would greet her dear mate. It was a year and ten months since their separation on that shocking day of his arrest on February 6th last year. After applying her make-up, she looked at herself over in the little mirror which hung on the wall over the little table which Mr. Kobayashi had made for her. She was 35 now and middle-aged, according to what people considered around her age. However, with her hair-do and light make-up, she felt that she still looked young, and her round face and soft, gentle features did make her look younger than her actual age. In fact, didn't she look just as young as when Yoshio was courting her? What will he think when he sees her now? The day dragged on with mixed emotions. People hearing about her husband's return congratulated

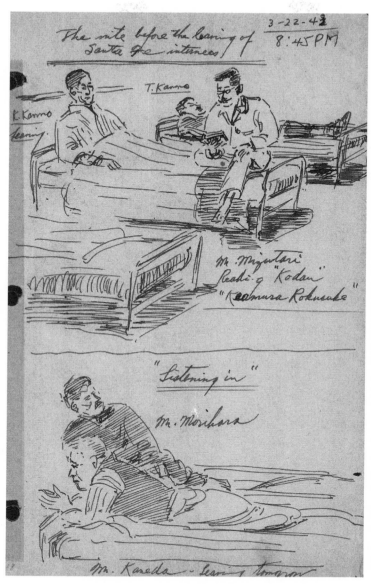

FIGURE 20.1. "The Nite before the Leaving of Santa Fe Internees,"
March 22, 1943. The departing men were clearly too excited to sleep.
George led a few friends on the long train trip from Santa Fe to Jerome;
traveling cross-country was no small feat for strangers from Hawai'i
who had rarely even left their own islands.

and at the same time teased her for the joy she must be feeling, not unlike that of a wedding day. Other women with their mates still back in the internment camp expressed their envy at Tamae's good fortune in being able to have her husband with her soon.

Daylight finally faded into early evening. Tamae counted the hours to midnight. The children kept asking her when their father will be coming home. But as night advanced toward midnight, the children, tired of waiting, dropped off to sleep one after another. Tamae, although lying in bed, could not sleep, listening for the knock at the door which may come any moment. Finally, toward dawn, she woke up from a light slumber to look at the clock which kept time on the little table near the bed. It registered some minutes after five o'clock. Surely something must have happened to delay him. But what was that? In the midst of her anxiety, she thought she heard some footsteps on the gravel path approaching her door! The steps came up the few steps to the little porch in front of the door; and then the knock!

Tamae leaped out of her bed and almost tripped. She raced to the door with her heart pounding so loudly she almost could hear it. She fumbled at the door lock and finally managed to open it! There the dark shape of her dear husband faced her in the dim light of predawn darkness! Then she heard his voice which she had yearned for so long! Tears blurred her vision as she looked up into her husband's face. "I'm back!" he whispered and took her trembling shoulders in his strong hands.

{George's point of view}

On December 4th, 1943, Yoshio finally walked out of the Santa Fe Internment Camp. It was farewell to internment life, and the long awaited family reunion at Jerome Relocation Center was about to materialize. Yoshio was paroled together with six other people, all to Jerome except one to Rohwer, also in Arkansas. One, Mr. Sukenoshin Nakano, was also a Hawaiian internee from Kauai and the others were all mainland people.

Yoshio had received notice of parole two days ago, although he was on parole list about a week before. Friends in his barrack helped him with the packing, and these were shipped out by express on the morning of the departure. The bus on which he and the others were to leave was departing from the city station at 3:00 PM so that they had to leave the camp on an army truck by 2:15. The bus at Santa Fe town left a little after 3 PM to Albuquerque—another city about 60 miles south—for them to board a train there. They had come through there on their way in this camp six months ago. The bus was full, and there were some soldiers in it too. One sat at Yoshio's side, and they soon got acquainted. He was also headed for Arkansas on the same train as theirs. Yoshio later met him, and other soldiers who came together, again at Albuquerque station and also at the Amarillo, Texas station. These soldiers were very friendly, and Yoshio didn't feel the hostility he felt from ones during the early days of internment.

They reached Albuquerque around 5 PM, and since the train wasn't due until 7:10 PM, they had supper at the bus station cafe. They had been given requisitions from the camp so that they didn't need to pay for them. Also, the Immigration Authorities had made arrangements to have their agents check on key points of the trip, and one of them was there to meet them and give them further information about the trip.

{On the train} There were several colored people sitting behind them. One of the internees had some oranges and offered one to them. Seeing these colored people being discriminated against by the whites brought feelings of kinship between these Japanese ex-internees and the dark-skinned unfortunate people. The colored people were very appreciative of this warm attention, and they soon opened up a friendly conversation.

While they were sitting there rolling along, a passing soldier spotted them through a little space in the short drape of the doorway. He poked his head through the drape and looked at them. He seemed to be a bit tipsy. He then asked, "Hi there! Are you Chinese or Japanese?" They looked at each other hesitating to answer but Yoshio finally replied, "We are Japanese."

He then looked them over and said, "No! You are not Japanese. I know Japanese and Chinese, for I was down in South Pacific and know them. You are Chinese." Yoshio was about to deny it but another nudged him from the side and whispered in to him in Japanese to acknowledge being Chinese. Yoshio, although he was not ashamed to say that he was Japanese, realized that it would be better under circumstances to be Chinese to avoid any unnecessary trouble with this drunken GI. So he acknowledged that they were Chinese. The soldier seemed to be satisfied with this and, after mumbling a few words, he waved at them and went on his way.

There were some rumors about Japanese parolees being beaten and injured, and Yoshio was a bit nervous about meeting with such incidents. This incident made Yoshio realize that to be honest sometimes may not be very wise and that he should use his judgment to avoid any unpleasant encounters.

There were some good-sized towns at intervals until they reached Amarillo, Texas which was designated to them as a point of transfer to Little Rock, Arkansas. They got off the train, and Yoshio went to the station master's window to inquire about their transfer. The station master informed him that the train which was to take them to Little Rock was delayed, and it would not be in until evening.

So there was nothing they could do but to wait. They found a little eating place nearby, and after lunch, went back to the station waiting room. Here the waiting rooms were divided into two sections—one for the whites and the other for the blacks, showing distinct discrimination. The parolees could go into the whites' waiting room, and the station master advised them to do so. But the men felt uneasy in there and preferred to go inside the blacks' room.

Finally, as dusk approached, a train pulled in, and the stationmaster informed them that it was their train. The train wasn't too crowded but, as in the previous one, the passengers were mainly GIs. However, they were friendly, and the parolees were able to relax and enjoy the trip through the night.

They had been given vouchers for meals to be used in the train. Then to their delight, one of the negroes who [had waited with them] at the station turned out to be a porter for this train and one who Yoshio had sketched. The porter came up to Yoshio and said that he had shown the sketch to his cook in the diner, and he had requested a sketch for himself too. Yoshio made a hasty sketch of the cook and gave it to the cook. The cook was delighted. He remarked how well it was done and shook Yoshio's hand in joy.

He showed his appreciation by serving supper before the diner was opened for the other passengers. The following morning and also at lunch until they reached Little Rock, the porter came for them and gave them special treatment before the other passengers came. It seemed that these black people, being discriminated by the whites, must have felt special kinship to them as fellow minorities, and this was one of their ways to show comradeship. The ancestors of these blacks [had been] captured in the jungles of Africa and brought here to be sold as slaves, and although they were now considered free, prejudices still persisted and they were still regarded as being subhuman, especially here in the south. Yoshio recalled the earlier days of Japanese immigrants and their treatment similar to these black people. This land of freedom and equality seemed to have a long way more to go before they could truly practice what they preached.

It was noon when they finally pulled into Little Rock. There a couple of people from the State Dept. were waiting for them. They took the parolees by car to a bus station where they were to board a bus to the Jerome Relocation Center on the last leg of the trip. But here too they learned that their bus was not leaving until late afternoon. They had their supper at a nearby cafe and boarded the bus for Jerome around 7 PM. The bus driver said that they'll be reaching "Little Tokyo"—the name they must have given Jerome Relocation Center—near dawn.

The bus stopped at the entrance to a side road where a sign identified the "Denson Relocation Center." There were some people waiting for them there. They were from the security office located further inside, next to the camp. Then one of them called out, "Hi there! Hoshida!" He had a khaki uniform, and Yoshio didn't recognize him at first in the dim light of the dawn. He then called out again and said, "I'm Yoshiyama! We've been waiting for you!" Yoshio recognized him at that as an acquaintance from Hilo and fellow inmate at the Kilauea Detention Camp and Sand Island.

The security headquarters wasn't too far from the entrance, and Yoshio and the parolees followed the security officers to the office. Yoshio walked along with Yoshiyama, both gushing with talks about the events after their separation at Sand Island. They waved at each other as they parted at the path to Yoshio's barrack. Dawn was now breaking in the eastern sky, and Yoshio could see the gravel which separated the two barracks facing each other. Yoshio's family apartment was the one at the end of the barrack and at the edge of the camp with bushes and some watchtowers silhouetted darkly in the background.

Yoshio's shoes crunched loudly over the graveled path in the quiet morning stillness as he passed the closed doorways to his family's apartment. To think that after almost two years of separation, he was about to meet his dear ones in a few seconds was so unbelievable that he felt as though he was walking in his dreams. There were lights showing through a couple of windows on the black walls of the barrack. He knocked at the door. At once he could hear rapid footsteps approaching the door. The door opened, and the soft round outline of Tamae's face stared up at him. The dim light of the electric bulb hanging from the rafters showed her little figure draped in a white nightgown. Yoshio's heart skipped a beat as he gazed into his dear wife's eyes, now brimming with tears. How he had longed for her during these two long years. Was this one of those dreams he had in the camp, with such emptiness which stabbed his heart when he awoke from them? This lovely vision now standing before him, was she real? They stood there for a moment, which seemed like ages, staring at each other—unable to speak.

Finally Yoshio heard himself speaking, "I'm back!" And they found each other in a passionate embrace. Her tiny warm body trembled in his arms and Yoshio felt the exquisite and long-sought dreamy ecstasy of love seeping through his body and hers. I've come home at last! This was real and no longer another dream!

Time stood still for them, until Tamae raised her face to him, her eyes streaming with tears. Their lips met and Yoshio felt the delicious sensation which he had tasted during their courtship so many years ago. Their two long years of agony, anxiety, and suspense of separation melted away into heavenly happiness. "We were waiting up from last night. I received your telegram from Amarillo but thought you may return during the night. The children couldn't wait up and they fell asleep. I stayed up as long as I could and finally fell asleep. But I woke up early this morning. Thought you'll never come."

"I thought we'll never make it too from the way we had to keep waiting at Amarillo and then at Little Rock. Seems my heart and mind had fled ahead of my body, and the trip really was like slow motion movie. Anyway, I'm back now, and we'll never be separated again. And how are the children?"

"Oh, they are all fine now. But they got sick one after another ever since coming here and sure got me worried and miserable. I didn't let you know because I didn't want to worry you. But you must see Carole! This will be the first time that you'll be seeing her! Come! She's sleeping here."

The interior of their apartment was about 20' by 30' and large enough for the family, but there were no partitions. A wood-burning heater about 18" in diameter and four feet tall, with a chimney going up straight through the gypsum board ceiling and roof, stood to the left of the entrance. It was on a concrete slab about four feet square with some cordwood piled near against

FIGURE 20.2. "Inside Our Apartment," March 4, 1944. The Hoshidas' "apartment" in Jerome, full of the children's paraphernalia. The all-important heater that was so difficult for Tamae to keep supplied with wood features prominently.

the wall. There was a storage cabinet about four feet high next to the heater section. Two army cots were placed against the wall, side by side, and Yoshio found the tiny face of their little baby girl above the blanket in the cot.

The baby's chubby face with rosy cheeks and long eye lashes glowed with the light from the electric bulb. She looked so peaceful and adorable. Her dark hair framed her face on the snow-white sheets. Tamae had covered her with a pink baby blanket topped with a gray army blanket. Although the heater was going, the room felt a bit chilly in this early dawn. Tamae said that it got really cold during the night and she had to get up a few times to replenish the heater with the cord wood.

Yoshio's heart stirred with a strange sensation as he looked down at this little life coming from him now lying there as his offspring. She had been born over a year ago but will she accept him as her father? He bent down to kiss her rosy cheek. It felt so delicate and warm. This little child coming into this world while her father was away, and only now meeting with her father who had given her life. She will be a memorial to this great upheaval which rocked the world bringing so much change to them too.

Yoshio looked around toward the other two cots where Mitsuko and Yoshiko lay sleeping. He approached them and bent down to kiss them in turn. They stirred but didn't wake up. Tamae said that they had been so excited and were constantly asking about their father's return. Then becoming weary of the uncertain wait, they had fallen asleep. It was around six in the morning now, but the winter dawn came late and it was still quite dark outside.

Yoshio and Tamae sat side by side on the cot and related some of their experiences from the time of their separation. Yoshio had suffered mainly from the pain of separation and worries about his family. But to Tamae, it was a succession of painful trials and physical and mental sufferings. She really had gone through difficult experiences, and it was a wonder that she was able to pull through them all.

CHAPTER TWENTY-ONE

A New Life in the Relocation Center

Readjustment to the new life in the relocation center was exciting and enjoyable. The two older children came to him as though he had never been separated from them, and to feel the warmth and the joy of holding his youngest daughter, Carole, was a new sensation which was the revival of the joy and wonder he felt when Tamae presented him with their firstborn, Taeko. Friends and acquaintances, as well as other fellow inmates here, came to visit and welcome him to this new life. As Yoshio became familiar with the work which had to be done in the maintenance of this camp, he followed the suggestions of the block manager to do his part. The main thing at present was to gather fire wood for the heater to keep themselves from the chills of winter, which was now coming. Yoshio went with several people to venture into the swampy forest to cut down trees and chop them into usable sizes. Heavy labor was quite strenuous, and evening found him with aches and pains which he had not experienced since those youthful days working in the fields and road construction.

Then after about three months at this camp, his fellow inmates at Santa Fe were released under parole to join their families who were here. Mr. Koide,

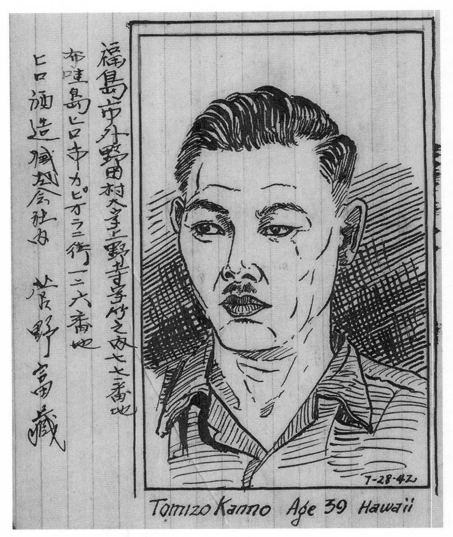

FIGURE 21.1. Tomizo Kanno, pictured here, and his wife Tsuruye were also close friends of the Hoshidas. Tamae wrote to George particularly that she wanted to live near the Kannos and Koides if they all went to the family camp. Koide and Kanno appear in many of George's drawings.

whose wife and daughter were living next to their apartment in the same barrack, was a professional carpenter, and he also joined Yoshio's group. Mr. Kanno, a close friend at the internment camp, also from Hilo, applied for the same group and became fellow workers. So with friends working together, they came to enjoy their life and company even in this unholy environment.

When May came, preparations were made to question people about their preferences of their destinations. The Relocation Center authorities, in order to cut down on the number of centers and eliminate expenditures, had decided on closing some of them. The Koides had an uncle at Gila Relocation Center in Arizona, and since the uncle wrote to them to come over there, they were thinking about going and suggested to Yoshio that they go together too. The climate there was hot but dry and not humid, and uncle had written that since they had devised a cooling system individually to cool their barracks, it was quite comfortable as long as they were inside. Being fed up with the humid heat of this center, they felt that Gila seemed to be most attractive and ideal, especially for Hawaii evacuees.

Even though this in fact was a concentration camp with most of their freedom taken away, it still held many memories to the thousands of people who had lived here. Struggling together to make this unsanitary hellhole more livable had been true hardship and misery. Strangers had become neighbors and friends so that parting into different camps and relocating outside meant possible permanent parting. And parting was always sad. Seeing departing fellow inmates at the train or bus meant tears.

DOCUMENT 6. TAMAE HOSHIDA'S LEAVE CLEARANCE HEARING

LEAVE CLEARANCE HEARING
Held April 11, 1944, 3:00 P.M.
Mr. Martin's Office 33–01-E
Jerome Relocation Center
Denson, Arkansas

April 28, 1944

MEMORANDUM

SUBJECT: TAMAE HASHIDA; Leave Clearance Hearing—Summary

Attached hereto is a WRA–261, Washington papers, and a transcript of the Leave Clearance Hearing of Tamae Hashida [*sic*], citizen, 35 years of age, Family No. H-75.

The Project records, the Washington records transmitted to us, and a transcript of the hearing reflects: that Mrs. Hashida was born in

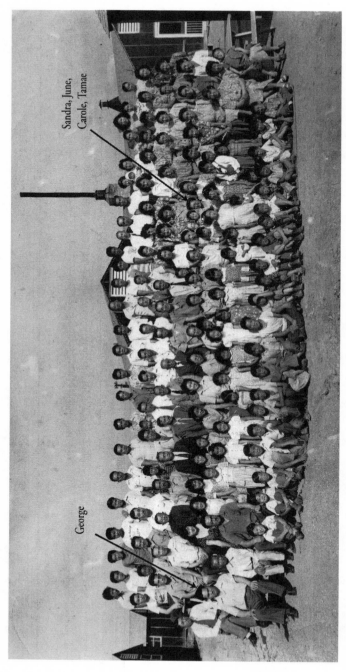

Sandra, June,
Carole, Tamae

George

FIGURE 21.2. A group photo from Jerome. According to June Hoshida Honma, this was taken in 1943 of Block 39 (one of the all-Hawaiian blocks), possibly as a memento before all the departures to other camps. The back of the photo lists Tom K. Okano as photographer; he took other photos of the camps in Arkansas for the War Relocation Authority around this time. Arrows indicate the Hoshidas. George is in the bottom left corner. The rest of the family is about seven from the right in the second and third rows. Carole is held by Tamae, next to Mrs. Koide. In the row below, Sandra is standing next to June, who has a big bow in her hair.

Hawaii and was living in Hawaii at the time of evacuation. She is not a dual citizen and has never been to Japan. She lives here in the center with her husband and three small daughters. All of her relatives live in Hawaii. Mrs. Hashida's husband was interned in 1942 and right after his internment he requested repatriation for himself and his family, but she wired him stating that she had no desire to go to Japan and advised him to withdraw the request. At the time of registration, Mrs. Hashida answered both Questions 27 and 28 with an unqualified affirmative and that is her answer today.

I recommend that Mrs. Hashida be granted leave clearance. The members of the Committee concur in this recommendation.

[Signed]
(Miss) Corine Key, Member
Vance Martin, Member
Leave Clearance Committee

FORM WRA–261 CONFIDENTIAL
WAR RELOCATION AUTHORITY
Washington
REQUEST FOR FURTHER INVESTIGATION
APR 5 1944
(Date)
To: Project Director E. B. Whitaker

In accordance with Supplement 12 to Administrative Instruction No. 22 (Revised), issued June 5, 1943, you are hereby requested to make further investigation of eligibility for leave clearance in the matters checked below. One copy of this form and attachments is to be returned to this office with your docket, report, and recommendations.

NAME Hoshida, Tamae Address 39–4-E

7/18/09

A confidential report states that the subject's husband, George Yoshio Hoshida, alien Japanese, was taken into custody and is interned at Lordsburg, New Mexico. In numerous letters to her husband since his internment, the subject has repeatedly urged him not to repatriate, expressing the feeling that he would be given a chance to start over if he remained in the U.S.

Since subject was apparently disapproved by the Joint Board because of her husband's internment, the reasons for such internment should be determined.

CHAPTER TWENTY-TWO

Gila Relocation Center

The camp took a large area, but the desert land stretched endlessly in all directions, and space was no problem. Their Block 61 faced a large open space in front with a stretch of rocky hills at the back. The adjoining blocks spread to both sides, then spread downward as they reached other high grounds which limited their advancing further. Thus their block had plenty of breathing spaces—unlike the crowded Jerome Camp.

Life in this camp was quite relaxed and enjoyable when compared to the tense years in the internment and early relocation centers. The personnel managing the camp came to understand the honest and sincere nature of the Japanese inmates and became very sympathetic to their plight in the camp. They were allowed to shop at outside towns and cities, and Yoshio remembered taking his family along a couple of times on the bus with other inmates for shopping trips to Phoenix, the capital of the state. They were also allowed to venture into the desert for picnics. Actually this was an Indian reservation, and about a mile to the east of the camp there was a canal which must have been constructed for irrigation purposes for farmlands to the south. Across

DOI: 10.5876/9781607323440.c022

FIGURE 22.1. "Hawaii People Picnic in the Gila Desert," March 11, 1945. Compared with the other camps, the Gila River camp was much better: less crowded, better food from the very successful camp farm, and a more lenient administration. Here, incarcerees enjoy a picnic. Sandra Hoshida remembers tossing oranges across the canal to some Native Americans on the other side.

the canal they could see Indian adobe huts. Many Indians, in fact, came to work in the camp to pick up garbage. They were very friendly to the camp people, and some made good friends since they could speak English and communicate quite well with each other.

The children were growing. June attained the age of eight on her birthday, June 23, 1944. Sandra was four on July 31st, and she started to attend preschool which was held at a barrack to the east across the open grounds in front of their block. She soon made friends. One of them was a cute little boy who lived to the west of the grounds and met her halfway on their way from the preschool. Yoshio or Tamae would stand at the edge of the block to watch her progress across the grounds until she reached the school at the other side. Sometimes some bully would get hold of her, and she would struggle to escape from his needling. At such times, Yoshio would shout at them to discourage the bully from harming her.

Food, especially farm produce, was in abundance since the inmates here, being mostly regular farmers from the coast, were experts in that line. They raised pigs also, and pork could be had most of the time. So here, unlike those lean and tense months in former camps, conditions were greatly improved.[1]

Although life in the camp became pleasanter as time passed, one sad and tragic [piece of] news confronted them soon after arrival at the camp. It came from Hawaii. In the later part of July, about a month after their arrival to these new living quarters, a letter came from the Waimano Home at Pearl City where Taeko was placed. A Doctor Chang wrote that Taeko had passed away on the 22nd of that month, caused by accident. It didn't contain any detail about what the accident was. A letter from Brother Raymond also came about the same time reporting the same, but he also said that they had not received any specific detail about the circumstances of Taeko's death.

Yoshio wrote back at once to Dr. Chang, requesting more detailed facts about the accident. The answer arrived with some delay, and it said that she was drowned in the bathtub while a nurse went away on something for a short time and left Taeko alone in the filled bathtub. It seemed that Taeko had convulsions during that short period when no one was in attendance.

Subsequent letters from Brother Raymond gave no additional information about the accident, except that Taeko's remains were sent to Hilo after being cremated by the institution, and funeral services were observed at the Hilo Hongwanji Temple with Mrs. Rev. Aoki officiating. Raymond also sent Yoshio a photograph taken after the services in the empty lot across the temple. It showed most of the relatives, friends, and people from Kaumana who came to the funeral.

This incident was a great shock to Yoshio and Tamae. They were truly saddened and shaken by the loss of their firstborn. Years later, after they returned to Hawaii, true details about the accident came to them through their niece Matsu. Matsu was working at the office of Hilo Memorial Hospital and at one time came in contact with one of the nurses from Waimano Home. The nurse, not knowing that Matsu was related to them, related this incident. The nurse said that the nurse in charge of Taeko was at odds for some reason with Dr. Chang, who also was taking care of Taeko. The nurse, in order to get back at the doctor, had intentionally left Taeko in the bathtub and caused her drowning. Yoshio's family doctor, Dr. Kutsunai, urged Yoshio to sue the Home for the cruel and criminal incident, but Yoshio decided against it since it wouldn't bring her back. Also, when considering the fact that having her alive at the institution, perhaps for her lifetime without any consciousness of what her life was about, may be more cruel for her and to Yoshio and Tamae. For them also this war had brought great changes in many ways. The tragic period of their life, they hoped, would end with this great upheaval, and a new life of hope and light would shine on their path that may be opening before them.

News came into the camp that Emperor Hirohito of Japan had accepted the terms laid down by the Allies at Potsdam on August 14, and all forces were directed to cease fighting. On September 2, 1945, the final surrender was signed. World War II had ended.

However, to the many older Japanese aliens in the camp, the war was not ended. They could not accept the fact that Japan had lost the War. It was all propaganda news made up by the Allies. Japan was god-country, descended from the gods, and had never in her history lost to any outside countries. If the war has ended, it wasn't because Japan lost but it could only mean the other way 'round, and the Allies were desperately trying to cover up their loss. Yoshio pitied these people who were so frantically firm in their belief but dared not offend them. He would just listen to what they had to say and gave answers which would not irritate them. Even about a year after the war's end, there were people in Hawaii who stuck to their belief. They formed a club and called it "Japan Won" and held meetings and exchanged rumors which they firmly believed.

After the end of the war, the relocation authorities announced their intention of closing the centers by the end of the year and urged all inmates to relocate outside as soon as possible. The day finally dawned when the Hawaiians themselves were given notice to depart. Yoshio prepared a simple breakfast for the last departing Hawaiian people and had barely time enough to rush over with his family to the administration compound where the last of the buses remained for departure. Because of the rushing, Yoshio never realized the nostalgia of leaving the place which was home to them for a year and a half, since moving there. But as the bus left the camp and Yoshio looked back to see the disappearing barracks fading into the distance, he felt an acute heartache for this desolate desert abode. It was also farewell to confinement in the camps and a flight into freedom which they had lost for four long years.

NOTE

1. Gila River, one of the WRA "Relocation Centers," was located in Arizona, partly on the Pima Reservation. Although the climate was drier and the winters were milder, the hot summers were difficult to bear, and George mentions elsewhere in the full memoir that the incarcerees rigged primitive air-conditioners. Gila River had the most flourishing agricultural program of the camps, partly because of climate and also because it was better developed when it was established, unlike some camps, where the incarcerees created farms out of entirely uncultivated desert land. Gila River, at its peak, held 13,348 incarcerees. It did not close until November 1945, well after the Hoshidas had left. (Iritani and Iritani, *Ten Visits Revised*, 10; *Relocation Communities for Wartime Evacuees*, 8–9.)

More information on life in Gila can be found in Hansen, "Cultural Politics in the Gila River Relocation Center, 1942–1943." A published memoir of life in Gila is Tashiro, *"Wase Time!"*

Farewell to the Camps and the Last Lap to Hawaii

They woke up when the bus stopped, and the driver announced that they had reached their destination. It was Santa Ana, near the coast of southern California. They were to be here for about three weeks, waiting for a ship which would take them across the sea to their home in Hawaii. But it was the most pleasant time of all the four years of their confined and turbulent life during this war. Since they were free now of any guards to restrict their movement, they planned trips to nearby Santa Ana town, fishing trips to the coast town of Newport and Balboa, and even trips to Long Beach and Los Angeles. However, Yoshio never dreamed that years later he and his family would be living here in Los Angeles.

After three weeks at the Santa Ana base, the evacuees were given notice that the ship they had been waiting for was ready, and they could be on their way. The old ship into which the evacuees were put was named *Shawnee*. The men folk were herded into the dark and gloomy hold of the ship below the water-line while the women and children were given rooms above with stacked cots. This was quite miserable, but having gone through many similar

FIGURE 23.1. "Santa Ana, Calif.," November 14, 1945. Santa Ana was the happiest time the Hoshidas spent on the mainland; they were on their way home. This drawing shows an unidentified woman, probably Mrs. Koide or Mrs. Kanno.

experiences, they felt little discomfort when they thought that this would be the last of their miseries and soon they would be released to the freedom and joy of their heavenly lives back at home in Hawaii.

Yoshio didn't remember how many days it took them to reach Honolulu. However, it must have been about six or seven days, although it seemed longer since they were so anxious to reach home port. Now at last the trip on the interisland ship awaited them. As the ship entered the entrance to the bay, past the Coconut Island, Yoshio could see a crowd of people gathered at the interisland pier waiting for the homecomers. The gangplank was lowered, but Yoshio and his family had to wait their turn to disembark. As he watched the homecomers filing down the gangplank, Yoshio's mind flashed back in panorama over the nearly four years away from this homeland. Now he was back with his family, but where actually was their home? The house they had purchased with so much dreams for the future was no longer their own! Had they lost everything of real value to them? Their eagerness and joy at being able to return to Hawaii had not given rise to such acute questions until now, and Yoshio felt a stab of confusion and sense of utter emptiness!

Then, just as suddenly, his wife Tamae's voice calling out to her relatives waiting down at the pier brought him back to reality. He also became conscious of his inner voice calling out, "Sufferings come from attachment to things impermanent." Those years of disappointments, longing for his loved ones, inner turmoil, deprivation, and periods of quiet thoughts and meditation had given Yoshio wisdom to awaken to the reality of life and true value of life. People of all ranks and position in ordinary life had all been stripped of their position, wealth, and power, and what appeared in the internment camp life were their bare naked selves which, compared to people with true spirit and sense of reality, were so pitifully shabby and inadequate. His years with the Teaching of the Buddha had reached out to awaken Yoshio to the true value of life at this moment of darkness and given him light to the true path to reality.

The path to the way to the gangplank was now opened for their turn to disembark, and Yoshio, picking up Carole in his arms, followed Tamae with June and Sandra down to the waiting arms of their loved ones. Now his steps were light and firm; the future, bright and gleaming with hope and inspiration, waiting for them.

Maps

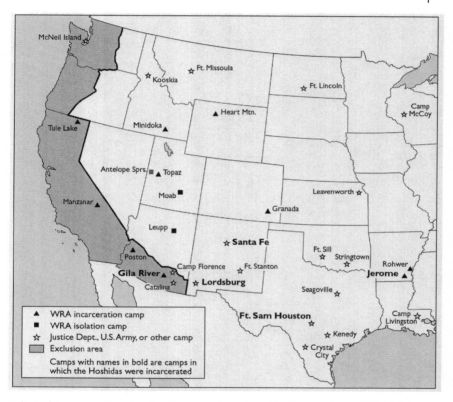

Selected incarceration sites for Japanese Americans in the continental United States.
Map by Bill Nelson.

DOI: 10.5876/9781607323440.c024

Map of the Territory of Hawai'i. This map shows some of the incarceration sites for Japanese Americans during World War II as well as locations important to Tamae and George's lives. Map by Bill Nelson.

Official Transcript of
George Hoshida's Hearing

RECORD OF THE HEARINGS OF A BOARD OF OFFICERS AND CIVILIANS CONVENED
PURSUANT TO SPECIAL ORDERS NO. 33, HEADQUARTERS HAWAIIAN DEPARTMENT,
DATED AT FORT SHAFTER, T.H., 2 FEBRUARY 1942, AS AMENDED BY SPECIAL OR-
DERS NO. 65, HEADQUARTERS HAWAIIAN DEPARTMENT, DATED AT FORT SHAFTER,
T.H., 7 MARCH 1942, AS AMENDED BY SPECIAL ORDERS NO. 80, HEADQUARTERS
HAWAIIAN DEPARTMENT, DATED AT FORT SHAFTER, T.H., 24 MARCH 1942,

IN THE CASE OF GEORGE YOSHIO HOSHIDA

ISN-HJ-1133-CI

REPORT OF PROCEEDINGS OF A BOARD OF OFFICERS AND CIVILIANS

Proceedings of a Board of Officers and Civilians which convened at Hilo,
T.H., pursuant to Paragraph 7, Special Orders No. 33, Headquarters Hawai-
ian Department, Fort Shafter, T.H., 2 February 1942, as amended by Para-
graph 24, Special Orders No. 65, Headquarters Hawaiian Department, Fort
Shafter, T.H., 7 March 1942, copies of which are attached hereto as Exhibit
A, A-1 and A-2.

DOI: 10.5876/9781607323440.c025

The Board met pursuant to the foregoing order at Hilo, T.H., on 22 April 1942.

Members present:

Mr. Frank McLaughlin, President

Mr. Alex J. Porter

Mr. Gavin A. Bush

Lt. Col. Victor R. Woodruff (05684) FA, Executive and Recorder.

The Board Recorder and Reporter were sworn; the Board was sworn.

PURPOSE: The hearing of evidence and making recommendations as to internment of enemy aliens, dual citizens and citizens.

GEORGE YOSHIO HOSHIDA, the internee, appeared before the Board with counsel.

The order appointing the Board and the substance of the regulations under which it was convened were read aloud by the Recorder.

Warrant of Arrest was received and read in evidence, and is hereunto appended as Exhibit B.

Except when Government witnesses were being heard, the internee, GEORGE YOSHIO HOSHIDA, was present during all open sessions of the Board, was afforded full opportunity to present evidence in his own behalf, to have counsel, to testify in person or submit a written statement and to submit a brief.

(Hideo Taguchi was duly sworn as Japanese interpreter.)

GEORGE YOSHIO HOSHIDA, internee, who being first duly sworn through interpreter, testified as follows:

Q. (By President) You are George Yoshio Hoshida?

A. Yes.

Q. Where do you live?

A. 483 Kalanikoa Street, Hilo.

Q. What is your occupation?

A. Salesman for Hilo Electric Light.

Q. How old are you?

A. 34.

Q. Of what country or countries are you a citizen or subject?

A. Subject of Japan. (By President) Very well, at this time you are excused and will be called before the Board subsequently.

(Internee together with interpreter leave the room.)

Lt. Farrell B. Copeland, entered the room and who, after being first duly sworn, testified as follows:

Q. (By President) Will you, in this case, state your name, occupation and reason for being here?

A. Lt. Farrell B. Copeland, First Lieutenant Cavalry, representing the assistant Chief of Staff, G-2.

Q. This internee has informed us that he resides in Hilo, salesman for the Hilo Electric Light Company, age 34 and a subject of Japan. If you have additional information, will you please present it?

A. Subject is married to an American born Japanese woman. Subject is a member of the following organizations: Kilauea Central Japanese Association, Waiakea Houselots Association, United Young Buddhist Association and the Hilo Young Buddhist Association, Hawaii Shimabuto Kyo Kai, Japanese judo expert.

Q. Is that the local one?

A. It is the judo, wrestling.

Q. No organization having headquarters in Japan?

A. It is an organization connected with the Hawaii Budo Kyo Kai. That is this Hawaii Budo Kyo Kai, which is translated "military arts" consisting of archery, rifling and kendo. If I am not mistaken, all those functions are carried on by the Hawaii Budo Kyo Kai.

Q. Which is purely a local outfit?

A. Purely a local outfit. As far as we can find out, we have no branch here of the Dai Nippon Kyo Kai, except that some of these people who are leaders of the Hawaii Budo Kyo Kai are members of the Dai Nippon Kyo Kai, except that in order to be a member you have to be given an order from Japan.

Q. All right.

A. As a member of the Hongwanji Mission, the subject admitted that he had donated to the Japanese war fund about $5.00 in 1939. When asked the question "who do you wish to see win this war," the subject replied, "I don't know which side I want to win, I don't want Japan to lose nor do I want America to lose. I have relatives in Japan as well as in America." Hoshida stated that he has a brother in Japan who possibly is in the Japanese army. From the files of our confidential informant, Letter A, it was learned that the subject, in 1939, was elected one of the three treasurers of the Hawaii Budo Kyo Kai. In 1938, he was elected Japanese secretary of the United Kyo Kai. In 1938, he was elected Japanese secretary of the United Y.B.A. for the island of Hawaii. In 1939, he was appointed a member of the entertainment committee for visitors of the Japanese merchant marine training ship, Shintoku Maru.

Q. Is that Y.B.A. something like the Y.M.C.A.?

A. Practically the same thing. In 1941, he was elected president of the United Y.B.A. of Hawaii. In 1941, he was elected second vice-president of the Hilo Y.B.A. Judo Club. An American citizen of Japanese ancestry employed by the Pacific Soda Works advised that he believed Hoshida to be pro-Japanese because of his activities on behalf of the Young Buddhist Association and the Hawaii Judo Society. Hoshida was closely associated with the Rev. Yetetsu Teramoto, formerly head of the Hilo Hongwanji Mission.

Q. Now in Japan?

A. Yes, he was to be picked up for custodial detention had he not returned to Japan just prior to the war. Because of his teaching judo, he was guided in his activities in this line by the Buddhist priest and who were directly under the supervision of the Japanese government according to this informant.

Q. On Mr. A's theory, anyone belonging to the Buddhist Church and any Buddhist organization, is a dangerous person, isn't that so?

A. More or less they are. He refers to this man working directly under this priest who themselves were under the supervision of the Japanese government. It is not the fact that he was a member of the church but the fact that he worked so closely in coordination with the Japanese priest.

Q. Buddhist priests are working closely in connection with the Japanese government?

A. Well, all priests are sent here from Japan.

Q. Well, it is one thing to be sent here by your organization and another thing to be sent by your government.

A. Well, let's look at it from a more missionary angle. Do priests also have the same function?

Q. Anyway, that is just Mr. A's opinion.

A. Another citizen employed by Ruddle Sales, American of Japanese ancestry advised that Hoshida was definitely pro-Japanese as shown by his activities with the Hongwanji Mission and his connection with the priest. Another salesman of the Ruddle Sales and Service stated that Hoshida was closely associated with Rev. Teramoto and states that everyone knew that Rev. Teramoto had been a Japanese leader and possibly an agent, that the subject entertained Japanese sailors and collected funds for the transmission to Japan. In his position as treasurer of the Buddhist Association, informant states, that the subjected collected $2.00 a month from him for the Buddhist Association but the informant states that he probably sent this money to the Japanese fund. The informant said, "I paid the money because of my mother, my mother's enthusiasm in the church." He goes on to say that the subject speaks excellent Japanese and is looked upon by the Buddhist priest as an intellectual.

Q. He also speaks English?

A. Well, in the capacity of a salesman, he did. I have here a report from Ho52, confidential informant. Hoshida arrived in the United States when an infant, speaks English fairly well but better Japanese, can get up and make a good speech in Japanese and is usually called upon as toastmaster. His associates are all Japanese. He was one of the leaders who formed a minority block in the Hilo Y.B.A. which constituted of over 90 percent of American born members. He was quite influential many years ago when there was about 25 percent alien members in the association but with the growing up of the citizens, his popularity is on a downward grade. This is on account of his pro-Japanese tendencies; capitalized on his church in Y.B.A. connection in selling merchandise and tried to make fellow members buy from him exclusively. He used to donate his commission on the sale whenever the church or priest bought from him. He was a big shot in the United Buddhist Association in Hawaii which controls the 12 local associations of this island. At the annual elections, he has always tried to maneuver the older alien members into directorship. He has taken part in jujitsu activity on this island for many years. His wife was formerly a Miss Takemoto, sister of Detective Takemoto, also sister of James Takemoto of the Hilo Drug Company. His wife was also a sister of Mrs. H. Hisanaga and she has a brother who does massage work and other light treatments on Piopio Street, Hilo. This informant feels that he is probably "sit on the fence type; if America wins, all right; if Japan wins, he will be the first to join."

(By President) Very well.

(Lt. Copeland leaves the room.)

(24 April 1942. All members of the Board being present, the Recorder and Reporter being present; the Board, Recorder and Reporter having been previously duly sworn, the following proceedings were had.)

(Internee entered the room without interpreter.)

Q. (By President) You are George Yoshio Hoshida?

A. Yes.

Q. When were you born?

A. January 13, 1908.

Q. Where?

A. Kumamoto, Japan.

Q. And what education did you receive in Japan?

A. None.

Q. When did you come to the United States?

A. When I was four years old.

Q. With your parents?

A. With my mother. My father was over here before us, you see.

Q. It seems that you have a brother who has requested Judge Harlocker to represent you?

A. I see.

Q. And if you wish to have Judge Harlocker, you, of course, may do so and he has sent a note to the Board asking if you can take note of the things we shall ask you.

A. Yes, I was thinking about Mr. Irwin, but Mr. Harlocker will be all right.

Q. You are willing to accept your brother's offering Judge Harlocker's services?

A. Yes, sir.

Q. However, don't let your note taking interfere with answering my questions.

A. Yes. By the way, I have a statement here that I want to show the Board.

Q. Possibly you had better show it to your attorney before.

A. All right.

Q. I think we had it you arrived in Hawaii when you were four years old?

A. Yes.

Q. Where did you live when you first came?

A. Kaumana, 5 miles.

Q. Where is your father employed?

A. In the plantation.

Q. Have you always lived on this island?

A. Yes.

Q. Have you ever been to the mainland United States?

A. No.

Q. Have you ever made trips to Japan?

A. No.

Q. Are your parents still living here?

A. Yes.

Q. And the wife was born where? Here?

A. Yes.

Q. When were you married?

A. April 23, 1933. Yesterday was the 9th anniversary.

Q. Does your wife still retain her citizenship in the United States, so far as you know?

A. I believe so, because that ruling went into effect before that time.[1]

Q. Well, they have changed it so many times, I have to look it up every time.

A. I think it was 1932.

Q. It is your understanding that she was a citizen of the United States?

A. Yes.

Q. Has she ever been to Japan?

A. No.

Q. Have you any children?

A. Yes.

Q. How many?

A. Three, one more coming.

Q. Born on this island?

A. Yes.

Q. How old are your children?

A. Eight, five and one year, plus.

Q. The child that is eight, is it a boy or girl?

A. Girl.

Q. Going to school?

A. No, she is cripple.

Q. Oh, I am sorry. She lives at home with you?

A. Yes.

Q. And the next child is a boy or girl?

A. Girl, all girls.

Q. And the five year old child does not go to school here?

A. She is going to kindergarten.

Q. Does she go to the Japanese language kindergarten?

A. She used to go to the Hongwanji Mission kindergarten so I think afternoon is Japanese.

Q. Do you intend to send her to the Japanese language schools if there were any?

A. Yes, sir.

Q. Why?

A. Because I think it is a good advantage to know more language than one.

Q. That is true, to know more than one language, and the little baby, of course, is at home?

A. Yes.

Q. How long have you worked for the Hilo Electric Light Company?

A. Ten years and about nine months.

Q. Prior to that, for whom did you work?

A. I worked two years for myself.

Q. In what business?

A. Salesman.

Q. And of what?

A. Household appliances, special, all kinds of various things.

Q. Do you have relatives living in Japan?

A. Yes.

Q. Who?

A. I do not know. We have so much. I don't know, only I know is one of my brother and sister.

Q. By the way, where are your parents? Are they living?

A. Yes.

Q. Are they living here with you?

A. No.

Q. Well, are they living on this island?

A. Yes.

Q. You never told me that before. But with regard to the brother and sister in Japan, were they born here?

A. No.

Q. Is your brother in the Japanese army?

A. I don't know. Maybe he is in but the last time I heard, he was not in.

Q. Do you have any relatives connected with the Japanese government or its armed forces?

A. I do not know because I don't know the condition of my relatives over there.

Q. Well, when last you heard from them?

A. I have not heard from any relatives except my brother and sister.

Q. By the way, was your wife ever expatriated from Japan is she was a subject of Japan?

A. No, she was not expatriated.

Q. Is she a dual citizen?

A. Yes.

Q. Have you registered the birth of any of your children with the Japanese Consul?

A. No, they are not registered.

Q. You have been active, have you not, in entertaining visiting Japanese officials and naval men?

A. No, only except judo boys when they come over. We usually arrange for practicing and contest and after the thing is over we give them several refreshments and sometime we take them around.

Q. Well, you were on a committee in 1939, which committee was organized to arrange entertainment for visiting Japanese officers and sailors from the Shintoku Maru?

A. I don't know, maybe they did, but I don't remember.

Q. You are a member, are you not, of the following organizations, Kilauea Central Japanese Association?

A. I was but not at present.

Q. What is the purpose of that organization?

A. To promote friendship among members and to cooperate in all sorts of social works and in general to . . . let's see, I can't say particularly but maybe those are the two I can say at present.

Q. Are you a member of the Waiakea Houselots Associations?

A. Yes, I am.

Q. Is that a Kumiai?

A. Kumiai.²

Q. Of the United Young Buddhist Association?

A. Yes.

Q. And of that organization, you have been secretary and presently, president?

A. Yes, I resigned after I was detained.

Q. Hilo Young Buddhist Association?

A. Yes.

Q. Hawaii Shimabuto Kyo Kai?

A. Yes.

Q. Is that a Judo Association?

A. Of judo, fencing and promoting that.

Q. Do you hold an office in that organization?

A. Yes, I think I was secretary in judo division.

Q. What other division does it have?

A. Kendo and fencing and archery but they haven't practiced archery, mostly kendo and judo.

Q. You were treasurer in 1937?

A. Yes, assistant.

Q. You are affiliated with the Hongwanji Mission?

A. Yes.

Q. That is a Buddhist church or temple?

A. Yes.

Q. Do you belong or have you been recognized or have you ever held membership or any other position in the Dai Nippon Butoku Kai?

A. No, the only thing I understand is when we get ranking for judo, in order to be recognized officially, we have to send application to the organization and when we send application there we have to pay a fee of, I don't remember exactly, about one dollar to three dollars and when we pay the fee, they consider us members. But it has first rank and second rank and I sent money and they considered me a new member each time so I believe that since I have not paid that, my membership is expired. I am not sure but that is what I think.

Q. So you hold two ranks in the Dai Nippon Butoku Kai?

A. Yes, first and second Dan.

Q. What does that mean? You are pretty good at judo?

A. Yes, that means that you have the power to instruct.

Q. Are you an instructor in this Hawaii outfit?

A. Not exactly instructor.

Q. What do you do?

A. Well, of course, I cooperate in any time that they hold tournaments and during the time that they hold tests for giving ranks or lower people, then, I guess they test for this Dan, too. Below Dan they have Kyo so we give the test once a year.

Q. Don't you participate in instructing the boys who are interested in judo?

A. Yes, I participate in instructing but this organization does not exactly, you know they take charge of instruction. We have different organizations that take charge of instructions and this organization mostly concern with tournaments, getting the people once a year for tournaments and then, once a year for ranking tests.

Q. Did you receive any literature from the Dai Nippon Butoku Kai?

A. No, I haven't the literature.

Q. (By Mr. Porter) Who does the instructing?

A. Well, these high instructors, they have their own places for instructions.

Q. Yes.

A. So high ranking people belong to the organizations take charge of this instruction.

Q. And they are nearly all aliens, if not all aliens?

A. Not all aliens. We have second generation who hold high ranking.

Q. And you know it is true that these aliens instruct, in addition, to instructing judo and kendo, also propagandize the young men of Hawaii, the spirit of Japan or Yamato Damaishi, as you call it?

A. So far as I know, they don't propagandize loyalty to Japan but they do stress Bushido.

Q. Yes, we have heard a lot about Bushido recently which usually involves the shooting of aviators who are parachuting to safety.

A. That is your understanding.

Q. Yes, and my understanding about teaching and the propaganda work of these instructors who have been members in the Dai Nippon Butoku Kai, is also very clear. They do propagandize the youth of Hawaii.

A. So far as I know, they have not propagandized in that way. Only thing is educate them physically as well as spiritually, because this judo is like a weapon, like a pistol held in the hand of people, do damage to some people while held in the right hand who protect that person. So judo is the same thing, if you just teach art, sometime they might misuse that, they use harmful. In order to prevent that, we have to teach judo is not to be used in such a way as to harm other people but to protect us and protect others. That is why we teach that Bushido. That is what I understand and Bushido is a kind of a sportsman, only it is deeper. For example, you fight with a person—.

Q. I don't think we need to go into that. It is quite obvious that Bushido is quite well propagandized.

A. Yes, I know, but I think you are prejudiced. What I understand, you fight to a person to a finish and if the person is defeated, he picks him up and restores him to health. That is Bushido rank, they hate crimes but they don't hate the person that commits the crime. So, if they fight and the person is knocked down and then he tries his best to bring him back and teach sense in him.

Q. Then, this spirit of chivalry, which you call Bushido, is it widely spread in Japan?

A. Yes, it is.

Q. They how do you account for the treatment that was given persons in China during the China Incident? How do you account for the treatment of civilians in Manila, in Hongkong, Java and New Guinea?

A. Maybe they have mistreated. I don't know about that because I haven't seen or I haven't heard about those things. But I believe if they were mistreated, it was not Bushido and if it was Bushido, they should not have mistreated.

Q. Hence my suggestion that Bushido is not very widely spread among the Japanese forces, because we have these reports from direct sources and from people who have written about it.

A. I am sorry that appeared but I know Bushido, that is the way I understand, is not that way. This thing here is all depends who the person uses but you hand this over to the child, he will waste all but if you used it, you will use it properly. So anything, even Bushido, it depends on the people who use it. Just because other people misuse it, doesn't mean that that thing is bad.

Q. It doesn't effect [*sic*] the good that may lie in the chivalrous spirit known as Bushido. Now we will get to your statement that because I know of these things which have been done by Japanese officers and soldiers and I voice them, you say I am prejudiced and yet you seem to admit that these have happened. Do you think that constitutes prejudice or knowledge of facts?

A. I don't know where you got those facts. I guess I was mistaken in saying that you were prejudiced.

Q. Well, I get my information from people like Pearl Buck and from the United States army and navy officers and United States officials who were in the Philippines and other government people all the way from the Philippines to Australia and that information is just as available to you as it is available to me. It is not a matter of prejudice. It is a matter of recognizing factual information.

A. As far as over here is concerned and what I understand Bushido is concerned, that thing that I have stated is what it is.

Q. You mean that is what it should be.

A. Yes.

Q. And not what it is. All right. You have contributed to the Japanese war fund, have you not?

A. Yes, I think about $5 or $6.

Q. And I presume you are loyal to your country?

A. I don't know exactly but I feel obligated to Japan to the extent that she had given me birth and 4 years of my life and I consider everything and I estimate myself and think that my 4 years is less than $5 or $10 or $100 so if I can, I will try to repay that obligation but at the same time, I am not blind to the fact that America has given me 30 years of my life so the obligation to America is about 8 times more than Japan and I will try the best I can to repay that obligation.

Q. Where do you stand in relation to that war which is going on?

A. Well, you see, since I was born in Japan and was raised there for 4 years, Japan is something like mother to me. And America have for 30 years adopted and she has given me also education, care, a home and livelihood and almost everything that she had given to her own children so I regard America as my adopted country. So you can understand that for adopted mother who gave birth and mother who have adopted me to disagree and fight is very painful and I further wish that they would not fight but it is beyond my control. But, as I have said, my obligation towards America is bigger than my obligation toward Japan so if you desire, I will fight against Japan, but, if possible, my desire is for America and Japan to come to an agreement as soon as possible and be on friendly terms again.

Q. Do you think that that can be done after that which happened on December 7?

A. I don't know.

Q. You don't know what happened on December 7?

A. Yes.

Q. By the way, where were you on December 7?

A. December 7, I was at home. In the morning I was out teaching Sunday School, I think, until about 10 o'clock.

Q. And what was your reaction when you first knew the war started?

A. I was shocked. I did not think it was real.

Q. You have been quite a friend, have you not, of the Rev. Teramoto?

A. Yes.

Q. Where is he now?

A. I believe he is in Japan, Tokyo.

Q. (By Recorder) Where were you educated, Mr. Hoshida?

A. Over here.

Q. (By President) But where?

A. Kaumana School and then Hilo Union School and then Hilo Junior High.

Q. Did you finish high school?

A. No. Junior High and then I had to leave and work to help my parents.

Q. Have you had any military training?

A. No, because I live here all my life after I came from Japan.

Q. No, to come back to this question of the Dai Nippon Butoku Kai, the grade that you mentioned there was the First Dan. Is that the highest honor that you can obtain in that organization?

A. No, the highest honor is, I don't know whether there is any limit but as I understand, the highest rank is either 9 or 10 Dan.

Q. Oh, it is reverse.

A. Yes, as Kyu, it is other way around. They go from the high number down to the lower.

Q. I believe you stated to the Board that you were an instructor in judo.

A. Yes, sir.

Q. Of the Hawaii Budo Kyo Kai?

A. No, I was not instructor but I instructed for Hilo Japanese High School for awhile, about half a year.

Q. Are you familiar with the number of instructors that may be on the island which belong to the Dai Nippon Butoku Kai?

A. I don't know whether they belong or not.

Q. How many instructors in judo would you say there are on the island now?

A. Let's see. I don't know.

Q. And do you consider judo and jujitsu the same as far as instructors are concerned?

A. No, different.

Q. So that the instructors would be different?

A. Yes, the instructors would be different.

Q. (By President) Judo is a modified form of jujitsu?

A. Yes.

Q. (By Recorder) Now, in this organization, you say, you have judo and kendo?

A. Yes.

Q. Did you also have jujitsu?

A. No, we do not have jujitsu. I don't know. So far as I know, there is no jujitsu because judo is a modification of jujitsu, so maybe I can say it is not included.

Q. This Bushido, is that written?

A. I don't know, not in Japan, but over here in Hawaii, I understand that they have a branch in Honolulu.

Q. Branch of what?

A. Of this Budo Kyo Kai and they have the separate constitution and by-laws so that they can apply to the conditions of Hawaii.

Q. Would that include that you were speaking about here, Bushido?

A. I don't think they have that inside. The only purpose is to build better citizens.

Q. I mean this Bushido code that you speak about that governs the sport of judo and kendo.

A. I don't think it is written in there.

Q. How do you teach that to students?

A. They do not usually teach by mouth. They just show by . . .

Q. By example?

A. Maybe example, but you know the sport of judo and the way they teach, naturally, you know, influence them, so that they can use the judo properly instead of improperly, so I don't know whether these instructors are actually and effectively teaching Bushido, but the main thing I get is they try to teach them the art, the way of using it properly.

Q. What I am asking you is this—Does the code that you call Bushido, does that exist on the island in a written form, in a textbook?

A. No, it does not exist in written form.

Q. Does it exist in any place in a written form? Does the Dai Nippon Butoku Kai have it in a written form?

A. No, I did not read it in the constitution.

Q. Did you expect to find it in the constitution?

A. Maybe, I guess so.

Q. (By Mr. Bush) In American boxing, we have the Marquis of Queensbury rules. That is a printed book telling how the games are conducted. You have nothing like that?

A. Yes, we have the rules of contest.

Q. (By President) But no particular rules as to the conduct of a good sportsman?

A. I don't remember so very well, but anyway, the ruling is made so they will conduct in a sportsman-like manner.

Q. Actually, Bushido is the code of a culture, is it not?

A. Well, in the olden day's sense, it was but that thing, I believe, has become to be meant a wider meaning than in the present days so it might be applied to our daily life, so that we could be more sportsman-like.

Q. It certainly has been modified since December 7.

Q. (By Recorder) Would you connect that code of Bushido as Yasukunijinsha?

A. I don't know if they have any relation. That is a shrine. I don't think they have any relation to that.

(By Mr. Porter) That is a Shinto shrine.

Q. (By Mr. Porter) Are you acquainted with Hideo Inouye? He lives on Hoku Street.

A. Yes.

Q. He is an instructor of judo?

A. Yes.

Q. Is he a member of the Dai Nippon Butoku Kai?

A. I don't know. I don't think so.

Q. Do you happen to know what rank he holds in judo?

A. I don't know if he is in the 4th rank.

Q. He is ahead of you?

A. Yes.

Q. Who is the highest ranking judo expert here?

A. Rev. Tsunoda, the 5th rank.

Q. What is the 10th?

A. No, 5th.

Q. That is the highest here?

A. Yes.

(By President) Very well, in view of your having an attorney, your case will stand continued until your attorney is ready to present your side of the case.

Q. (By Recorder) May I have another question, please?

A. (By President) Yes.

Q. (By Recorder) How do you attain the rank of judo? By competitive tests?

A. Yes.

Q. And matches?

A. Yes, all we hear. The high ranking instructors recommend us by judging us by our daily practice. Of course, that is not the rule, but sometimes we do it that way, sometimes by gesture.

Q. (By Mr. Porter) Generally speaking, the man who wins the match is the man who attain the rank?

A. Not exactly, daily practice too.

Q. Daily practice in judo or method or form of life daily?

A. No, judo.

Q. In judo only? That is they observe you on the floor and watch your form and action and so on so that if you showed up constantly in a period of time, you might request a rank and still obtain a higher rank?

A. Yes.

(By President) Very well, you may now confer with your attorney and when you are ready, will you notify us?

(Internee leaves the room.)

(After a short recess, Mr. Harlocker, attorney for internee, entered the room with internee and testified as follows:

Q. (By President) Case 144, you represent the internee, Judge Harlocker?

A. Yes, I would like to have my appearance entered in this case.

Q. Very well. You may proceed to present the internee's case.

Q. (By Mr. Harlocker) Mr. Hoshida, in connection with the Budo Kyo Kai, the organization in which you made application for rating in connection with your judo work, have you made any payments to that organization within the last few years?

A. Only when I had my ranking. I paid a fee of between $1 to $3. I don't remember the amount exactly.

Q. How long ago was that?

A. About 3 or 4 years ago.

Q. Are you a member of that organization at the present time?

A. I am not sure because when we send in that application for ranking, we do not send it as intentions as membership but they take it as membership fee and consider us as a member at that time so I do not believe that I am anymore their member.

Q. Do you consider yourself a member?

A. No.

Q. Have you ever had any intention of returning to Japan to make your home?

A. No.

Q. Do you own your own home in Hilo?

A. Yes.

Q. And when did you buy that home?

A. About 2½ years ago.

Q. Where?

A. Waiakea Houselots.

Q. What did you pay for it?

A. $3,500.00.

Q. Is there a balance due on it at the present time?

A. Yes, there is a balance of about $2,200.00

Q. Do you own any other property?

A. No.

Q. Do you own any property of any kind in Japan?

A. No.

Q. Have you ever had any intention of returning to Japan to make your home?

A. No.

Q. Have you ever purchased any Japanese bonds?

A. No.

Q. Have you purchased any bond of the United States government?

A. Yes.

Q. When and how much?

A. Around November, $25 bond.

Q. Have you ever done anything else in connection with the sale of United States Savings defense bonds?

A. Yes, through my activity, I encouraged the various Y.B.A. people and members to purchase defense bonds.

Q. Were any purchases actually made?

A. Yes, the United Y.B.A. headquarters purchased $100 bond and the Y.B.A. organization here, too, purchased a $1,000 bond but I don't know because their funds were frozen after the war started and I don't know whether they were free to purchase or not, and there are various organizations who had purchased or were about to purchase defense bonds.

Q. Do the various associations to which you belong and which you participated in support any activity against the United States government?

A. So far as I know, I have not noticed any of these activities.

Q. Do you know whether or not there are such activities?

A. I am positive that there are no such activities.

Q. Is there anything in those activities which support the policies of the Japanese government?

A. No.

Q. If you were to be released from custody, as between Japan and the United States, whom would you support and cooperate with?

A. I support the United States of America.

Q. Is there anything at all in your mind which would cause you to doubt your ability to do that?

A. I have no doubt of my ability if only I was allowed.

(By Mr. Harlocker) I believe that is all the questions I have.

Q. (By President) Very well, have you any witnesses?

A. (By Mr. Harlocker) No. In this particular case, gentlemen, the detainee himself has prepared a statement which I believe, being in his own words, reflects his own attitude better than any line of questioning which I could make. It includes a lot of irrelevant material, material which I do not believe the Board necessarily would be interested in. I would like to ask permission either for the detainee to read this statement or that it be admitted in evidence and later perused by the Board or in view of the fact that there are some irrelevant parts to it, I would be permitted to make extractions from the statement in typewritten form and attach them to the original as a whole, and submit it, or if you prefer, have the entire statement be put into a typewritten form and later perused by the Board.

(By Mr. Bush) Could we submit this, that the detainee be allowed with his attorney to mark the most important passages and submit it?

(By President) Supposing then, you take it and mark the portion that you wish to stress and return it to us and we will receive it as internee's Exhibit A.

(By Mr. Harlocker) I suggest that, gentlemen, because I believe it being an expression in his own words, that probably presents in better form his real attitude.

(By President) Very well. All right and when you are ready to present it, if you will just bring it in and we will accept it and the internee's case is continued pending further action.

(Internee together with attorney leave the room.)

(A recess was had and later Judge Harlocker presented the statement and it was marked as internee's Exhibit A.)

Exhibit A

"STATEMENT

To the Honorable Gentlemen
of the Board of Inquiry:

I wish to submit to you the following statement as proof of my innocence against your charge of my being an undesirable enemy alien:

First, I wish to make clear my position and attitude toward America and Japan.

I was born in Japan and lived there until four years of age, and then came to Hawaii, where for the last thirty years I have been living without once having stepped out of these islands. So, to me, Japan is like a mother who had given me birth and reared me up to four and then had given me up to the willing hands of America for her to adopt. America had willingly adopted me and had most generously cared for me, educated me, given me livelihood and home, and in fact had lavished on me practically everything as she would have to her own.

Now, Japan and America are at war—my country or mother who had given me birth against my country or mother who had adopted me. What could be sadder and more painful? I had fervently wished that they would not come to this, and although I have heard each others reasons for entering into this war, the real reasons are beyond my comprehension.

To see my two loved countries injuring each other is very painful, but to be suspected of intentions of taking part on one side and injuring the other is more painful. I would not like to take part on any one side if it is injurious to the other but if I am allowed to take part, I wish to do all I can to help ease the pain, instead of contributing to it. Or better still, I would like to see these two nations come to an agreement as speedily as possible and return to friendly terms again. Nevertheless, since it is plain that by far the greater part of my obligations is toward America, it is my duty to do what America bids me. So, although I cannot truthfully say that I shall like it, I will not hesitate to take arms against Japan if America so desires.

Secondly, I would like to state that I sincerely believe I had been a very good and loyal resident of the United States.

I had tried all I can to conform to the Constitution and Laws of the United States and to the best of my recollection, had not committed any crime or broken any law, except a few minor traffic regulations. I had paid my taxes regularly, and in fact, I was, at one time refunded the Territorial Gross Income Tax amount to eighty some odd dollars which I had paid during a period of three or four years through not being rightly informed of its regulations. I had contributed my bit in keeping the wheel of industry moving through my work as electrical and gas appliance salesman for the Hilo Electric and Gas Companies for a period of over ten years and also through other occupations that I had been able to perform. I had pursued my occupations honestly and to the best of my ability. I have done also my share of the social works contributing to the welfare and progress of the community and its people. I have given my contributions—though so small, but nevertheless, the best that I could do in my poor financial condition—to the Welfare, the Tuberculosis Society, the Red Cross and the purchase of U.S. Defense Bond and stamps. I had obeyed the rules and regulations set forth by Martial Law after the war started, and would have willingly contributed my services to any defense work within my ability and means, if the army authorities had allowed. I did try to contribute a little when I went to the Hilo Memorial Hospital for blood test intending to add my share to the blood bank, but was unable to do so because I was detained a couple of days after the test and before the hospital could approve my blood.

So, summing it all up, I believe, I could rightly say that I had done all that I could as a good and loyal American resident, although of course I realize that it is but a very small return for all that America had done for me. And, if there were any of my actions that had offended my adopted country, I can only say that it was purely unintentional and would humbly beg that you accept my sincere apology and forgive me with the same generous heart that had welcomed me into you bosom.

Thirdly, and last, I wish to present my family and its conditions as a positive proof of the impossibility of my doing anything undesirable or injurious to my adopted country.

I have a wife and three children—all girls—who are all American citizens by right of birth. I, myself, would certainly have become an American citizen if only she had allowed, but still I feel that I am ninety per cent American when figuring from the length of my life here, and eighty per cent American if I am to represent my family.

Of my three children, the youngest will be two years old on July 31st this year, and is at an age when she is getting into all sorts of mischief and danger and requires constant attention. The second child will be six this June and is at an age when parent's words mean nothing. The eldest girl was eight last January 30th, coincidently the President's birthday, and is a big burden to the family as she is a total invalid, caused through a serious car accident when she was only three months old. Judge McLaughlin of this board is, I believe, familiar with her case, as her case was presented to his court around the beginning of March, this year—after I was detained—in order that she be placed in the Waimano Home, the home of the feeble-minded.

[. . .] But, after the permission was granted by the court, we found that there were no opening for her there. I have heard that it is very hard to find an opening on account of its crowded condition and many waiting applications. So, at present, my wife is doing all she can to take care of her, with occasional helps from our relatives.

But the worst part is that my wife is in no condition to assume this heavy burden, as she is pregnant and she herself, also, is a cripple. Besides that she is a type that worries too much, although it can be considered natural in her case, as she have had more than her share of suffering throughout her life. [. . .]

Now, with this war and my detention, I am afraid that the strain of these heavy burden and responsibilities might be too much for her to stand up long. We have no savings and there is no source of income except what the Welfare Department had promised but had not carried out as yet to this date of writing. The relatives are doing their best to help her but they themselves have their responsibilities and cannot care for her long. Furthermore, since our house is located in a section less than half a mile from the Hilo air field, I am very much worried about their safety in case of an unexpected enemy attack. I do not mind my suffering but I cannot bear to see my loved ones suffer and to be helpless to do anything about it. So, this is the main reason why I am trying to have myself cleared and released.

You have the general picture of my family's conditions, now, and I would like to ask you how anyone in these conditions, with his life and the fate of his family at stake, can consider doing anything harmful or undesirable to the country to which he is so deeply indebted. If he does, he is worse than a fool, and I am, I believe, not such a fool. I believe that any man with a family for which he has any affection, can understand that. Furthermore, since my sole desire is to protect my family and since they are all American citizens, I believe that I will be performing a highly desirable and essential service for America by protecting her subjects, provided, that she really believes in her own Constitution and considers my family as still being American citizens.

Therefore, in just and honest considerations of my past actions and present conditions, I firmly believe that I am not an undesirable American resident.

I, now, sincerely beseech you, Honorable Gentlemen of the Inquiry Board, and whoever are responsible for my future fate and the fate of my family, to give me honest and fair judgment and considerations, remembering: that I am your fellow human and an individual, that every man is given his life to use for good or for evil, and that he should be judged only by his own deeds, his own faith, and his own efforts and not by any label of race, nationality, or creed. And, allow me to close with the firm belief that if America is truly a land of Equality and Justice, I shall also be given Freedom.

> Written Apr. 20, 1942
>
> Respectfully submitted,
>
> This 24th day of April, 1942.
>
> (Sgd.) George Yoshio Hoshida"

(5 May 1942. All members of the Board being present, the Recorder and Reporter being present, the Board, Recorder and Reporter having been previously duly sworn, the following proceedings were had:)

FINDINGS:

The Board, having carefully considered the evidence before it, finds:

1. That the internee is a subject of Japan;
2. That the internee is loyal to Japan;
3. That the internee's activities have been pro-Japanese, though not necessarily subversive.

RECOMMENDATIONS:

In view of the above findings, the Board recommends:

That the internee, GEORGE YOSHIO HOSHIDA, be interned for the duration of the war.

> [Signed] Frank McLaughlin
> (President)

> [Signed] Victor R. Woodruff Lt. Colonel, FA.
> (Recorder)

> [Signed] Alex J. Porter
> (Member)

> [Signed] Gavin A. Bush
> (Member)

Notes

1. George and the questioner are referring to the amendment of the Cable Act of 1922, which repealed a previous act that decreed that a female U.S. citizen lost her citizenship if she married a foreigner. However, the Cable Act allowed women to keep their citizenship only if they married foreigners eligible for citizenship. As Asians were not permitted to naturalize, this meant that marriage to a non-citizen Asian would result in a woman losing her U.S. citizenship. This provision was repealed in 1931, so Tamae was indeed able to keep her citizenship upon her marriage in 1933.

2. An informal social organization within a neighborhood, through which members would support one another with financial help, services, etc. and also hold some recreational activities.

Memorandum for Col. Karl R. Bendetsen re Pro-Japanese Activities

(excerpted)

March 12, 1943

MEMORANDUM TO: Colonel Karl R. Bendetsen

SUBJECT: Notes re Pro-Japanese Activities

(2) ORGANIZATIONS: There are in excess of 750 local Japanese organizations which have participated in pro-Japanese activities (About 150 different organizations). Roughly fall into following classes.

(a) PATRIOTIC COLLECTORS OF WAR AND DEFENSE FUNDS:

Example: HEIMUSHA KAI (Japanese Military Service Association). Organized in 1937 in the United States. Over 10,000 known members. Each member pledges a minimum of $1.00 per month for Japanese Army and Navy (known to have collected over one million dollars).

(b) MILITARY SOCIETIES:

Example: BUTOKU KAI (Military Virtue Society). Purpose was to "uplift the Imperial Spirit of Japan as well as the Military Virtue." Organized to interest the nissei in taking their education and military training in Japan. Taught arts of war and defense. Many thousands of members.

DOI: 10.5876/9781607323440.c026

Timeline of Major Events

October 23, 1907. George (Yoshio) Hoshida is born in Kumamoto, Japan

July 18, 1908. Tamae Takemoto is born at the Waiakea Plantation outside of Hilo

Summer 1912. George, with his mother Eno and brother Matsuo, arrive in Hawai'i.

1922. George leaves school to go to work.

1931. Tamae and George start dating.

April 23, 1933. Tamae and George are married.

January 30, 1934. Taeko, first of four daughters, is born.

May 1, 1934. Tamae and Taeko are seriously injured in a car accident. Taeko is left blind and disabled.

June 23, 1936. June Mitsuko is born.

July 31, 1940. Sandra Yoshiko is born.

December 7, 1941. Pearl Harbor is attacked by Japan.

DOI: 10.5876/9781607323440.c027

1942

February 6. Yoshio is arrested and taken to Kilauea.

Late February. Tamae learns she is pregnant.

April 24. Yoshio's military hearing is held.

May 1. Taeko is sent to the Waimano Home.

May 7. Yoshio is taken away from the Island of Hawai'i.

May 24. Hawaiian men are sent to the mainland.

June 9. They arrive at the Fort Sam Houston Internment Camp.

June 19. They arrive at the Lordsburg camp.

October 20. Tamae and George's fourth child, Carole Aiko, is born.

December 27. Tamae and the children depart Hawai'i on the second military transfer.

1943

January 5. Tamae, June, Sandra, and Carole reach Jerome.

April 23. Tamae and George's tenth wedding anniversary.

June 14. George is moved from Lordsburg to Santa Fe with 350 other men.

October 21. George's friend, Kinzaemon Odachi, passes away.

December 7. George is paroled to Jerome, and the family is reunited after nearly two years.

April 11, 1944. Tamae has an Exit Clearance hearing.

May 1944. The Hoshidas and their friends are transferred from Jerome to Gila River.

July 22, 1944. Taeko drowns in the Waimano Home in Pearl City, Hawai'i.

September 1945. The Hoshidas spend three weeks in California before departing the mainland for Hawai'i.

Bibliography

ARCHIVAL MATERIALS

George Hoshida's artwork and his correspondence with Tamae (and other members of the family) are available for viewing at the Hirasaki National Resource Center of the Japanese American National Museum (JANM) in Los Angeles, California. Documents 5 and 6 are filed within the correspondence. A photocopy of the original memoir is also held there.

Two pieces of his artwork (figures 11.1 and 13.2) were previously published in the 1983 volume *Poets behind Barbed Wire* by Bamboo Ridge Press. This book is currently out of print.

Documents 2–4 (and figure 16.2) are from the Japanese Internment and Relocation Files in Hamilton Library at the University of Hawai'i at Manoa. An oral history and transcript that George Hoshida did for the university's Ethnic Studies Department are also kept there. It largely overlaps with the memoir.

Documents 1 and 7 are from the National Archives. Document 1, George Hoshida's hearings transcript, is from Record Group 389 (Provost Marshal General), Enemy POW Information Bureau Reporting Branch, Subject File,

DOI: 10.5876/9781607323440.c028

1942–46; Hawaii—Civilian Internees, held at National Archives II in College Park, Maryland. Document 2, Tamae Hoshida's exit clearance hearing transcript, is from Record Group 210 (Records of the War Relocation Authority), the Japanese American Internee Data File, File #957414, held at National Archives I in Washington, DC. Her file there contains some originals and duplicates of petitions for reunion that are also held at the JANM.

References

More background information about the government's policies and handling of the incarcerees from Hawai'i can be found in the 1980s Congressional Commission's report published as *Personal Justice Denied*, Tetsuden Kashima's excellent introduction to Soga's memoir, Ogawa and Fox's essay, and Okihiro's *Cane Fires* (which quotes from Hoshida's 1981 oral history), all cited below. Robinson's *By Order of the President* gives a highly detailed account interwoven with the other aspects of incarceration.

For general history of the incarceration, Daniels's *Prisoners without Trial* is the best short introduction. Weglyn's *Years of Infamy* is still an excellent account that includes reproductions of several primary sources. Robinson's *A Tragedy of Democracy* is a highly detailed comparative study of the incarceration of ethnic Japanese across North America.

The notes within the text contain some suggestions for further reading on specific topics. However, I have not cited sources on the individual camps and detention centers except where particularly detailed information is offered. General background information on the camps can be found in Kashima, *Judgment without Trial*; Burton, *Confinement and Ethnicity*; and Iritani and Iritani, *Ten Visits Revised*.

For other artwork by incarcerees, there are several good publications, of which Okubo's is the most famous. Estelle Peck Ishigo published an account much less famous than Okubo's, which served as the foundation for the Academy Award–winning documentary short film about her life in camp, *Days of Waiting*. *Topaz Moon* is an edited volume collecting letters, contextualizing essays, and artwork by Chiura Obata, an assistant professor of art at the University of California, Berkeley, whose painting of the Topaz camp was presented to Eleanor Roosevelt in 1943. The recently published *Stanley Hayami, Nisei Son* reproduces some of the drawings by this gifted teenaged artist who was drafted into the army in 1944. He was killed in action with the 442nd at the very end of the war in Europe.

Anderson, Charles R. *Day of Lightning, Years of Scorn: Walter C. Short and the Attack on Pearl Harbor*. Annapolis, MD: Naval Institute Press, 2005.

Asahina, Robert. *Just Americans: How Japanese Americans Won a War at Home and Abroad*. New York: Gotham Books, 2007.

Austin, Allan W. *From Concentration Camp to Campus: Japanese American Students and World War II*. Urbana: University of Illinois Press, 2007.

Azuma, Eiichiro. "Brokering Race, Culture, and Citizenship: Japanese Americans in Occupied Japan and Postwar National Inclusion." *Journal of American-East Asian Relations* 16, no. 3 (Fall 2009): 183–211. http://dx.doi.org/10.1163/187656109793645670.

Borch, Fred, and Daniel Martinez, eds. *Kimmel, Short, and Pearl Harbor: The Final Report Revealed*. Annapolis, MD: Naval Institute Press, 2005.

Burton, Jeffery F. *Confinement and Ethnicity: An Overview of World War II Japanese American Relocation Sites*. Seattle: University of Washington Press, 2002.

"Catalogue of the University of Michigan for 1919–1920." *University Bulletin* 21, no. 39 (May 15, 1920).

The Cats of Mirikitani, dir. Linda Hattendorf. New York: New Video Group, 2010. DVD.

Coffman, Tom. *The Island Edge of America: A Political History of Hawai'i*. Honolulu: University of Hawai'i Press, 2003.

Commission on Wartime Relocation and Internment of Civilians. *Personal Justice Denied*. Reprint, Washington, DC: Civil Liberties Public Education Fund / Seattle: University of Washington Press, 1997. Originally published as two volumes in 1982–83.

Culley, John J. "Trouble at the Lordsburg Internment Camp." *New Mexico Historical Review* 60, no. 3 (July 1, 1985): 225–48.

Daniels, Roger. *Prisoners without Trial: Japanese Americans in World War II*. New York: Hill and Wang, 2004.

Days of Waiting, dir. Steven Okazaki. Berkeley, CA: Farallon Films, 2000. DVD.

Federal School of Commercial Designing. Advertisement. *Photoplay* Feb. 1924: 108.

Federal School of Illustrating. Advertisement. *Photoplay* Jan. 1924: 102.

Felipe, Virgilio Menor. *Hawai'i: a Pilipino Dream*. Honolulu: Mutual Pub., 2002.

Franks, Joel S. *Crossing Sidelines, Crossing Cultures: Sport and Asian Pacific American Cultural Citizenship*. Lanham, MD: University Press of America, 2002.

Gannon, Michael. *Pearl Harbor Betrayed: The True Story of a Man and a Nation under Attack*. New York: H. Holt, 2001.

Goldstein, Richard. "Kazuo Sakamaki, 81, Pacific P.O.W. No. 1." *New York Times*, December 21, 1999. http://www.nytimes.com/1999/12/21/world/kazuo-sakamaki-81-pacific-pow-no-1.html.

Hansen, Arthur A. "Cultural Politics in the Gila River Relocation Center, 1942–1943." *Arizona and the West* 27 (Winter 1985): 327–62.

Hayami, Stanley. *Stanley Hayami, Nisei Son.* Ed. Joanne Oppenheim. New York: Brick Tower, 2008.

Hisanaga, Kazuma. "Dedication Ceremony Remarks by Kazuma Hisanaga." *Puka Puka Parades,* August 1995. 100th Infantry Battalion Veterans Education Center. http://www.100thbattalion.org/archives/puka-puka-parades/mainland-training/camp-mccoy/dedication-ceremony-remarks-by-kazuma-hisanaga/.

Honda, Gail, ed. *Family Torn Apart: The Internment Story of the Otokichi Muin Ozaki Family.* Honolulu: University of Hawai'i Press, 2012.

Houston, Jeanne Wakatsuki, and James D. Houston. *Farewell to Manzanar: A True Story of Japanese American Experience during and after the World War II Internment.* New York: Houghton Mifflin, 2002. First published 1973.

Howard, John. *Concentration Camps on the Home Front.* Chicago: University of Chicago Press, 2008. http://dx.doi.org/10.7208/chicago/9780226354774.001.0001.

Inouye, Ronald K. "Yasuda, Frank." In *Encyclopedia of Japanese American History: An A-to-Z Reference from 1868 to the Present,* updated ed., ed. Brian Niiya. New York: Facts on File, 2001.

Iritani, Frank, and Joanne Iritani, *Ten Visits Revised: Brief Accounts of Our Visits to All Ten Japanese American Relocation Centers of World War II, Internee and Non-internee Recollections, Struggle for Redress, Internment of Other Groups, Our non-Nikkei Friends, and Other Essays.* Los Angeles: Japanese American National Museum, 1999.

Ishigo, Estelle. *Lone Heart Mountain.* Los Angeles: Heart Mountain High School Class of 1947, 1972.

Kashima, Tetsuden. *Judgment without Trial: Japanese American Imprisonment during World War II.* Seattle: University of Washington Press, 2003.

Kumamoto, Bob. "The Search for Spies: American Counterintelligence and the Japanese American Community 1931–1942." *Amerasia Journal* 6, no. 2 (Fall 1979): 45–75.

Lane, James B. "Joseph B. Poindexter and Hawaii during the New Deal." *Pacific Northwest Quarterly* 62, no. 1 (Jan. 1971): 7–15.

Layton, Edwin T. *"And I Was There": Pearl Harbor and Midway—Breaking the Secrets.* New York: W. Morrow, 1985.

Lyon, Cherstin. *Prisons and Patriots: Japanese American Wartime Citizenship, Civil Disobedience, and Historical Memory.* Philadelphia: Temple University Press, 2011.

McNaughton, James C. *Nisei Linguists: Japanese Americans in the Military Intelligence Service during World War II.* Washington, DC: GPO, 2007.

"Memorandum, The Spanish Embassy to the Department of State." In *Foreign Relations of the United States, Diplomatic Papers, 1944,* vol. 5, 1104–6. Washington, DC: GPO, 1965.

Michaelis, David. *Schulz and Peanuts: A Biography.* New York: HarperCollins, 2007.

The MISLS Album 1946. Camp Snelling, MN: Military Intelligence Service Language School, [1946?].

Miyamoto, Kazuo. *Hawaii: End of the Rainbow.* Rutland, VT: Bridgeway Press, 1964.

Miyasaki, Gail, ed. *Japanese Eyes, American Heart: Personal Reflections of Hawaii's World War II Nisei Soldiers.* Honolulu: Tendai Educational Foundation / University of Hawai'i Press, 1998.

Muller, Eric L. *American Inquisition: The Hunt for Japanese American Disloyalty in World War II.* Chapel Hill: University of North Carolina Press, 2007.

Nakano, Jiro. *Kanda Home: Biography of Shigefusa and Sue Kanda.* Honolulu: University of Hawai'i Press, 1996.

Ochoa, Holly Byers. "Another Day of Infamy." *Pomona College Magazine*, Spring 2002. http://www.pomona.edu/Magazine/PCMsp02/DEyears.shtml.

Odo, Franklin. *No Sword to Bury: Japanese Americans in Hawai'i during World War II.* Philadelphia: Temple University Press, 2004.

Ogawa, Dennis M., and Evarts C. Fox Jr. "Japanese Internment and Relocation: The Hawaii Experience." In *Japanese Americans: From Relocation to Redress*, ed. Roger Daniels, Sandra C. Taylor, and Harry H. L. Kitano. Seattle: University of Washington Press, 1991.

Okawa, Gail Y. "Putting Their Lives on the Line: Personal Narrative as Political Discourse among Japanese Petitioners in American World War II Internment." *College English* 74, no. 1 (Sept. 2011): 50–68.

Okihiro, Gary. *Cane Fires: The Anti-Japanese Movement in Hawaii, 1865–1945.* Philadelphia: Temple University Press, 1992.

Okubo, Miné. *Citizen 13660.* Seattle: University of Washington Press, 1983. First published 1946.

Putney, William W. *Always Faithful: A Memoir of the Marine Dogs of WWII.* Dulles, VA: Brassey's, 2003.

Relocation Communities for Wartime Evacuees. Washington, DC: Government Printing Office, 1942.

Robinson, Greg. *By Order of the President: FDR and the Internment of Japanese Americans.* Cambridge: Harvard University Press, 2001.

Robinson, Greg. *A Tragedy of Democracy: Japanese Confinement in North America.* New York: Columbia University Press, 2009.

Rosenberg, Emily S. *A Date Which Will Live: Pearl Harbor in American Memory.* Durham, NC: Duke University Press, 2003. http://dx.doi.org/10.1215/9780822387459.

Sakamaki, Kazuo. *I Attacked Pearl Harbor.* New York: Association Press, 1949.

"Setsuo Richard Takemoto." Military Experience Database. *Discover Nikkei.* http://www.discovernikkei.org/en/resources/military/12772/.

Smith, Susan Lynn. *Japanese American Midwives: Culture, Community, and Health Politics, 1880–1950.* Urbana: University of Illinois Press, 2005.

Soga, Yasutaro (Keiho). *Life behind Barbed Wire: The World War II Internment Memoirs of a Hawai'i Issei.* Honolulu: University of Hawai'i Press, 2008.

Sone, Monica. *Nisei Daughter.* Seattle: University of Washington Press, 1979. First published 1953.

Spickard, Paul R. "The Nisei Assume Power: The Japanese Citizens League, 1941–1942." *Pacific Historical Review* 52, no. 2 (May 1983): 147–74. http://dx.doi.org/10.2307/3638793. Frequently cited with a subtitle reflecting the correct name of the JACL: "The Japanese American Citizens League, 1941–1942."

Sterner, C. Douglas. *Go For Broke: The Nisei Warriors of World War II Who Conquered Germany, Japan, and American Bigotry.* Clearfield, UT: American Legacy Historical Press, 2008.

Stinnett, Robert B. *Day of Deceit: The Truth about FDR and Pearl Harbor.* New York: Free Press, 2000.

Takaki, Ronald. *Pau Hana: Plantation Life and Labor in Hawaii, 1835–1920.* Honolulu: University of Hawai'i Press, 1983.

Takemoto, Paul Howard. *Nisei Memories: My Parents Talk about the War Years.* Seattle: University of Washington Press, 2006.

Tashiro, Kenneth. *"Wase Time!": A Teen's Memoir of Gila River Internment Camp.* Bloomington, IL: AuthorHouse, 2005.

Taylor, Paul A. "Report from Jerome Relocation Center, Denson, Arkansas, Sent to Dillon S. Myer, Director WRA." Photocopy typescript, February 28, 1943. Japanese Internment and Relocation Files, Folder 101. Hamilton Library, University of Hawai'i, Manoa.

Thomas, Dorothy Swaine, and Richard S. Nishimoto. *The Spoilage.* Berkeley: University of California Press, 1964.

Waller, Anna M. *Dogs and National Defense.* Washington, DC: Dept. of the Army, Office of the Quartermaster General, 1958.

Waseda, Minako. "Extraordinary Circumstances, Exceptional Practices: Music in Japanese American Concentration Camps." *Journal of Asian American Studies* 8, no. 2 (June 2005): 171–209, 231. http://dx.doi.org/10.1353/jaas.2005.0044.

Weglyn, Michi. *Years of Infamy: The Untold Story of America's Concentration Camps.* New York: Morrow Quill Paperbacks, 1976.

Whitehead, John S. *Completing the Union: Alaska, Hawai'i, and the Battle for Statehood.* Albuquerque: University of New Mexico Press, 2004.

Page numbers in italics indicate illustrations.